FROM POVERTY TO [...]
FROM AFRICA TO AMERICA,
AND FROM CHILD SOLDIER
TO U.S. MARINE

Born into the Congolese wilderness, Tchicaya Missamou became a child soldier at age 11. As a horrific civil war loomed across his country, Tchicaya began using his militia connections to ferry jewels, cash, computers, and white diplomats out of the country. By 17, he was rich. By 18, he was a hunted man, his house destroyed, his family brutalized in front of him by his own militia. By 19, he'd left behind everything he'd ever known, escaping to Europe and, eventually, to America.

Incredibly, that was only the start of his journey.

In the Shadow of Freedom is the uplifting story of one man's quest to achieve the American Dream. Tchicaya Missamou's life is a shining example of why America is a gift that should not be taken for granted, and why we are limited only by the breadth of our imagination and the strength of our will.

IN THE SHADOW

❖ OF ❖

FREEDOM

A Heroic Journey
to Liberation, Manhood,
and America

TCHICAYA MISSAMOU

with Travis Sentell

ATRIA PAPERBACK   New York   London   Toronto   Sydney

This work is a memoir. It reflects the author's present recollections of his experiences over a period of years. Certain names and identifying characteristics have been changed and certain individuals are composites. Events have also been compressed.

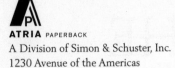

ATRIA PAPERBACK
A Division of Simon & Schuster, Inc.
1230 Avenue of the Americas
New York, NY 10020

First Atria Paperback edition August 2010

ATRIA PAPERBACK and colophon are trademarks of Simon & Schuster, Inc.

For information about special discounts for bulk purchases, please contact Simon & Schuster Special Sales at 1-866-506-1949 or business@simonandschuster.com.

The Simon & Schuster Speakers Bureau can bring authors to your live event. For more information or to book an event contact the Simon & Schuster Speakers Bureau at 1-866-248-3049 or visit our website at www.simonspeakers.com.

Designed by Dana Sloan

Manufactured in the United States of America

10 9 8 7 6 5 4 3 2 1

Library of Congress Cataloging-in-Publication Data

Missamou, Tchicaya, 1978–
    In the shadow of freedom : a heroic journey to liberation, manhood, and America / by Tchicaya Missamou ; with Travis Sentell. — 1st Atria pbk. ed.
        p. cm.
    1. Missamou, Tchicaya, 1978– 2. Congo (Brazzaville)—Biography. 3. Congo (Brazzaville)—History—Civil War, 1997—Personal narratives. 4. Immigrants—United States—Biography. 5. Marines—United States—Biography. 6. United States. Marine Corps—Biography. 7. Iraq War, 2003—Personal narratives, American. I. Title.

    DT546.283.M57A3 2010
    956.7044'345—dc22
    [B]
                                                                                        2009013264
    ISBN 1-4391-1629-6
    ISBN 1-4391-4912-6 (ebook)

This book is dedicated to educators, parents, and all the servants of freedom—wherever they are found.

In loving memory

Bobby Thompson
8/30/65–7/10/08

James P. Williams, U.S.M.C.
5/31/32–3/19/66

and

Mama Ntsiangani Therese
"Coco ya Koni"

In the SHADOW of FREEDOM

PART 1
MUNDELÉ

Born with less, but you still precious . . .

— *TUPAC SHAKUR*

Brazzaville, Congo
August 19th, 2004

Thursday

I am almost home.

The plane skims the treetops and I stare down at a country that is no longer mine.

Slowly, the shadows solidify into shacks, primitive buildings, run-down streets, and I feel excitement coiling in my stomach like a snake. The air around me charges and pulses with electricity as my seat begins to shudder. Flying into the Congo is never commonplace. It is never ordinary. It is never easy.

The plane touches down with a series of thumps and my heart pounds a rough counterpoint.

As the door swings open, the heat covers me like a blanket, but it's not the heat of the Middle East or California. It is the heat of Africa. It burns my eyes, and I mistake the sharp stinging sensation for the onset of tears as my feet touch what passes for a tarmac.

The light feels strange against my skin, tangible, warm, thick, and I imagine for a second that a different sun shines here.

I smile and step into the terminal.

The noise explodes into my ears and the heat doubles, triples in this contained space. I notice the lack of air-conditioning and suddenly wonder how different I really am, how far I've really come.

I queue in the immigration line for foreigners and see Mama Nicole, my aunt, standing on the other side of the dusty glass. She waves at me, leaping up and down like a small child. I smile back, excitement swelling my chest. White people step ahead of me and are waved through the line, but I don't let this bother me today.

"*Passeport,*" says the man in French. Like most of the Congolese police and government personnel, he wears civilian clothes. Dark sweat stains creep across his yellowed shirt.

I plaster a wide smile onto my face and pull out my American passport.

He stares at the blue document for a moment, his face wrinkled in confusion. He turns it over. There aren't many Americans who venture this deep into the Congo.

"American?" he asks.

I nod.

"Next," he says, placing my passport to the side and assisting the man behind me. I take a step to the right and wait patiently. I will not cause any disruptions.

He picks up my passport again. "I have to check this out," he says, then disappears into the crowd. I stand there, separated from my people by a thin glass barrier. I watch as if they were a television show, moving and shouting and hustling for money in a cacophony of languages. It is more desperate than I remember, more violent.

The man doesn't come back.

My aunt waves at me again, a confused look on her face. I raise my hand for reassurance, but her expression makes me nervous. I try to ask another immigration officer for help, but am ignored. Minutes pass. My aunt comes close to the glass. "What's going on?"

"The man needed to check something with my passport."

"Congolese?"

"American," I say, shaking my head.

She clucks at me. "An American passport in the Congo is like gold. You should not have even let him leave the counter. There's no one to be trusted here." I start to answer, but she turns to the man beside her and says something. He walks off, returning a few moments later with the commandant of the terminal. My aunt is a strong woman, but it's not permitted for her to express anger to a man such as this, so she keeps her mouth closed. Her friend discusses the situation with him instead, and I watch my aunt closely to determine exactly how worried I should be.

Minutes later, employees are lined up and threatened, and somehow my passport magically appears. The commandant attempts an apology, but I simply nod and move into the twisting, black cloud of the main terminal. I'm happy to let others do the talking for me. It never crossed my mind to brush up on languages I spoke for nearly twenty years.

I struggle not to touch the soft skin on my face. I'm as dark as anyone in the room, but seven years away from the dirt, the dust, and the winds has changed my complexion.

My aunt runs toward me and wraps her arms around my neck. I say hello to the man beside her, who turns out to be the boyfriend of my other aunt, Mama Julice. His name is Batsimba.

"He pretended to be a colonel," says Mama Nicole, smiling. "They managed to find the passport very quickly after that."

I look at Batsimba, and he shrugs. "They don't know better," he says. "Is it not good to get what you want?"

I nod and shake his hand.

"Last week, I was a captain," he says, a slow grin overtaking his face. I feel my mouth mirroring his and pat his shoulder. I'm thankful for his presence, for his ability to deceive.

"Come," says my aunt, "stay close."

She sees me widening my eyes against the crowds and smiles. "American and European flights bring more people. More money to be made."

I pull my satchel tightly against my back.

I'm wearing jeans and a T-shirt and heads turn as I walk. People reach out to touch me. Children point. No one who sees me counts me as a local and, for some reason, this makes me angry. My clothes would be nothing in America, but here, they set me apart.

"So is it everything you remember?" asks my aunt.

I speak softly, slowly, hesitant in my native tongue. "It is crowded," I say.

She laughs, her teeth reflecting the dull halogen lights above us. "It's always been crowded. It's you who take up more space."

I allow myself to smile, but can't shake the twisting snake in the pit of my stomach. I can't tell if it is fear, nervousness, or excitement. Possibly all three.

Beggars surround the crowd like a fence, and I wonder if there was always such poverty, such sadness. Children do not notice such things, but my new eyes are attuned to suffering.

I pull my Nalgene bottle out of my backpack, unscrew the top, and take a long swig. Stares accompany the gesture, and nearby children reach out to touch my legs as they pass. One little boy stops, his eyes bright, his mouth gaping.

"What's that?" he says.

"It holds water," I say, suddenly aware of this alien technology that I've brought into my homeland. It's okay for a white man to carry such an object, but for a black man to hold this device is strange, foreign, confusing. I put the bottle away and resolve to keep it stowed until I get home.

The boy moves on, pulled by the endless tide of skin and sound.

"Find your bag," says my aunt, and points to a line of tattered men and women dragging luggage into the terminal, sweating from the heat of the tarmac. Some are unable to see thanks to the sheer number of suitcases piled in front of their faces. A few push wheelbarrows full of other people's possessions. Others have staked their fortune on one or two pieces of expensive-looking baggage. I pat my pocket to make sure I still have my money.

I spot my suitcase and tip the man a few extra francs, causing him to smile and pat my arm.

"I take it for you," he says, and I nod.

There is an entire assembly-line operation here, from beggars to baggage handlers to porters to cab drivers. It's a strange economy, thriving on the meager offerings of tired travelers. Again, it's the same as when I left, but more desperate, scared, crowded.

The customs official grabs my bag from the handler, dismissing him with a wave. My face betrays no emotion as the squat man rubs his hands across an old, tattered shirt and pats his big belly. The woman next to him, dressed in an identical faded yellow uniform, glances at the bag.

"Remove the lock, please," she says, and I do. She yanks the zipper with a harsh, practiced motion. The crowd presses against my back. The constant wash of voices weighs against my eardrums.

My face is still and calm.

She lifts the top and I watch her expression closely. Her eyes widen and she nudges the fat man. He glances into the bag, then looks at me.

Two officials come around the table to pat me down. This part, I remember watching as a child, and keep a careful eye on my wristwatch. They touch my chest and pockets, and then they move away. I double-check my possessions, finding cell phone and wallet intact. I move them both to my front pockets, where they are more difficult to steal. This, I should have done earlier, but I have never before carried a wallet on African soil.

The man behind the table reaches into the suitcase and pulls out my cover—my hat. I have purposely packed this item on top. The woman slides closer to him and together they pull out my uniform and lay it on the table. I approve of the way they have handled my second skin, my new life.

"What's this?" they say.

"I'm a U.S. Marine," I say, watching their eyes scan me from head to toe.

I feel my aunt behind me, her hand on my shoulder, but she says nothing. The customs officials work faster now, nicely repacking my jeans and tennis shoes, my carefully folded T-shirts, the small trinkets I've purchased for my family.

A crowd has gathered around us, and we are swept out to the taxi stands. Ten different voices clamor for our attention, offering services, help, advice, all for the smallest of fees. This is the Congolese economy at work. The freest of markets.

I raise my arm to signal for a car, but the man who grabbed my bag from the airplane resurfaces, gesturing toward a cab. "Best driver," he says, smiling largely. "Already booked for you." I follow him. My aunt sighs as if I have done something foolish, but I continue, giving him another hundred francs for his efforts.

"Hey, *mokondzi*," says the driver in Lingala, a regional dialect from the north. "Where you going?" He wears a Kangol hat like Samuel L. Jackson and a shirt that looks older than me. The sweat from his armpits has stained the shirt a dull yellow.

My aunt speaks to him so I don't have to. Here, I am *mokondzi*. Here, I am boss. Here, I am somebody.

"Moungali," she says, directing him to one of the northern sections of Brazzaville, and chills spring up between beads of sweat. I haven't heard that word spoken aloud in seven long years. I clench my fists, picturing my mother's face, trying desperately to block out the last image I have of her, the one permanently etched into my brain.

I force my mind to happier thoughts.

Brazzaville, Congo

1978–87

CHAPTER 1

The grass reached all the way to the sky.

I moved through it, a ghost, a whisper.

To my left, the stuttering swishes of the other hunters assaulted my ears and I cursed their clumsiness.

The sky was clear, hot, bright, and I wiped tiny beads of sweat away from my forehead. I parted the grasses for a better view.

There, in the distance, approaching the Djoué River . . .

"Shhh," I said, but no one could hear me amongst the clattering of feet and murmuring of mouths. "Shhh," I said again, muscles tensed, focused on the prey not ten feet from me. It stopped and cocked its head.

Silence.

We all watched as it slowly pivoted, smelling us, hearing us, sensing our presence in the air. My stomach growled.

The monkey turned and ran for the river. Its tail was rigid, stiff, a finger pointing at us as it sprinted away.

The grasses exploded and we all charged the fleeing animal, tiny spears held high. Blood pumped in my ears. The ground disappeared under my feet as I pulled away from my friends. My mouth opened and a joyful howl erupted.

The monkey reached the river and spun to its right, sprinting along the bank.

I raised my arm high and pushed my legs even harder. Tiny

clouds of dirt sprang up with every step, and I squinted my eyes against the dust, sweat, and sun. My world narrowed to this moment. I could hear the breath filling my lungs.

The monkey turned its head as it ran and we locked eyes. I smiled, delighting in the fear that crossed its face, reveling in the power that surged through my limbs.

Five steps.

Four steps.

I raised my stick high and issued my best approximation of a battle cry, the one I heard the men in the village make when they returned triumphantly from the hunt.

Three steps.

The monkey was nearly in arm's reach, and I could make out the streaks of mud coating its fur, the sheen of moisture across its arms. Time slowed and I watched the muscles coil and release under its skin.

In this moment, I felt alive.

Two steps.

I reached out my arms and grazed the tip of its tail.

It moved even faster, pulling away from me.

One step.

The monkey leaped, spinning toward the jungle, and my hands grasped only air. I turned back toward the grasses to avoid falling into the river. The other kids would never let me hear the end of it if I came back wet.

I stopped, breathing hard, panting in the thick heat. The other kids arrived, wheezing, smiling, laughing.

"You almost had him, Tchic!"

"That was the closest ever!"

I smiled, happy because I'd seen fear in the eyes of the prey. I didn't catch it on that day, but I knew that I would. It was inevitable.

"Come on," I said. "We don't want to miss dinner."

. . .

Matsimou is a small village in southern Brazzaville. It was, at least
to my memory, nearly communal in arrangement. There were no
walls, no gates, no locked doors. If I was hungry, there was no house
that would not feed me. If I was thirsty, there was no woman who
would not give me water.

When we approached from our hunt, the women were gathering coconut shells full of water for their husbands. Some walked
from the river, carrying buckets on their heads, babies strapped to
their backs, while others stoked the fires for the large amounts of
meat the hunters were sure to bring home. A twinge of regret rang
through my body as I pictured the closeness of the monkey.

I jockeyed for position with the other children as the deep
voices echoed from the tree line. Dinner was upon us.

Huge monkeys, nearly five times the size of the one I'd chased
along the banks of the Djoué. Stalks of cassava. Snakes. *Mpuku-
mbendé*. The women carried baskets of fresh vegetables, and my
mouth began watering.

The men set down the prey in front of their wives, who kneeled
in return, holding out coconut shells full of fresh water. Boys ran to
their fathers, clasping them around the leg and exclaiming about
the size of the day's catch.

I was surrounded by singing and dancing, the celebration of a
successful hunt.

The sun edged toward the horizon.

I walked over to my grandmother, Mama Ntsiangani, and
smiled.

"Did you have a good day?" she asked. I nodded, and she smiled
back. "Good. Now run along while I get dinner ready."

We sat on a dusty floor, crammed together, shoulder to shoulder,
naked, sweating, dirty. The sharp edges of the *kouala* rug tickled

the bare skin on my legs and butt. I quivered in excitement as my mother raised the lid of the pot.

A thick white smoke poured out, filling the room with the rich smell of smoked monkey stew, and I giggled in anticipation. The other kids in the house looked at me, smiles on their faces. The house was full, bustling, complete, with two of my grandmothers, my mother, about ten aunts and uncles, and nearly twenty other children.

My mother dipped the long wooden ladle into the pot and pulled out scoops of meat and fresh vegetables, placing them on the huge tray in the center of the room. An appreciative murmur erupted as it always did when such a dish was served. Outside, the fire pits crackled in the night air and I inhaled deeply, sucking the smells into my body.

Everyone gathered around the tray, reaching in with mud-covered hands, stuffing handfuls of food into their gaping mouths. Sighs of contentment merged with grunts of approval and my mother smiled. I licked my fingers, tasting the smoked monkey, imagining the hunt, feeling the warm broth as it raced down my throat and into my belly. I grabbed a piece of hot cassava from the tray and chewed it, letting the juices trickle over my teeth and chin.

A thousand different conversations happened around me as I sat there in the heat and smoke of my grandparents' house, but I did not join any of them. I sat and I ate and I listened.

Pépé, my grandfather, stoked the flames of the fire pit high and we all gathered around him, laughing at his wild eyes and frantic movements. He lowered his voice and we crammed in even tighter, silent as he whispered stories of *mundelé* and black magic, of myth and legend.

I curled close to my mother, smiling to myself as her fingers traced mystical patterns up and down the bare skin of my back.

Chills sprang up along my body, illuminated by the flickering sparks of fire in front of us.

Pépé was now just an outline, a shadow, a ghost flitting in front of the pit, and I stared, letting my eyes unfocus and drift, letting the gods reach into my head and steal my thoughts away from this moment.

My stomach gurgled gently, my muscles sore from the day's play. My mother kissed the top of my head and the fire faded.

Sleep surrounded me like mist and I did not fight it.

Saturday meant cowboy movies, episodes of *Dallas*, or *Rambo*.

As the boys arrived from around Matsimou, I watched as Miekoutima, my uncle, picked up the small black-and-white television and ran the tangled wires over to the car battery that sat in the yard. He connected the frayed ends and watched the screen intently, breaking into a smile as bright rays splashed his face. I sat in front of the screen, marking my territory. Without a front-row seat, there was little chance that I would be able to hear the strange American accents or see the gunfights. Often, I'd be late to the movies and would get stuck in the back, hopping up and down to catch scattered glimpses of the flickering images, laughing when everyone else laughed, but not knowing why.

Right now, the screen showed only static, the strange jumbled hissing of black and white specks violently merging together. Amidst much grumbling, Fanfan, my cousin, was elected to hold the antenna. He climbed the nearby *sapele* tree and waved the thin wire around in the air.

"Wait!" I said as an image formed itself out of the random hissing, then disappeared. "Go back!"

I watched closely, giving him instructions, narrowing in on the cowboy clawing his way out of the background noise. Fanfan finally found the spot, then looked for a way to make himself comfortable. Tonight, he would only be able to listen to the movie and watch the glow of the tiny set reflected against the faces of his friends. It was a thankless job, but we'd all done it at one point or another.

The movie started, one we'd all seen countless times, and we crowded in for a better look.

"Shh," said somebody as the first gunshot rang out.

American movies were what kept us in line, week after week. If a mother decided that you had done something truly deserving of punishment, she would deny television time. It was an action with far-reaching repercussions. The Saturday movie was all we talked about on the five-mile walk to school Monday morning. Sister Antoinette, the teacher, would watch it at her own house and make references repeatedly throughout the day's lessons. If you hadn't seen the film on Saturday, the dismay lasted until at least Wednesday or Thursday of the following week. In the life of a child, this might as well have been a year.

In addition, so much of our slang derived from American sources—Ninja, Cobra, Stallone, Schwarzenegger—that if you didn't watch the movies, you could expect to be left out of countless conversations. Eventually, even our militias and political structures came to be shaped around these American idols.

"*Gringo!*" shouted Sazouka, throwing his head back in delight, and all the children laughed.

Gringo was what the bad guys called *mundelé*, and it made us happy to know that other people in the world had special names for the white man. The sounds of gunfire filled the air, and all the boys giggled to themselves and pushed and talked about what they would do when they had their own guns.

"Pow," said Sazouka.

"Pow," I said.

"Tchic! Voumbouka!"

The cold water hit my head like a fist and I sat up, sputtering. My mother smiled, holding an empty bucket. My grandmothers, Mama Loukoula and Mama Ntsiangani, nodded, the latter kicking my leg.

I was late for school. Again.

Hopping up, I stood still as my mother flattened my hair and hung the *ardoise*, the blackboard, around my neck. She shoved a piece of charcoal into my hand and kissed my forehead.

"You come back with this filled, do you hear me?" she said. "Every time you write something down, you remember it. The man who writes will be remembered forever. The man who talks is forgotten."

"Okay," I said, heading for the door. She always said these things before I went to school.

Mama Ntsiangani followed me outside, a machete in one hand and a half-burned cigarette in the other. She began chopping wood, grunting as the sun rose, and the strange sounds followed me deep into the jungle.

It was a five-mile walk to the baobab tree where school was taught. The tree was large and hollow and, when it rained, would allow all the students and Sister Antoinette to fit comfortably inside. I caught up to Loko, Bakala, and Taty, laughing and quoting Schwarzenegger movies.

I liked these boys because they hated school as much as I did. I'd skipped school only once in my life. My mother found out and told Pépé (who was illiterate himself), Mama Loukoula, and Mama Ntsiangani, and I'd been beaten with sugarcane until my blood ran thick. Now I went, but didn't enjoy it.

There is nothing more powerful than a man with knowledge.

I knew my mother meant well, but to a young boy, nothing was more exciting than hunting or fishing. Some days, when the village was hungry, we would have to miss school in order to hunt small game for our families. If the hunger pains weren't especially bad, I almost always enjoyed this more than my lessons.

"You'll never guess what happened to my Pépé," I said to the boys as I caught up, breathlessly interrupting them.

"He got drunk again?" Taty laughed.

"Yes," I said, "but listen." The boys quieted down, and the only sounds were the crunching of leaves under our feet and the chatter of birds. "He was visiting all of his palm trees two nights ago, collecting the wine."

"How many trees does he have?" asked Loko.

"At least a hundred," said Taty, shuffling his feet in the moist dirt.

My grandfather, Pépé, would use a rope made of roots to climb to the tops of palm trees and leave cups to collect the sweet palm wine. Every so often, he would go from tree to tree, collecting his prizes and getting extremely intoxicated. This habit was well known around the village.

"He got drunk and fell asleep in the middle of the jungle, next to the river. When he woke up, a boa constrictor had swallowed his leg all the way up to his waist!"

The boys laughed and jumped up and down. I smiled, quieting them.

"So my Pépé stared at the boa constrictor, who couldn't go any farther, and said, 'You should have started at my head.' And then he pulled out his knife and cut both of the snake's eyes out. He slit the boa's throat like this." I mimed cutting around my thigh with a knife, severing the imaginary snake's head from its body. "And then he took the boa home for soup!"

Taty shook his head. "Your grandfather is crazy."

"He tells me to always carry a knife."

"I guess so!" said Bakala. "And maybe you shouldn't drink any of the palm wine!"

The boys laughed. It was good advice.

To this day, I have had only one sip of alcohol.

CHAPTER 2

The first time I saw a white man was on a golf course.

I stared, impressed by the muscular arms of this stranger, by his easy, confident gait, by the power he exuded. Never before had I seen a man carry himself in this way.

His shoes were gleaming white and the crease in his trousers was so sharp that I could have sliced a mango on it. It seemed to me that he was dressed for a date or a ceremony, not to play golf.

The other boys ran over to the lakes, but I held back, apprehensive, excited.

He was joined by two other men, dressed in similar clothes and colors. They laughed and patted one another on the back and smoked cigarettes, waving their golf clubs around as if they were made of twigs.

These were men who I'd expected to see only on the television or in my imagination—not this close. Not in my hometown.

"Tchic! Come on!" shouted Taty, and I ran to join the others before the first ball landed with a resounding *ploop*.

After years of watching the older boys come back from the courses with fistfuls of money, I'd finally been allowed to participate in the games. The white men would show up and hit balls into the water, sometimes on purpose, sometimes not. We would race each other, diving into the lakes, holding our breath, hoping to come up with a white-dimpled sphere or two. If we did, we'd run back to the men, breathlessly returning the balls in exchange for a few francs. It was good fun, but at seven years old, it was also my only hope of earning any money at all.

The men laughed as we ran and dove, our naked bodies shimmering in the warm waters of the resort. Those who spoke our language called us *"mwana ya ngando"* or "crocodile kids." Sometimes, they would pick us up, smiling and letting us touch their hair. I remember patting the head of this one man, twisting the thin billowy strands of gold between my fingers, feeling the sinews and muscles tensing in his arms as he held me. He laughed, his teeth blinding white, his eyes a piercing blue. I wondered if everything he saw was coated with a blue tinge and resolved to ask my mother this vexing question.

"How can I be like you?" I said in my best French.

He smiled and put me down, playfully slapping the back of my head. "You're never going to be like me," he said. "You have to be an American before you can become a Marine."

"What is a Marine?" I asked.

He replied, the smile never leaving his face. "It's too complicated for an African boy."

"But what is it?"

"Why, we're the saviors of the world," he said.

"Like *Star Wars*?"

He thought for a moment, then said, "Yeah. Like *Star Wars*."

"I want to be like you," I said again.

He laughed, turned me around, and gave me a little push. "Not a chance. Now get back over there."

I ran back to the lake to wait for the next errant ball, the sun beating down upon us in waves, the men pointing and laughing as we chased their mistakes.

We began going out to the Djoué River to watch the white tourists play. We stared, openmouthed, as they rode motor scooters across the river, gaped as they kicked off their skis and skipped barefoot across the water.

It was magic.

It was power.

I couldn't get enough of it.

I hid in the bushes, watching as they took out frozen pieces of meat and threw them onto open flames.

"What is that?" whispered Loko.

"I think it's a chicken," I said.

"Not a real chicken."

"I don't know. Maybe."

"No. Not a real chicken."

I never tired of the adventure or the constant surprises. Bottles of milk. Real milk. Ours was either powdered or warm and sticky from the teats of the goats. These strangers drank cold milk in the middle of the jungle as if it were an everyday activity. Endless supplies of it.

And the shoes! All *mundelé*—even the littlest ones—wore shoes, no matter where they went.

"Do you think it makes them walk faster?" asked Bakala.

"Maybe," I said doubtfully, "but they can't be comfortable."

"Or all those clothes on your body," added Lema.

"Then why do they do it?" I asked.

Loko shook his head. "Because of their chicken skin. The sun would burn them, the bugs would eat them. They have to wear these things so they don't get injured. They don't have strong skin like us."

We all nodded. This seemed to make sense.

They would leave such amazing things behind after their excursions, and I remember the excitement we'd feel as we rummaged through their garbage cans. Incredible treasures like water containers made of hard plastic or strange metallic cups with ridged handles. There was no end to the things we could find if we dug deep enough. Every night during *Mbangala*, or the hot season, we would return with our prizes and present them proudly, beaming as our parents examined the day's haul.

"Why would they get rid of this?" wondered my mother, turning over an unopened container of fresh water. I could only shake my head and smile, happy to study this mystery with my mother. The garbage cans of golf courses, riverbanks, and *mundelé* houses in the nearby village—these were the places I found the greatest treasures of my youth.

Remote-control cars.

Electronic games.

Bicycles.

It became our goal to befriend as many of the *mundelé* children as possible.

The only toys I'd ever played with were the ones constructed by my older brothers and sisters. Now, staring at the incredible array of gadgets and equipment carried around by nearly every white child, my mind began to spin, my mouth to water.

We became bold in our approaches, striding right up to the whites sitting along the banks of the Djoué. Many of them spoke French, so we were able to communicate without difficulty, and when in doubt, we found that a large smile would go a long way. More often than not, they would laugh and offer us anything we asked for, grinning and taking pictures of us as we rummaged through their boxes. It became an understood exchange—we'd pose for the bright flashing cameras, exposing our naked African butts, and they'd bring toys for us to play with.

Many of these activities, we kept secret from our parents. Our whole lives, we'd been given the impression that white people were gods, that the French had given us life. After all, they were the ones who had come to Africa and taught us to read and write, given us government, taught us civility. Everything the French touched was gold, but everything we touched was nothing. It was like seeing perfection from a distance, like living in the shadow of freedom. Still, children have no respect for history, and we were shameless in our quest for fun and excitement.

We became experts in knowing when and where to find *mundelé*, and in knowing which ones were likely to have the best toys.

One of our favorite games was football, what Americans call soccer. We'd take a hollowed coconut and wrap it in plastic, kicking it with our bare feet across the sticks and sand. We usually went down and played at a local park that was a favorite hangout for many of the richer families in the area. If no one showed up, we played football. If they did, there was no telling what incredible toys we might have access to.

One day, a strange boy showed up at the park while we were kicking the coconut around. He was dressed in all the proper apparel, even down to the cleats and shin guards. He carried a real soccer ball that looked as if it had never touched the ground. Staring at us, he slowly set the ball on the ground and halfheartedly kicked at it.

We played for a few more minutes, watching this *mundelé* out of the corners of our eyes, waiting to see if he had other toys with him. He stayed in a small corner of the park, kicking his regulation ball forward and backward, running across the ground in his black spiked shoes.

"Hey," I shouted.

He looked up.

"Come over here and play with us."

"Bring your ball," shouted Lema.

He smiled, picked up his ball, and ran over.

"What's your name?" I said.

"Gervais," he said, out of breath from the short jog.

"Do you want to play with us?"

He nodded.

"I'm Tchicaya," I said. "You can be on my team."

We stood there, six naked African boys and one *mundelé* in a full football uniform. One by one, we all began to smile.

· · ·

We became inseparable.

People began to expect us to arrive in pairs. If you wanted to find Tchicaya, all you had to do was look for Gervais, or vice versa.

His French was perfect, eloquent, measured, and I attempted to sculpt my voice like his, form my words in his accent. He was half-black and half-white, which, in the Congo, made him *mundelé*. In America, I came to learn, it is the opposite. His mother was a beautiful Russian woman named Olga, who accepted everything my friends and I did with a quiet smile. She also never greeted us without first offering a piece of candy or a cookie. We loved her immediately.

And the toys . . . Gervais had everything a child could ever want!

Board games, electronics, remote-control vehicles, balls, bats, gloves, fishing poles, gadgets, gizmos, things even he couldn't figure out how to work.

He lived nearly ten miles away, and during the summer, it became a habit for me to walk to his house in the morning and run back at night, racing the rapidly falling sun. The jungle was not a safe place to be after dark, and my mother was not a safe person to talk to if I was ever late.

We would walk through the jungles of Matsimou, talking for hours. I would regale him with tall tales of my father, who'd been away on military training in Romania ever since my birth. I would tell him of the strongest hunters in our village, how they could kill a leopard with their bare hands. I would tell him about my brothers and sisters and their crushes and hopes and dreams. And he would listen, nodding thoughtfully.

This *mundelé* was my best friend, my closest companion. We came from different worlds, but there is no racism in children and we quickly grew to love each other.

. . .

"Want to come to my house for lunch tomorrow?" asked Gervais as we marched out of the jungle.

"All of us?" I said.

Gervais shrugged. "Whoever you want. The four of you can come. My mom said it's okay to invite as many people as I want." I looked at the other boys, all of us struggling to contain our excitement. My mouth twitched, imagining the foods I'd be stuffing into my face in less than a day. "Do you have to check with your mom?"

I spat on the ground and rubbed it into paste with my foot. "I don't have to check with anybody. We can come. I know it."

Gervais smiled. "Okay. I'll tell my mom you're all coming."

As he ran to his mother's waiting car, the four of us began to laugh and jump around. Eating a meal with *mundelé*! There was no one in the village who wouldn't be jealous.

The next day, we showed up at Gervais's door and waited until his mother came to answer it. I'd been to his house many times, but we'd always played outside, so I had never actually gone in before. I carefully wiped my feet on the rug, as I'd seen Gervais do. His mother smiled, and the other boys followed my example. We'd been playing, so dirt and mud caked our naked bodies as we slowly stepped onto the gleaming wooden floors of the main room.

It was enormous.

Paintings covered the walls and colorful rugs were carefully positioned every few feet. The house smelled of cinnamon, and my mouth watered in anticipation. Gervais ran down the staircase, smiling.

"*Salut!*" he said and we waved, awkward in our new surroundings. The floor felt strange against my feet—cold and hard.

His mother led us from room to room, explaining what everything was for, where everything went.

"This is where Bony sleeps," she said, opening the door to a gigantic room.

I tried to keep my mouth from dropping open, but couldn't help it. The dog slept inside the house. It had its own room.

In my village, animals stayed outside. I mentally recorded everything so I could report back to my mother. She wouldn't believe me. I'd have to get the other boys to support my story so she wouldn't think I was making the whole thing up.

"What's that?" I asked, pointing to a large plate on the floor.

Gervais's mother smiled, shutting the door. "Her food bowl."

The dog had its own plate. I was beginning to feel a little dizzy. Even I didn't have my own plate. Even I didn't have my own room.

Bony walked up, apparently upset that we were intruding on her space.

"Sit," said Gervais's mother, and the dog sat.

I shook my head. The white man told animals what to do, and the animals listened. It was beyond anything I could have imagined.

"Go away," she said, and the dog lowered its head and walked toward the back of the house.

I was careful not to make eye contact with the other boys. I thought my head might explode. Truly, *mundelé* was magic.

Gervais pointed us to the enormous television in the center of the room. It was easily ten times bigger than the one we used to watch our cowboy movies.

"Wow," I said.

"Watch," he said, and picked up a tiny black stick. He pointed this at the television and pressed a button.

The screen growled and sprang to life, and the four of us murmured in shock. It was in *color*. Vibrant pictures, not much different from the world around us, played in front of our eyes. The images were so clear that they could have been inside the huge box itself and I never would have been able to tell the difference.

"Color," said Bakala.

The rest of us watched silently, thinking that we could stay in this house forever.

My brothers and sisters were going to be so jealous.

In the dining room, we stared as Gervais's mother gestured for us to sit. Eight chairs were placed around a dark wooden table.

We looked at each other. In our eight years of existence, none of us had ever sat at a table for dinner, and we had assumed that we would be eating on the floor as we normally did. Gervais smiled and climbed onto one of the chairs, his chest barely reaching the table. I hopped up on the seat across from him, my heart thumping, my bare butt scratching against the fibers of the cushion.

Gervais's mother disappeared into the kitchen, leaving us to sit in silence, waiting for the meal to begin. No one spoke, but I saw Gervais grinning.

After a few minutes, she returned carrying a small container of oily liquid and a large bowl of water. She had a towel draped over her arm.

"Here," she said, extending the bowl toward me. "You must wash."

Wash, I thought, surprised. *She must think I'm too dirty to sit on her nice chairs. Maybe I offended her by coming to her home with so much mud on my body.* I plastered a serious, apologetic expression onto my face.

"Here?" I said.

She nodded and extended the smaller container. "I brought soap for all of you."

"This is soap?" I said, staring doubtfully at the strange oil.

She smiled and squeezed a tiny bit into my hands. It smelled of flowers.

I reached into the bowl, my eyes widening as I encountered warmth. Only *mundelé* used warm water. I smiled, cupped my hands, and poured a large handful of water over my head.

"No!" shouted Gervais's mother, but it was too late. Water was everywhere. It dripped off my body in brown rivulets, falling in streams onto the white stitching of the chair. Droplets littered the carpet. I stared up at her.

"Your hands," she said. "You need to wash your hands. For lunch."

I felt my cheeks begin to burn. I had never been asked to wash only my hands. I opened my mouth to apologize, but she just shook her head. "Wash your hands. I'll dry the water."

I stuck my arms back into the warm water, watching the clouds of dirt spiral around the bowl. I could have kept my hands in that water forever, rubbing them over and over again with that magical liquid soap. In my village, we bathed with sand from the river, using it to scrub the grime off our bodies. This strange soap smelled of perfume and felt smooth like palm oil. I smiled, even though the heat on my cheeks reminded me of my mistake.

I resolved to wash my hands again after lunch and to rub that soap all over my body so I would smell good the whole way home.

Soon, the table was laden with bowls of salad, fine cuts of meat, fresh vegetables, and a strawberry cake. I stared at the food, swallowing more and more to control the watering of my mouth. My arm moved toward the nearest dish, but I stopped myself, remembering to look around first. Gervais's brother came into the room and took a seat across from me, beside Gervais. Their father, a black man who acted like *mundelé* and worked in a bank, entered last and sat at the end of the table across from his wife. The four guests sat side by side on plush chairs, our dirty legs dangling against the polished wood. Gervais's father picked up the bowl of salad and spooned some onto one of the three plates in front of him. He picked up a fork and stabbed a raw tomato, placing it gently into his mouth. He looked at his wife and let a slight smile play across his face.

I'd never seen anyone eat a raw vegetable. Everything my mother made was boiled, cooked, heated. It seemed reckless and exciting, but I couldn't quite bring myself to risk it. Raw lettuce, raw carrots, raw tomatoes—the crisp crunch of the vegetables in Gervais's mouth made me smile.

In front of me, a large plate sat beneath a smaller plate, which sat beside an even smaller plate. A folded napkin lay on top, and a glass full of clear water was to my right, tiny beads of moisture dripping down its sides. Not only had I been given my own plate— I'd been given three of them! And they had provided me a blanket for my hands! My mother would never believe any of this, and I wished that she were there, sitting beside me. It didn't make any sense. If everything went to one stomach, what was the point of separating the food as you ate it? I made a mental note to ask Gervais this question the next time we were alone.

The plates were almost at chest level, and I was nervous to reach up, afraid that I would break something, scared that I would drop food onto the already damp rug below. It was awful, having so many delights in front of me, but being too nervous to take them!

I picked up my fork, staring at it, observing the others out of the corner of my eye. How should I hold it? The metal was cool and heavy against my fingers, and I suddenly felt clumsy. Why did *mundelé* use such things after washing? Was it not faster to use hands and fingers? Stabbing the food, putting it onto the fork or the spoon, cutting it with a knife—the process was unnecessarily complicated, and it forced them to eat so slowly! The other boys appeared just as perplexed as me, and fiddled anxiously with their forks or spoons.

"What would you like to eat?" asked Gervais's mother, reaching over and grabbing the largest of my plates.

The strawberry cake was staring at me. There had never been an opportunity to taste such extravagant *mundelé* treats before,

and the smell was overpowering everything else in the room. I
pointed to it.

"Cake?" she said, cocking her head. She looked at her husband,
who shrugged. Had I done something wrong? She looked back at
me. "That is an excellent idea, Tchicaya." She cut a large piece of
cake and lifted it onto my plate. "Perhaps we should all start with
dessert tonight. Who wants a piece of cake?"

Everyone raised their hands, even Gervais's father, and I took
a bite of the softest, sweetest bread I'd ever tasted. I smiled and
grunted my appreciation.

"Good?" she said, lifting a bite to her mouth.

"It's the best thing I've ever had in my life," I said, truthfully.

She smiled. "I'm glad to hear that. Eat up. There's plenty."

And I did, slowly stuffing my mouth with succulent meats
and boiled vegetables. I quickly gave up on the fork and knife
and began using my hands to pile these delicious treats into my
mouth. I pulled my feet up onto the chair, giggling as I felt my
stomach pushing against my thighs. I worried that it would take
me until the next day to walk home with this much food in my
body.

Bite by bite, they chatted and sipped and chewed while I
stayed quiet, eating and listening. In my village, cooking was a social event, but eating was something done as efficiently as possible.
In Gervais's world, it appeared that the opposite was true. There
was a discipline, a structure to their eating, specific rituals and
meaning and purpose behind their movements that I could not
immediately discern.

I wondered if all *mundelé* lived this way.

I wondered why Gervais and I had such different lives, though
we lived so close to each other.

Bony poked her head into the dining room and stared at the
strangers one last time before being sent away.

·   ·   ·

Every boy in my village learned to swim, fish, use a spear, and paddle a canoe. These were the things I taught Gervais.

In return, he taught me about something called cartoons.

Tom and Jerry was our favorite. It became a ritual—every afternoon, after Gervais got out of his *mundelé* school, I would meet him at his house and he would put in the nearly worn-out tape while we decided what to play with that day. The seemingly limitless pranks never ceased to amaze me. The way they ran, the way they talked—I couldn't get enough of it.

The other show that Gervais and I grew to love was an adventure program about a boy named Tom Sawyer. Here was a *mundelé* with my life! Tom spent his days swimming and fishing, avoiding school, making fun of grown-ups and falling in love with Becky Thatcher.

These were things I could understand.

We were in the den one afternoon watching Tom Sawyer. I was silently mouthing the words while Gervais spun a remote-control car around the wooden floor.

Gervais's mom came into the room holding some clothes.

"Tchicaya, do you want these?" she asked.

I stared at the bright red pair of shorts.

"Well?"

I sat there.

"Here, try them on." She handed them to me, and I stood, feeling the rough fabric between my fingers. I bent over and slipped one leg in.

"This way," she said, turning the shorts around. Gervais smiled, watching silently from the corner, the car remote dangling from his hands.

I nodded, pulling them up. She fastened them and took two steps backward. "A perfect fit!"

Gervais clapped, and I smiled, spinning around, showing off all sides of my first pair of shorts. I glanced toward the television and saw my reflection standing beside Tom Sawyer. My new clothes were even better than his! I felt my grin widen even farther.

"I have other clothes for you, too, Tchicaya. Things Gervais won't wear anymore. They would look great on you."

Wide-eyed, I took the gifts with thank-you after thank-you after thank-you.

That evening, I came home wearing my new clothes. My mother looked at them, then hugged me. She said nothing.

I took off the shorts.

At eight years old, I was continually getting into fights, always causing trouble. I didn't mean anyone harm, but this was fun for me, playful.

If I ever complained to my uncle, Miekoutima, that someone had beaten me up, he would slap me across the back of the head, turn me around, and send me back outside.

I quickly learned to finish what I started.

I quickly learned not to be afraid of anyone.

My uncle convinced my family that I needed an outlet, somewhere to spend all that excess energy, something to keep me out of trouble. With my grandparents' blessing, he signed me up for martial arts classes—an African style called "Mpongo."

The first day my uncle dropped me off, I stared at the circle of sand and bit my lip. The other kids stared at me. I wanted to be somewhere else, anywhere else.

The instructor brought me into the ring with a much older boy, and I proceeded to swallow half the sand in the area. I was slammed onto the ground, hit, twisted, bruised, and battered for over an hour.

I limped to my uncle's car, crying all the way home.

The next day, my uncle sent me back again.

And again.

Mpongo became part of my life. After a year of this, I didn't feel right unless I exercised every day. Cuts turned into calluses. Soreness turned into strength. Fear turned into confidence.

I would teach Gervais the moves of the snake, or the leopard, or the monkey. He would take off his shoes and shirt when he played with us, but I noticed he always left his shorts on.

Gervais became quick, lithe, agile. For a man of the Congo, he was nowhere near capable, but for a *mundelé*, he was amazing.

He became like a brother to me.

I assumed that we would be friends forever.

CHAPTER 3

Come with me. We're going to meet your father."

I stared at my aunt, Mama Nicole, not comprehending her statement.

"Come on," she said. "Your father is back and you should meet him."

I ran to get my red shorts, feeling the comforting scratch against my thighs.

"Pack your things," Mama Nicole called out, and I gathered a few of my belongings into a plastic bag. Would I be staying the night?

My father.

It had been eight years since he'd left. I'd never met him.

My father.

Suddenly, I wished I were taller, stronger, different. Mama Nicole smiled at me as we walked down the dusty roads of Brazzaville. I wished for my nervousness to disappear. Why had he waited so long?

"Where are we going?" I asked.

"Potopoto."

The sun was hot, and my shorts began to itch as they rubbed against my butt.

What would my father be like?

What would he look like?

Sweat formed and rolled across my body. Mama Nicole walked with a steady gait, a neutral expression on her face. Had she ever met my father?

All I knew was that he was a lieutenant in the National Police and had been away, training in Romania for many years.

We traveled over ten miles before stopping at the outskirts of Potopoto. I stared up at the minarets obscuring the skyline and listened as a strange voice sang unrecognizable words over a loud-speaker. The city was quiet.

"Shh," said Mama Nicole and stepped forward. "Keep your head down."

I did.

We stood in front of an enormous apartment complex while Mama Nicole examined the scrap of paper in her hand. She grabbed my arm, and led me to a staircase. Higher and higher we climbed, three flights of stairs, my anxiety growing with every step. Only rich men lived this high off the ground. Did my father live like *mundelé*? I replayed everything I'd learned from Gervais over the last few years, the placement of the forks, the proper way of greeting a stranger.

My aunt knocked on the door.

"Come in."

She smiled at me, turned the knob, and stepped into a carpeted living room. Children played on the floor.

"Is your father home?" asked Mama Nicole.

The kids shook their heads.

"Ah," said Mama Nicole and looked over at me. Something flipped through her eyes. Finally, she pulled me over to a corner of the room. "Wait here," she said. "I'll be back."

She walked out of the apartment, leaving me alone on the strange carpet. The other kids stared and played around me. After a few minutes, an older girl walked up.

"I'm Mireille," she said.

"I'm Tchicaya," I said.

"Are you our brother?"

"I think so."

"Okay.

She walked off. Another girl took her place. "I'm Brigitte."

"Tchicaya."

"How old are you?"

"Eight."

No one else approached me. I sat against the wall for over two hours, growing increasingly despondent. Where was Mama Nicole? What had happened to her? Was I stuck in the apartment with a group of strangers?

The doorknob turned, and I stood, ready to leave. Instead of Mama Nicole, a towering man with a gigantic mustache entered. He looked around the room, stopping on me.

"This is Tchicaya," said Brigitte. "He's our brother."

The man nodded and walked over, scanning me from head to toe. I nodded back, unsure what we were agreeing upon.

"You are my son?" he said.

"Yes," I said, straightening my back as much as I could, awaiting his judgment with a stoic expression.

Still staring, the man opened his mouth and shouted, "Kids! Everyone come here. There's someone I'd like you to meet."

Slamming doors, trampling footsteps, murmuring voices, and then we were surrounded by children. I scanned the room, quickly adding up the brown bodies. Twelve, not including myself.

I rocked from foot to foot. My father stepped closer, his muscles evident even in the semithreadbare shirt he wore.

"I want you to meet your new brother. He—" Here, he paused and leaned in close to me. "What's your name?" he asked.

I cleared my throat. "Tchicaya," I said. "Just like you."

He frowned, and I tried to keep the disappointment off my face. Was he embarrassed that someone like me shared his name? Had I done something wrong?

"That won't do," he said. "We'll call you Tchico instead. Is that okay?" And here, he smiled and winked at me. A rush of joy swept through my body.

Tchico.

My father had given me a nickname.

"Tchico is going to be staying with us during the school months. Does everyone understand?"

The children nodded. There were six boys and six girls, nearly all of them older and taller than me.

I struggled for a consistent expression. Nervousness and excitement writhed inside my body, competing for dominance. I hitched up my red shorts and tightened the grip on my bag. Mama Nicole had left me. I was moving in with my father.

"Someone show Tchico to his room," said my father, patting me firmly on the back.

I had to fight to keep my mouth from dropping open. It was too strange to comprehend, and I found my body doing its best to laugh and cry at the same time.

Two boys came and smiled at me. I forced a smile in return, following them into a long hallway, counting the rooms as I went.

My father was a rich man, maintaining a third-story apartment with three bedrooms and an actual bathroom.

I felt unprepared for such a drastic move, and suppressed a flash of anger at my aunt.

"Where are you from?" asked one of the boys.

"Matsimou," I said.

"I'm from Brazzaville, too."

I smiled at him. "Do you visit?"

"During vacations we all go back and stay with our mothers. We're only here for the school year."

"Oh," I said, nervous that I now had two homes to worry about.

"It's not so bad," said the first as he walked into the last room on the right. "This is where we stay."

I forced another smile.

I hitched up my shorts and followed my new brothers into my new room.

Life was suddenly moving very, very quickly.

PART 2
LE FILS DE L'HOMME

Education is the most powerful weapon which you can use to change the world.

—NELSON MANDELA

Brazzaville, Congo
August 19–20, 2004

Thursday–Friday

The road is a disaster and the potholes begin to numb my body with their repetitive thumping. The drive reminds me more of an Iraqi desert than the Congo, but somehow the sand has been replaced by thick, stagnant water. There is no more irrigation here, and liquids sit festering in the fierce heat. The driver swerves this way and that, but you can't avoid an enemy who is on all sides. My thighs hurt from holding my legs up, but there is no place to set them down. Rough driving has ripped holes in the floorboards, and I watch the ground crawl by underneath my hovering feet. A journey that would take fifteen minutes in America takes over an hour. My impatience grows.

My mind takes in images of this strangely unfamiliar city and slowly the changes become more apparent. Bullet holes mark the doorframes, windows are smashed. Garbage rises high alongside the roads.

I wave to a group of boys on bicycles and try to contain my nervous energy.

Finally, I see the street sign in the distance.

Avenue Mayamaya.

Memories of childhood flash before me in frozen pictures, and the sand-covered street becomes a whiteboard of images.

Soccer.

Dzango.

Silicoté.

Wrestling.

War.

I stop remembering and focus on the fast-approaching house. The walls are gray stone, the frame still exposed from the fire so many years before. I spot my mother's room, the living room, the kitchen. Children I don't recognize sit in the front yard playing cards. They look up, find nothing of interest, and return to their game.

My heart reaches out to this shell of a home, this sprawling concrete monstrosity, and I am in love all over again.

For safety reasons, my visit is a surprise.

"Thank you, Mama Nicole," I say to my aunt.

"Go," she says, and I step out of the taxi, watching as realization slowly dawns on the faces of the older children.

They run inside, only to return again with four of my brothers and sisters.

Kinata comes out first, his face lighting up in the bright sun. Sandra and Mabakani follow, their hair gleaming, their teeth white. They've grown strong and beautiful, and my heart sings. Sazouka runs down the steps of the house, wearing a tie despite the heat, and wraps me in his arms.

"You're here," he says, squeezing the life out of me.

"Ya-Tchic!" shout my cousins, screaming with glee. I can't help but smile. My family, whom I have missed so much, whom I have dreamed of for so long, whom I have stayed alive for, are here, touching me, hugging me, crying over me. I am the eighth of sixteen children, but few of my siblings remain in the Congo. We have spread across the world like seeds blown by the wind. Unfamiliar young faces pour out of the house, surrounding my legs, poking me, shouting.

"Where is Mama?" I ask. "Where is Mama?"

The teenagers scream, and the children not old enough to understand the circumstances shout along with them. It's an event. Something is happening.

I walk into the house, overwhelmed by the familiarity of the smell, the feel of the air, the sounds of padding feet on the dusty floor.

My mother limps out of the back room, a wrap tied around her waist, only one sandal on. She hurries, dragging her foot.

"Mama—" I say, my voice breaking on the word.

She comes to me as if I were risen from the dead, her arms outstretched, and I grab her, pressing her body to my own.

Tears coat my cheeks as my mother pulls my head down and murmurs into my ear. I know her dreams have come true on this day. I know this, because our dreams are one.

Five minutes pass in an instant until the children pull us apart, anxious for stories, eager for gifts. My mother stares at me, pride in her eyes. She keeps touching my arms, my chest, unable to believe their size. When I left, I was slight, scrawny, young.

"You are like Rambo," I hear someone say.

The family still crowds close, touching me, squeezing my skin, hugging my body, and I feel like a king.

"Bring him a chair," someone shouts.

"Ya-Tchic, tell us a story," says another.

The clamoring begins, and we all move to the back room, away from the street. More of the family has arrived now, about twenty-five people in total. They sit on the floor and stare at me as a *ta-bouré*, a long, flat bench, is brought in. I shake my head. "I will sit on the floor like everyone else."

No one disagrees.

We sit.

Kinata says, "You talk like *mundelé*."

I shrug, unable to escape what's happened to my voice. I live among the whites now. I don't doubt that I've become like them in more ways than I can fathom. That is one of the reasons I've come back.

The stories flow out, unprompted. The magic sliding doors and self-rising stairs. The food, the cities, the people, the fashions. There is so much to say, and I suddenly feel the press of time against my chest.

I tell stories until almost midnight, stumbling over phrases, asking for help with forgotten words. The children laugh at this hulking man amongst them without the language for even the simplest of objects. My mother just sits, staring quietly, the largest of smiles hung upon her face like a painting.

My voice grows tired, and I realize that we're all reluctant to end the night. It's too perfect, and if we disperse, the dream may never come again. But as the children begin breaking into yawns, it spreads to my own mouth and my mother slaps her leg.

"Tchic has traveled far and must be tired," she says. "Everyone to their rooms. My son needs to rest."

The grumbling begins and my cheeks ache. I'm not used to smiling. My mother grabs hold of me again and I squeeze her back.

"How's your foot?" I ask her.

She shakes her head and pulls me into a room where a bed has been set up for me. It's covered by mosquito netting, and has a thin mattress lying on it.

"No, Mother. Let the children sleep with the netting. I'll sleep on the floor with the others."

She shakes her head and pushes me onto the bed, smiling, proud that she can offer her son this luxury. "You're not used to the malaria anymore," she says. "This will keep you safe."

I know better than to argue, and watch her limp away, my heart swelling with a confusing mixture of love and anguish. I've missed her more than I'm able to say, but she is my mother and she knows this without the exchange of words.

The bed is awkward for me, painful, uncomfortable, even though it's more luxurious than anything I ever had growing up. Still, my exhaustion is great and I quickly fall into a dreamless sleep, the sounds of Africa flitting against my consciousness like down feathers against my skin.

The rooster crows and I stare at the beam of light entering the room, noting where it hits the floor.

Six o'clock.

The house is quiet, and the ghosts of past memories begin to scurry through my consciousness like rats exposed to the sun. I drop to the ground and do fifty push-ups, loosening the kinks from my weary body.

Grandmother Loukoula is outside, clearing the front yard with a *ballet*. I try to take it from her, but I am a *mopaya*, a guest, and am no longer allowed to help with such menial chores. I watch as she waters the ground to prevent the dust from flying up, and smile.

It's the small details of living that create the sensation of home.

A few of the younger children arrive with two full buckets from the river. It's important to get water early, before the river is dirtied with animals and other people from farther upstream. The same water is used for washing clothes, washing bodies, drinking, and cooking, so it's imperative that it be fresh. I reach for the buckets, intending to help my grandmother water the ground.

"No!" says a young cousin I'm meeting for the first time.

"It's for you," says another.

"We brought two, because one wouldn't be enough," giggles a third.

I grin, thanking them. Never before have I needed two buckets to clean myself, but the children are right. Things have changed.

I carry the water through the kitchen and into the outhouse, gagging at the smell. At least a hundred flies circle the hole, buzzing in and out, teasing the maggots that infest the piles of dung left by my family members. I squat over the hole, attempting to figure out how to get low enough without scraping my knees against the decrepit door. Holding myself up by wedging my elbows against the walls, I nearly pass out from lack of breath. I try to block out the sound of my falling shit.

It's strange the things you forget.

The walls of the "shower" come up only to the middle of my chest, and the children gather around as I scoop cup after cup from the quickly emptying buckets. I wash my body and my underwear, feeling the grime and dirt of travel sloughing away. I'm remembering the routine of life in the Congo, the feel, the flow, the ritual. Home is beginning to have a face again.

My mother is in the kitchen, and I grab her leg. It doesn't look good, but I maintain a neutral expression. She tries to shake me away. "Tell me," I say.

"They want to amputate," she says, not looking me in the eye. "But there is no safety here for such a procedure."

I put her foot down slowly, ashamed. I will save her. I'll get her to America, where she can receive proper treatment. For now, this is impossible.

I sit and force a smile as she brings me my breakfast.

There is no official United States embassy in Brazzaville, so I walk north to a tiny, cramped cubbyhole in Mpila where I find an American representative. He sits silently with a local man, smoking, surrounded only by papers and dust. They look up when I enter, but don't change expressions.

"I want to alert you to my presence," I say. "I'm an American Marine here in the Congo." This is something that I was instructed to do by my Marine unit commander, simply as a matter of pre-caution. I don't believe it to be necessary, but I do not want to disobey a direct order.

They mask their surprise well and make copies of my passport and military ID. They do not ask any questions.

"Be careful," they say.

I nod.

I walk home the long way through central Brazzaville and stare at the city where I grew up. A child's eyes are always colored with expectation and hope, and I cannot help but compare the sagging frames and third-world facilities to the shining perfection of America. No one is well served by comparing their past to their present, but the two are shoved together in close contrast here. It's difficult to dismiss the feeling that I've escaped, moved on, progressed. This is what I want for my family. This is what I want for the Congo, for Africa.

The bullet holes are many, the signs of progress few. Barefoot children chase one another around crumbling buildings. Aimless piles of rock dot the landscape like strange punctuation marks. People smile at me as I pass, but I can see the strain, feel the gears turning in their brains. It seems that my home is falling apart, that somehow, I was a key beam in the frame of this place—that by leaving so suddenly, I disrupted the very foundation on which it was built. I shake my head and return the smiles. I'm here to spread happiness. I'm here to spread love.

A woman walks past, a basket of cassava balanced on her head, a baby strapped to her back. With her free hand, she holds the tiny arm of her son, who, like her, is barefoot. I watch as they notice my Timberland shoes, and I wonder if I'll ever walk again without shoes on my feet. I wonder if I'm still able. Her head is held high, her eyes clear, but they are empty, lifeless, without hope. I walk on, strangely moved by the changes to my homeland. Food, water, shelter—all of these can come and go, but once hope leaves a region, it is dead.

I walk into the house, go to my suitcase, pull out my Marine uniform, and lay it on the bed. The dirt on the mattress suddenly stands out, the brown tint of the walls, the dust floating through the air. I sit beside my uniform and remove my shoe polish and cloth. My shoes are shined to a crisp gleam before I notice the audience I've attracted. They mimic my movements, fighting for space in the tiny room. I shine each of my uniform buttons until they are as blinding as miniature suns. I strip down to my shorts and T-shirt, then slip on my socks and shoes. My trousers follow, the wrinkles falling away into the sandy floor. I don't look around me, but I hear every breath, every murmur. The sleek lines of my blouse, my shirt, fit tightly around my chest, leaving little space for air or dirt. The ribbons press against my left breast and I tuck the shirt in, aligning the seam with my belt buckle. I pull on my dress coat and finger the tiny gilded eagles on the buttons.

As the cover (hat) grips my forehead in its cool, leather ringlet, the children stare, and I snap to attention, savoring the moment. The roof of my cap brushes the ceiling, and I feel that I've grown three feet in the last twenty minutes. I gaze at the reflection in the long mirror beside the door and see myself transformed.

I am a warrior.

The dusty walls have faded away, the dank air has dissipated. I am the mirror, and cannot look away from this strange image.

My mother enters the room and stops, stunned. A spoon drops from her hand, and she grabs her face.

"My son," she says, tears filling her eyes. I walk to her, the children parting around my legs like mist. This time, I do not cry. I grab her by both shoulders and look into her eyes. "My son," she says again.

She pulls me outside so that she can get a better look. I explain to her what my ribbons mean, taking the time to answer each and every one of her questions. I've been many places, fought many battles, seen many things. I want to impart all these memories to my mother's brain, for it is she who has made me.

"This is my expert rifle badge," I say.

"This is my expert pistol badge," I say.

"That is for marksmanship," I say.

She nods, though she doesn't understand the words. I think that maybe it is better if she never does.

Potopoto, Congo

1989

CHAPTER 4

Education occurs in two places.

Your home teaches you moral lessons, respect, and life skills. The streets and your peers teach you everything else.

At age eleven, I began carrying a pistol to school.

I did this because it was expected.

At recess, all the boys would gather around and brag about the weapons they had at home. Pistols. Rifles. AK-47s. RPGs. I quickly discovered that my father's name carried a great deal of weight in these conversations. As captain of the local police, my father was at the front of every military parade, the face of every military exhibition.

He would lead hundreds of soldiers through the streets of Brazzaville in Russian style, legs kicked straight out, arms swinging cleanly like hands on a clock. I rarely missed a parade, rarely missed the opportunity to see my father in his perfectly pressed uniform, his insignia gleaming brightly amidst the sun and camera flashes.

My father's reputation was my protection.

It also was a target on my back.

I constantly felt the need to prove myself in school, to show that I was more than the son of Tchicaya Missamou, that I was a man in my own right.

• • •

The tension in school was palpable, but few of us discussed it. We all knew what it was.

In less than a year, we would be considered men.

I was eleven years old.

I would go home to my grandparents' house, where I lived during the summers, and take part in the ritual designed to ensure that I was fit to be a man of the Mukongo Wa Boko tribe. Every boy, at some point between his eleventh and fourteenth birthdays, depending on the judgment of his father, would be subjected to this series of trials testing his hunting, swimming, and fighting strengths. It was rumored to be the most difficult thing a young man would ever go through. The women's trials were different, and were constructed around cooking, cleaning, childbirth, and running a household. These occurred when a woman reached marriageable age—usually around twelve or thirteen.

None of us talked about the upcoming test in anything but the vaguest of terms, for fear of displaying our nervousness.

Our guns could not help us in the jungle.

I was especially nervous because of my father's reputation. My performance would be a direct reflection on him. In effect, my father's parenting skills were being analyzed by the entire tribe.

I wasn't sleeping well.

One morning, my father grabbed me by the arm as I stepped into the bathroom.

"No more showers," he said.

I nodded, my chest tightening.

It was beginning. Boys were instructed not to bathe for a month before the trial, so their bodies would acclimate to the animal world. The best hunters were those who could blend into any surroundings. Animals could smell a clean human from a great distance, and our natural odors were the best camouflage we could ever develop.

My father began to pay more attention to me during this time, which served only to increase my anxiety. Maybe he wasn't confident in my abilities. Maybe he was worried that I would fail him.

"You're good with a slingshot, yes? Show me," he said, and handed me an old Y-shaped piece of wood wrapped with rubber. Heart pounding, I demonstrated the classic attack position.

"Good," he said, taking the slingshot back. "Very good."

There were three main weapons used by a hunter: the slingshot, the knife, and the spear. The slingshot was good for knocking monkeys or birds out of trees from a long distance, the spear for long-range face-to-face combat, and the knife for slitting the throat of your prey. I would be required to demonstrate proficiency in all of these weapons.

My dreams became filled with violence and death, with snarling animals and starlit hunts. Tom Sawyer gradually disappeared.

The day arrived and we set off. There were nearly thirty of us, accompanied by our fathers and a host of *Ndoki*, or medicine men. A train took us from Brazzaville to Loubomo, the third-largest city in the Congo. As we entered the region, we watched the dirt change from brown to yellow, mirroring our own rising fear. This was the farthest I'd ever been from my home. A bus took us from Loubomo to the outskirts of Mayombe, where we disembarked and continued on foot.

We headed into the heart of the Mayombe jungle, one of the fiercest in the world. It was stuck in a nearly permanent state of rainfall and, as a result, was overgrown with incredible amounts of tangled plant life. It hid some of the most dangerous animals in Africa, and I shuddered, knowing that I would be expected to face them alone. I wondered what Gervais would think if he knew what I was about to accomplish.

Hours passed as we marched deeper and deeper into the undergrowth, eventually stepping into a large clearing where a central wooden structure had been set up. In front of it was an enormous fire pit filled with glistening coals and piles of fresh wood.

My father placed his hand on my back.

An *Ndoki* gestured for everyone to gather around the clearing, then ignited the fire, replacing the rapidly fading sunlight with towering flames. The sound of the *bôda* echoed loudly in my ears as the dance of the warriors began.

Chills sprang up along my body, but I did not look to my father. An *Ndoki* strode to the front of the circle, his head shaved and his face painted, clothed only by a leaf across his crotch. He was the controller of the black magic, and I feared his power. In his right hand, he held a bottle of *tsabá*, or wine of the palm tree. In his left, he held a live black mamba, the deadliest snake in the jungle. It writhed and hissed against his arm, but the *Ndoki* paid it no notice, dancing and leaping around the fire in frenetic circles. The drums pulsed, driving him to greater heights of frenzied movement. The shadows danced around his limbs like birds.

The men began singing.

Mama Cria, hey hey.
Zambi ya poungou.
Mu koubu, ya tata.
Mu koubu, ya mama.

Their voices reached the sky and the fires licked the stars.

The *Ndoki* poured the wine into his mouth, then spat it into the face of the mamba. The snake hissed above the sound of the drums, twitching its tail in a strange counterpointed rhythm. My heart knocked against my chest as I clapped. The trees were dark shadows now, pressing in against the circle, and I imagined for a second that we were the last people on earth.

The yellow dust from the ground exploded in tiny puffs as other *Ndoki* joined in the dance, singing words straight from their guts, the words forming and erupting one by one.

Ya Tilouti
Ya santou
Amen

The boys joined the song, clapping along, wild-eyed in the firelight. We prayed to Ntiya, the god of the fire, and Vouala, the god of the rain. We asked for their blessings in the coming trials, we asked them to support us in our journey toward manhood. I pictured them high above us, examining our bodies and our souls, deciding if we were worthy to worship them in such a way.

The painted faces of the *Ndoki* whirled faster now, the sparks of fire shooting high into the air.

Time slowed.

I stared through the flames at the master *Ndoki*, an old man with the power to control the wind and rains. He sat still, his face the original painted mask of the tribe, and I felt the weight of his age. I imagined he stared directly at me, discussing my fate with the gods themselves.

I shuddered.

The dance grew.

Zambi ya poungou
Mamé
Ehey hey
Mama
Ehey hey

Time flew away until five or six hours had passed. The ground was hardened into gritty paste, and still the rain had not come. The fire burned as brightly as ever, and my voice was raw from singing and shouting.

The other boys were tired, fidgeting, ready to sleep, but I felt powerful.

I felt alive.

I clapped even louder, sang even harder. My father looked down at me again, surprised, and I sang the words with all my might.

Ah mon colonel
Muwashi
Ah mon general
Muwashi

I would not fail in this task.

I would leave as a man, or I would not leave at all.

The eldest *Ndoki* stepped to the front of the circle and held a squirming rooster in front of him.

The *bôda* grew quiet and we all leaned forward.

With his right hand, he grabbed a leg of the gurgling rooster and snapped it to the left with a sharp *crack*.

"When this rooster walks, your journey will be over," said the *Ndoki*, setting the injured bird on the ground and watching it flap its wings in helpless bursts.

Everyone nodded.

"Now sleep," said the *Ndoki*. "You have much training to accomplish."

CHAPTER 5

Two weeks passed in the blink of an eye.

We rose every morning with the sun and followed our fathers into the jungle. We swam in the rivers and tracked animals in the dense foliage of the Mayombe.

Every night, we gathered around the fire and learned the songs of our ancestors, singing and dancing to the pulsing beat of the *bôda*.

It was exhilarating.

It was exhausting.

My father was a man of few words, but when he spoke, I listened.

"Remember, son, a good warrior must not show fear. Read the leaves of the tree. Listen to the direction of the wind. You will discover your prey."

I would repeat his words to myself over and over again.

I knew that this was the most time I would ever spend with my father and forced myself to pay attention to every moment, every sound, every touch.

My muscles were tight, my hands raw.

I threw the spear thousands of times, climbed hundreds of trees, swam miles and miles through the waters of the Djoué.

The chief gathered us around the campfire.

"Your three-day test will begin tomorrow," he said. "You will be sent into the jungle on your own. You will hunt your prey. You will return as men."

We nodded, serious, fear no longer present. I would succeed. I knew this. I had no other choice.

Every child was given two chances to succeed at this trial. If the first three days ended without a kill, he was allowed to rest, then try again for a second three days. If he failed this second attempt, he would not be considered a man in the Mukongo tribe.

My father pulled me aside that night. "Tomorrow, we will rise early. You must succeed quickly. The other fathers are watching me. The other boys are watching you. Do you understand?"

"I'm ready, Papa."

He patted my head. "I know you are. Remember, a warrior fights stronger when he is not desperate. Kill on the first day. Do not leave it until the third, for you will not fight well with the pressure of time weighing you down."

I nodded, my knife gripped tightly between aching hands.

"Sleep. I will wake you."

I curled up beneath the stars, heart beating loudly in my chest. Tomorrow, I would fight in the jungle. Tomorrow, I would make my father proud. Tomorrow, I would become a man.

The stars twinkled in the fading smoke of the fire pit, and I forced my mind to relax. I knew I wouldn't sleep that night, but my muscles needed rest.

Somehow, my eyes found their way closed.

That night, I dreamed of cartoons and river rafts, of exploding dynamite and whitewashed fences.

"Tchico," said my father, shaking me gently. "Come. It is time."

The night was warm and sticky, the scent of burned embers rich in my nostrils. I stood, grabbing my spear, slingshot, and knife. I looked around the circle at all of the other boys and fathers still sleeping soundly. The sun had not yet risen.

I followed my father to the edge of the jungle.

"It is best to hunt animals before they wake. You can follow their trails, you can lay traps for them. They will not be prepared to fight after they have just woken. Do you understand?"

I nodded. He turned to me.

"You will succeed, Tchico. You are my son. Fight to win. Kill to survive. Look straight into the eyes of your prey as you are killing it. The eyes do not lie."

"Yes, Papa."

He squeezed my arms. "Go. I will watch to make sure you stay safe."

I turned away and stepped into the darkness of the jungle.

I walked for a while, calming my heart, slowing my breath.

There was plenty of time. I had to pick the perfect location.

I forced my eyes downward, using the training my father had given me. Scratches on the ground became footprints. Broken branches became trails. I felt the blood pumping hot in my veins.

When I was deep enough into the jungle, I stopped and scanned the area with a hunter's gaze, searching for a tree with easy access to neighboring branches. One that was tall enough to offer a complete view of the surroundings, but not too high to leap down from. One that would comfortably allow hours of stillness and silence.

There.

A mango tree stood a few meters away from a natural clearing, blending into the surrounding foliage. I gathered a few fallen bananas and scattered them around the base of the tree before climbing into its branches.

Then, I waited.

I knew my dad was somewhere nearby, following me, but could neither see nor hear him. The only sounds were the slowly wakening birds and the rustle of hidden animals taking their first steps of the day.

I sat.

Light began to creep in through the treetops, and I watched the leaves dancing in the growing breeze. I scanned the area upwind of me, where my scent wouldn't be as strong.

My breath caught in my throat.

A gorilla, one a little larger than me, ambled down the path I had spotted hours before. I forced my breathing to slow and tightened my grip around the spear, resting my slingshot on a nook in the tree branches.

Wait.

Wait.

A true warrior does not rush if he does not have to.

I had three days.

The gorilla walked down the path, clearly unaware that anyone was watching him. He had just woken and was probably looking for breakfast.

He sniffed the air. I did not breathe.

The bananas.

He ambled over, spotting the food I'd laid out for him.

An opportunity was presenting itself and I had to take advantage of it. Another one might not come.

I'm not ready, I thought.

A million reasons not to attack ran through my head. The size of the animal. The early hour. The danger. The fear.

But all of this trickled away as I gripped my spear and thought of my father watching nearby.

I was a warrior.

I waited for the gorilla to begin eating. An animal concentrating on food is not an animal that is aware of its surroundings. Enjoyment and comfort breed complacency.

He grabbed two bananas and stuffed them into his mouth.

He turned, scanning the ground for more food. I could see only his back, his finely muscled shoulders, and his sleek gray hair.

I held my breath.

Don't show fear.

Control your breathing.

Attack without hesitation.

I leaped, spear pointing downward.

Over five feet below, I landed on the back of the gorilla, thrusting my spear into the base of his neck. It was a perfect shot, but a gorilla is a mighty animal. He roared and spun around.

I clung to him, thrusting the spear deeper and deeper, smelling the blood pouring from the wound, listening to the wild ripping heartbeat of my prey. His breath erupted in ragged gasps, and I felt his legs spasm. I gave the spear one last twist and leaped down, facing him, staring him in the eyes.

Fear.

Confusion.

Anger.

The gorilla roared and stumbled toward me.

I pulled out my knife and leaped, staring him in the eye as I cut his throat.

His breath was hot against my face as I pushed the knife in, drawing more blood from my prey. His eyes were wide, full of fury and hate.

I felt his heartbeat against my chest, fading fading fading, and still I clung to him, tearing his hard flesh with every ounce of my strength.

Again the gorilla roared, weaker this time, and wrapped his arms around my body. I pulled my hands away, leaving the knife embedded in his neck, the spear in his back. I pushed against his throat, trying to choke him, struggling to close his airway.

I did not look away.

We were both fighting to win.

We were both killing to survive.

I pulled the knife out of his throat, releasing a red torrent onto my arms and face.

He looked at me and I saw the fear return.

I watched as he gave up.

My father was right.

Eyes never lie. They show weakness. They show desperation. They show death.

I stepped back as he sank to the ground, a moist rattle escaping his mighty body.

The silence of the jungle screamed against my ears as I stared at my conquered prey. His blood seeped into the jungle floor, coating a half-eaten banana.

In that moment, I resolved to never give up. I had seen first-hand the effects of despair.

I was fearless.

I was powerful.

I was a man.

My father strode up behind me, staring at the lifeless body. He turned me around, gazing at me with a serious expression. "*Tu es le fils de l'homme,*" he said.

You are the son of the man.

I hugged him.

We stayed there beside the body in silence, listening to the quiet caws of the birds and the rustling of nearby snakes. It was peaceful, the quiet after the war, the dawn after the storm. I took a deep breath, unable to believe that my trial had ended so quickly.

It was not yet eight o'clock on the first day and already I had felled my prey.

I did not smile, but my heart was filled with joy, for I knew that I had made my father proud.

"Come on," he said. "Pick him up."

I arrived at the circle, muscles aching, sweat pouring from my body. The village elders stared at the mighty gorilla and nodded approvingly.

I placed the animal by the fire pit and stepped back, lowering my head.

My father put his hand on my shoulder. "Go and wash," he said. "There is one more thing you must do."

I walked down to the river, no longer fearful of solitude. I stepped into the cool waters, gasping as the current whipped my aching legs. Kneeling, I picked up handfuls of sand and scrubbed the weeks of grime from my body.

Birds flew overhead and the sounds of nature filled my ears.

I imagined I was a snake shedding its skin, a butterfly emerging from its cocoon. I had entered the river as a boy, but was leaving as a man. My feet felt solid against the earth as I returned to the circle. My chest felt large.

When I arrived, the village elders were gathered around a long wooden table. The *Ndoki* were there, the eldest standing silently behind them.

My father approached. He shook my hand, handed me a wrap to put around my waist, then blessed me. "You must not show pain, Tchico," he said. "You must be brave."

I nodded, staring at the elders. The gorilla was gone.

"As long as you have suffered, you will never fear. Pain is your friend. It tells you that you are alive. The day you stop feeling pain is the day you are dead. Do you understand?"

"Yes," I said.

"You can't run from pain. It follows you. You must embrace it." My father squeezed my arm, then disappeared into the crowd.

Two of the elders led me to the table. I lay down, inhaling deeply as I felt hands pressing against my legs, immobilizing them. Two more men came behind me and pushed my arms flat against the ancient wood.

The sound of the *bôda* erupted from somewhere nearby. The other children were still hunting. I was here. I was a warrior.

I stared into the sun, listening to the sound of a knife being sharpened.

A shadow fell across my face as the singing began. An *Ndoki* appeared, holding a live mamba above my head. It writhed and hissed, but I showed no fear.

The *Ndoki* pulled a knife out of his waistband and slit the throat of the mamba, sucking its blood into his mouth and spitting it over my body.

I watched him chew a *makazou* root, listened as his teeth ground against the tart bark. Again he sucked the blood from the mamba and spat it onto my face.

He began to preach, overpowering the deep voices echoing across the circle. He prayed to the god of fire, the god of rain, the god of the sky.

He sucked the blood and spat it onto my legs.

He prayed to the god of the jungle, the god of pain, the god of the earth.

He sucked the blood and spat it onto my loins.

He prayed and prayed and prayed, chewing the *makazou* root and sucking the mamba dry. The voice echoed in my ears, drowning out everything around me, reaching a frenzy above the pounding thump of the *bôda*.

Above me, he passed the limp mamba to an assistant and received a bottle of palm wine. Chanting faster and faster, he poured half of the bottle onto the ground, giving drink to the gods of the earth. The rest of the wine, he drank, letting it pour over his chin and chest.

I forced my eyes to stay open.

The voices grew louder, and I felt the cloth being removed from my waist, felt the sun against my naked body.

The sound of the sharpening knife grew in my ears, and I steeled myself.

I felt a hand grasp my penis, the screaming, preaching, and pounding assaulting my ears. My foreskin was pulled taut.

The *Ndoki* raised his arm, then cut through in one swift motion.

I bit down hard.

Do not show pain.

Do not show pain.

Tears erupted, but I did not blink, refusing to let them fall. I stared into the sun, willing the bright rays to dry my eyes in front of my father.

Blood spilled over my legs and still I did not move.

Pain throbbed through my body like nothing I had ever experienced.

No one knows himself who has not suffered.

Man is a slave. Pain is his master.

I let my mind float up into the sky, removing itself from my body. The only way to beat pain is to not think about it, to distance yourself from it, and I floated high above the clouds. My mind was everywhere but in that circle. I dreamed of worlds and galaxies and let my consciousness fly like an eagle above the ocean.

Slowly, my tears dried, and I sat up.

I blinked.

I swung my legs over the table and stepped down, wrapping the now-red cloth around my waist.

I looked to the village elders, nodding at them. They nodded back. I stepped toward my father, my legs weak. He took my arm and squeezed it.

"I am proud of you, Tchico," he said, whispering into my ear. "Come. You must rest."

He led me over to a pallet that had been set up. I lay down, careful of the bleeding.

"Drink this," he said, giving me a cup of frothy, bitter liquid. I did as he asked, and felt the warmth creeping into my body.

The pulsing heat began to fade.

The aching of my muscles became a memory.

Blackness overtook the sun, and I fell into a deep, dreamless sleep.

. . .

The march home was triumphant, filled with singing and cheering.

Thirty boys went into the jungle, but not a single one returned.

In their place were warriors.

Men.

Though my voice joined in as I walked, I allowed my mind to float through the events of the previous weeks. I felt a confidence I'd never imagined possible. I had learned how far a man could push himself, and I truly believed that I was capable of anything my mind could create. My limitation was not body, it was imagination, and I began creating the most luxurious future possible.

I stared at my father as he walked, head held high, proud, shouting along with the music. I had given him honor that week, and this meant the world to me. I would grow to be like my father. With success comes confidence, and with confidence comes leadership. I would lead like my father. I would be confident and compassionate. I would never be fearful, because fear is contagious.

Leaders are not born. They are made.

Warriors are not born. They are made.

They are made by their family and by the streets.

Both of these would continue to educate me.

When we arrived in Matsimou, the women were waiting for us with food, drink, and dancing. Pride filled my chest as my mother came to me. Though I would always be her son, I was no longer her little boy. I kissed her on the cheek, then joined the men around the bonfire.

We performed the songs we had learned over the previous weeks, joining our voices together, singing from our guts. Though I wanted to appear to everyone as a warrior, I could not keep the smile off my face.

We danced until the sunrise, then fell into an exhausted sleep. The smile did not leave my face until I woke.

Late that afternoon, a village elder came to check my healing process. I removed the thin wrap and lifted my penis. After confirming that I was healthy, he moved on to the next house.

Pépé showed up that evening with a gift for me. He was leaping from foot to foot, excited, anxious to show me what he had purchased.

"What?" I said, smiling, pleased that my grandfather had thought to bring me something to commemorate this day.

From behind his back, Pépé pulled a pair of shoes—the nicest ones I'd ever seen. Gleaming white and shiny blue, they reflected the rays of the sunset, and I grabbed them, feeling the smooth plastic between my hands. Though worn by *mundelé* only in the showers, they were extremely desirable amongst boys my age.

I placed them on the ground and slid my feet in, the rubber straps gliding between my toes. It was the first time I had worn shoes. They felt strange, but powerful. This was something I would have to get used to.

Though I wanted to hug my grandfather, I did not. I stood straight in my new shoes and I nodded, thanking him. His eyes twinkled in the fading light, and I could tell that he was pleased by my reaction. His blood ran in my veins, and it was simple for him to guess my thoughts.

I carefully tucked my shoes away, excited to show them off at school. A good warrior was recognizable by the way he walked and ran, by the way he took care of his feet. Now I would have protection against the hot sands and sharp rocks of the city streets. I would be strong, untouchable, safe.

I was reborn, a man of the Congo, and somehow these shoes became the final piece of my new persona, something I didn't know was missing until I had become complete. This gift from my grandfather gave me more confidence than any pistol or AK-47 ever could, for it reminded me of the power contained inside my own heart.

This could never be stolen, for it was my birthright.

This, I had earned.

This, I deserved.

My father and I walked back to Potopoto in near silence, as there was little that needed to be said. I could feel his approval, his happiness, and that was enough.

I did not glimpse the worry behind his eyes, could not hear the bullets whizzing through his imagination.

I smiled, feeling the weight of the shoes against my back, not missing my pistol at all.

PART 3
BECKY THATCHER

During your life, never stop dreaming.
No one can take away your dreams.

— TUPAC SHAKUR

Brazzaville, Congo
August 20–21, 2004

Friday–Saturday

My brother Sazouka arrives with a 4x4 that he borrowed from our great-uncle, and we drive to see our grandfather. Pépé is too blind to see the sparkling rays reflecting off my uniform, but as he touches me, his mouth drops wide.

"You are a mountain," he gasps, squeezing my arms.

I hug him tightly, aware of how frail he feels against my chest.

I lead him away from the harsh sun and into the house, listening as his mouth overflows. "I've heard about your fighting for the Americans. Have you seen Saddam Hussein?"

"No, Pépé, I haven't."

"What is this we hear about George Bush? Have you found the weapons of mass destruction?"

"Not yet, Pépé. We're still looking."

"Ahh, I knew it. We knew there would be no weapons. What do you think about this George Bush?"

"I think he's a good man. Why do you ask so many questions?" I can't keep the smile off my face.

"You were always a good hunter, Tchic. You are a good soldier, yes?"

"I am. You taught me well, Pépé."

"What about Osama bin Laden?"

"No, Pépé, I haven't seen Osama bin Laden. Let's talk about you."

"Me? I am boring. I am nothing. You're traveling the world, my Tchic, you're saving lives. You fight for the Americans. You are the one who changes the world."

I smile, but he doesn't notice. He talks, and I watch his face, wrinkled and browned from decades in the African sun. I'm lucky to have so much family alive. So much of my past is here, contained, waiting for me. The chaos of the last seven years spirals into focus and I push it away. I want to be here, now, sitting beside my brother whom I love, listening to my grandfather.

I have come all this way precisely for moments like this.

On the way home, I see that they're rehearsing for graduation at my old military school, and I convince Sazouka to stop.

"Why do you want to go there?" he asks, frowning.

"I want to see my old friends," I say, and he turns the wheel.

My stomach aches as we pull into the driveway and I swallow hard.

My brother says nothing.

This is where I learned to fight.

This is where I became a member of the Congo National Army.

This was the first step toward my life as a Marine, and I want to understand my journey in greater detail. I didn't expect to feel this way, but I can't ignore it.

The faces are strangely familiar and they surround me, taking in the cut of my new uniform, eyes envious behind shaded lids.

Old friendships flood my mind, along with petty rivalries and ancient grudges. It all seems so meaningless now, such a waste of the precious little time I had available to me. I hug the ones who remain, and watch the backs of the ones who leave. It's easy for me to forgive, for I'm the one who has escaped. Grudges fester when they are left stationary, stagnant, unmoving.

Two soldiers walk up, their eyes unmistakable even though their faces have changed.

"Lieutenant Colonel Okoko. Lieutenant Colonel Nkoyi. It's

good to see you!" I address them by their new rank to honor them, to demonstrate my respect for their positions. They are instructors now, and deserve to be addressed as such.

They hug me, these friends of my past, and they call me *ki-amwu*, brother. I feel my body relax, and hold their hands tight in my own.

"You must come tomorrow to the ceremony," they say. "You must wear this uniform. You'll be an inspiration to the students. An American Marine. They will learn to expect great things from their lives."

"No," I say. "I came to spend time with my family and I will stay with them. My mother is not well."

"Two hours," says Lieutenant Colonel Okoko, his eyes twinkling beneath a deeply furrowed brow, his hands tracing intricate patterns in the air. "It would mean a great deal to the students. You're different now. They should see the changes that are possible through the military life."

I agree to come, and they shake my hand, pleased. I understand that I'm merely a feather in their cap, but a large part of me is happy to serve this role. As they walk away, another figure approaches, and I stand ramrod straight, saluting him.

"Colonel Niama," I say.

His eyes scan up and down my uniform, and I see the specter of jealousy floating between us. I hold my salute steady. Disgust fills his face and he walks on, ignoring me, dismissing me.

I drop my hand, squeezing it into a fist.

My brother glares at me as I slide into the passenger seat. "You should stay away from this place," he says.

"Why?"

"They don't respect you here. They're jealous. We shouldn't have stopped at all."

"Well, I'm coming back tomorrow. I've been invited."

My brother lets his silence answer for him.

I realize that though I'm cautious, there is little here that I fear. I have brought a new kind of power with me.

The next morning, I rise early and go through my calisthenics in front of the children. A number of them follow along, exhausting themselves quickly with push-ups and sit-ups. I try not to smile, wanting them to remember this as a serious moment.

"You must hurry back," says my mother.

"Of course, Mama," I say, tucking my shirt in even tighter against my skin.

"I'm making *sakasaka*—your favorite."

"I'll be back in a short time, Mama. You won't even know that I've gone. You just cook and when you look up to call us in for lunch, I'll be sitting at that table, wondering why lunch has taken so long."

She laughs and hugs me again, unable to keep her hands away for longer than a few minutes. I smooth the wrinkles from my shirt and get into the 4x4 with my brother.

I do not think to look back at my house.

I do not think to memorize its outline.

I do not think to say good-bye to my brothers, sisters, cousins, nephews, aunts, or uncles.

I do not think about any of this.

Potopoto, Congo
Brazzaville, Congo
1990–95

CHAPTER 6

Enough is never enough.

This, I learned from my father.

He never seemed to rest, and was always searching for a bigger and better deal. When I was twelve, he bought a tract of land in the Bakongo area, built an enormous house, and moved us all into it. The debt he incurred didn't appear to bother him at all.

"A man who takes no risks is a man who has no future," he would say.

I watched his every move with careful attention, trying to guess what business he would venture into, what chance he would take next.

This, I thought, *is how a man should act.*

Around that time, strange things began to happen in Brazzaville. Men would come into local bars carrying briefcases, buying drinks for everyone, acting cavalier with incredible amounts of cash. Invariably, they would speak Lingala, designating them as part of the M'Bochi tribe from the northern region of the Congo.

At night, my father would come home and talk to me about it, choosing my ear and counsel over that of my brothers and sisters. "There is a lot of this oil money around, Tchico," he would say. "The country is getting very wealthy, but we are not seeing any of it, because we are not from the north. Sassou-Nguesso will never let the money trickle down this far. We are not his people."

Denis Sassou-Nguesso, our president, had been in power for thirteen years, controlling the country under a Marxist-Leninist regime. Using the oil profits from the twenty-five thousand barrels a day produced by offshore wells thirty miles west of Pointe-Noire, Sassou-Nguesso created a large network of businessmen and militiamen throughout the Congo. He poured substantial amounts of money into the Congolese infrastructure and built a great number of schools, and thus faced little opposition. This would change as Western countries grew increasingly insistent that the Congo democratize.

My father sensed this and was determined to take advantage of the upcoming democratic elections.

"When democracy comes," he said to me, "the market will be open. Tourists will come. Money will flow. Do you understand?"

"Yes," I said.

"If you're confident in yourself, then risk is nothing."

I watched him spend more and more time with Gervais's father, a wealthy banker who was buying up property along the Djoué River. On these trips, I would spend hours sitting and fishing with my old friend while my father scouted the area, searching for something. The constant moving had made it difficult for Gervais and me to see each other as much as we had in our childhood, but every summer, when I returned home, it was as if nothing had changed. My father's new house was much closer to Brazzaville than Potopoto, and allowed me to begin spending time with Gervais during the school year—something that pleased me greatly.

One morning, my father woke me up and took me to the national bank, leaving my brothers and sisters behind. He was dressed in his full police uniform, ribbons flashing and medals jangling. My father looked like a painting, a statue, and my heart swelled, proud to accompany such a man in public. I slipped on my shower shoes and kept my head high as we entered the austere brick building.

My father took off his cover and looked around.

"Hey!" shouted a *mundelé* from across the bank. I felt my father tense. He didn't like to be addressed in this manner by anyone, let alone a white stranger. He cleared his throat, and I worried that he might cause a scene. "Come over here!" yelled the stocky, pale man, and my father raised his shoulders, consuming the bank floor in huge strides. I hurried to keep up.

The man stood and extended his hand. My father took it.

"Mr. DeSeize, bank director. I've seen you before. You're the guy who leads all the parades, right?"

My father nodded, eyes gleaming. "Yes, sir. I am."

"You march just like a German. You remind me of my grandfather—he was a Nazi captain. Have a seat."

My father sat. "Thank you."

"Pleasure to have you in here. What can I do for you?"

My father asked this Mr. DeSeize for a loan of 60 million francs ($120,000) to build a hotel resort on the banks of the river. It was the first I'd heard of the idea, and my ears popped with the amount of money they were discussing so casually—60 million francs!

I forced my leg to stop shaking against the hard plastic of the chair.

My father, using our house as collateral, as well as his status in the community, secured the loan and began construction on a luxury resort along the banks of the Djoué River. He decided to name it the Oasis.

As police captain, he had access to prison labor—and he made the most of it. The prisoners would work day and night, happily straining themselves to the limit. My father paid them all a decent wage and fed them well, and soon there was a list of inmates fighting to be on the construction detail for my father's new riverfront property. The entire resort was completed in only 225 days.

It was beautiful.

I watched everything my father did—how he talked to people, how he dealt with the bank, how he treated his employees. I was mesmerized by his energy, by the way he floated from meeting to meeting, from deal to deal.

Some days, he would sit me down and open his brain.

"This hotel, Tchico, it is right on the flight path to the Mayamaya airport. Everyone will see it, especially visitors to the country. Even the president does not have a mansion like the one I am building. There will be jealousy. There will be talk that I have stolen this money. People will say that I am a traitor. But none of this is true. I am a risk-taker. And the world belongs to the risk-takers. Do you understand that?"

"Yes," I would say, soaking in every word.

He was right . . . about everything.

The rumblings around town were loud, even reaching my young ears from time to time. People called my father a criminal, a cheat, a liar. They claimed he was embezzling money from public funds, that he was stealing oil profits from the government. But my father ignored all this talk and continued his business plans.

One morning, government inspectors arrived without warning, hoping to shut the Oasis down. I shadowed the group as my father took them around the property, showing them the proposed layout, explaining his ideas for the white tourists. As they passed close to the river, a hippopotamus lifted his mighty head from the brown waters and roared. The inspectors jumped back, but my father simply laughed.

"Nestor!" he called out, his voice reverberating against the thick wall of foliage facing us. The hippo responded by yawning loudly and flipping over in the water, creating an enormous splash. The inspectors clapped, as my father had made it appear that he had control over nature itself. I jumped up and down, not afraid to show my excitement.

They nodded and shook his hand, satisfied. In fact, as my father told me later, they even offered to invest in the property themselves, supplying my father with much-needed finishing costs. The resort opened, and *mundelé* began pouring in from across Europe. For a time, life was good.

For a time, I saw my father smile.

CHAPTER 7

Election day.

There are three main ethnic divisions in the Congo, roughly divided along geographical lines: the M'Bochis from the north, the Laris from the central part of the country, and the Niboleks from the south. Each of these came to have their own leader, and subsequently, their own candidate. Sassou-Nguesso was from the north. A man named Bernard Kolelas represented the Lari population. The south was represented by a former professor named Pascal Lissouba.

As my family was from the Bakongo region of Brazzaville, I was and am a Lari.

We have never constituted a majority.

Due to the relatively sparse population of the northern regions, Lissouba won an easy victory. But governing in the Congo was not simply a matter of exchanging one leader for another. Sassou-Nguesso had built up a lifetime of strong alliances among the elite members of the country, and many of these men resented the intrusion of Lissouba into their circles. In one of his first acts as president, Lissouba dismissed all high-ranking M'Bochi militiamen and sent them back to the north. He surrounded himself with an independent security force from the south, the Réserve Présidentielle.

None of this should have mattered. None of this should have bothered my father. After all, he maintained his job as captain of the police force. He maintained his booming resort business. But others were displeased. After helping Lissouba get elected, many Lari felt slighted that their tribe was not represented in the government.

On November 30, 1992, the Lari population marched on the capitol building in a peaceful protest. Lissouba responded by sending out the Réserve Présidentielle, weapons raised. The resulting conflict left two Lari dead, with another thirty to forty severely injured.

Word spread like wildfire around Brazzaville. The Niboleks had fired on a group of unarmed Lari. Lissouba had betrayed the very people he'd been elected to govern. Rioters took to the streets. Sassou-Nguesso, sensing an opportunity, met in private with Kolelas and supplied him with weapons to use against Lissouba.

Civil war had begun.

My father's business instantly became unprofitable.

He left central Brazzaville and began staying at the hotel in order to protect his investment.

As a result, I discovered that I had an incredible amount of freedom.

One day after school, I was sitting on a dusty road, playing with a group of friends. As usual, we were discussing girls. At fourteen, we thought of little else.

We heard the sound of a revving engine and Taty shut his mouth.

A jeep pulled up, loaded with weapons of all types—AK-47s, RPGs, land mines, grenades. We all leaped to our feet.

Three men got out and came over to us. They wore a strange mix of military and civilian clothes. Each of them had a red bandana tied around his forehead, with a smaller red sash around each biceps. They looked like black versions of Rambo.

"Come here," they said.

We looked at each other, then approached the jeep.

They handed us each a gun, some ammunition, and a few grenades.

"Take these," they said. I squinted, staring at the AK-47 I'd been given. For some reason, it felt much heavier than others I'd held. "We need warriors to protect the neighborhoods against Lissouba's people. They're coming to hurt you and your families. They want all the Lari dead. Are you going to let that happen?"

We all shook our heads, but no one spoke.

"We need you to set up checkpoints around the neighborhood, okay?"

We nodded.

"Check IDs. Don't let Niboleks or M'Bochis into the area. They want you dead. You don't know who is Cocoyes and who is safe."

Cocoyes was the name that the Nibolek militants had given to themselves.

Chills ran along my arms, even though I was sweating buckets. I looked at the faces of my friends as they gripped their new weapons. None of them were smiling.

The sun baked our skin.

The men took us out to the jungle and gave us a five-minute lesson on how to fire an AK-47, how to throw a grenade, and how to set a land mine. A few seconds later, only a dust cloud floated where they'd been, and the sound of the jeep faded away like the strangest dream.

We stared at each other, suddenly feeling enormous weights on our shoulders. I couldn't for the life of me remember what we'd been talking about not fifteen minutes before.

In my father's absence, I designated myself man of the house, ahead of even my older brothers, from whom I was growing increasingly distant. As part of this new, primarily self-defined role, I set up a checkpoint with a few of my friends.

We began examining IDs and asking irrelevant questions of anyone who felt the need to walk down our street. Besides the obvious linguistic differences, it was relatively easy to distinguish the Laris from the Niboleks or the M'Bochis. Northerners had names that started with O, I, E, Y, or W. Southerners had names that started with M, T, S, N, or K. If we were suspicious or bored, we would ask people questions based on regional dialects. For example, there is a rat in the south nicknamed the *"fufu"* and there is a cassavalike plant called a *"fou-fou."* We would ask strangers, "Can you eat *fou-fou* with *fufu?"* If they were truly from the south, they would know to answer yes. If they were confused by the question, we knew that they were from the north. Niboleks were turned away or shot.

I began to realize how powerful a man can be when he is holding a gun.

It felt good.

Things changed very quickly. The neighborhood was no longer filled with the sounds of commerce and children. Silence reigned over everything. Food became scarce. Reports reached our ears of Nibolek raids on nearby towns, or successful Lari raids on southern villages.

Since most of us were only thirteen or fourteen years old and had school during the day, we were usually put on guard duty after darkness fell. My friends would smoke weed and drink liquor, casually toying with the safeties of their weapons, discussing exactly how they would kill a Nibolek if one had the nerve to approach the checkpoint.

I took my responsibility very seriously and was rarely late. The first time that I was, I found only Loko there, looking glum.

"Where are the others?" I said.

He stared up at me, but something was strange about his eyes. They were glazed over, confused. I thought that maybe he was high. "In *le petit matin.* A woman didn't have ID and they wanted to search her body for weapons." *Le petit matin* was the name we used for the abandoned house behind the checkpoint where we would "interrogate" potential suspects. Usually, this involved asking ridiculous questions until we grew tired of them. Sometimes, it involved more.

I walked over, opening the door.

Inside, a woman lay on her back. Her baby screamed beside her, abandoned. Bakala was raping her as the others looked on, slowly nodding. A haze of blue smoke filled the air, and the smell of liquor permeated everything. The woman was silent, staring, and her eyes bored into me as I entered the room.

She was crying.

My friends looked at me. I looked at them. They laughed. I turned around and left.

I couldn't confront them, I didn't know how. I was too weak to stand up for what I thought was right, and that image is forever ingrained in my memory. The helplessness on that woman's face, her calm acceptance of a rape by boys younger than her own sons.

I walked back to the checkpoint and sat in silence with Loko.

The night grew cold and I went home.

CHAPTER 8

The Lari militiamen came nearly every day to check on us, encourage us, give us more ammunition, weed, alcohol, whatever we requested. They praised our diligence and reminded us how much we were protecting our people. They gave us updates on the fighting in other areas of the country and let us know that the whole thing would be over shortly.

Lari soldiers were encroaching upon southern regions and were torturing, raping, and burning the bodies of Nibolek villagers. These actions pleased us, as we knew they were only retaliation for the even worse atrocities committed by the Cocoyes militia.

Our power slowly grew, and soon we were the de facto warlords of the streets. Villagers feared us. Grown men and women cast their eyes down when they approached our homemade checkpoints, or *bouchon*.

I saw Gervais less and less.

Lissouba, in response to the rebellion, cut off water, electricity, and communication to the southern sections of Brazzaville. Food shipments were halted into the Bakongo/Makelekelé regions, which had garnered the nickname "Sarajevo."

We grew hungry and began stealing food from people as they crossed our checkpoint.

In response to the desperate plight of his people, Bernard Kolelas began using the Congo River to ferry shipments of food from Congo-Kinshasa to the Lari people in "Sarajevo." This cemented his role as leader of the Lari tribe, and we praised him for his noble actions.

Food was distributed by the red-sashed militia members, and my people began to welcome their arrival instead of fear it.

Not long after, they provided us with our own sashes to wear around our heads and arms. "You will be bulletproof," they said. "These sashes will protect you. They will make you invisible to the enemy."

"Like ninjas," we said.

They nodded.

So the Lari militia, under the distant command of Bernard Kolelas, became known as the Ninjas.

We gave each other nicknames from American films, names like "Rambo" and "Commando" and "Al Capone." We embodied our new role as warlords. We grew to love the power that it offered.

We began looting nearby businesses, enforcing the curfew that we had mandated. The Ninjas patrolled the streets, looking for rule-breakers. I didn't want to loot, but I was hungry, and far from perfect. It was a way to fit in, to reassure everyone that you were a part of the group. My brothers and sisters stayed inside or visited their mothers in other cities. I'd quickly become the sole source of authority in my father's house during his absence. I began to enjoy the power.

Eventually, civilians stopped driving their cars through our street, because it was nearly guaranteed that they would leave on foot.

We were feared, even by our own people. Some of the child soldiers had been taken from their parents and fed a constant diet of alcohol and marijuana, until they were nearly unrecognizable. Others volunteered to fight, leaving their parents behind. Usually, the parents were too frightened of potential retaliation to face the militias and reclaim their sons. Some boys, when confronted with a direct choice, didn't hesitate to turn their weapons on their own mothers or fathers.

"If you die for your tribe, you go to paradise," we were told. "Do not regret your kills."

And we believed it.

We believed every word.

I saw awful things during this time.

Things it pains me to remember.

I watched as a Nibolek woman without ID was stopped at our *bouchon* by the chief, a boy named Matsaga. I watched as he removed the firing pin from a grenade and handed it to her.

I watched as she was led over to a corner beside *le petit matin* and chained to a tree. I watched her stare at the strange object, not understanding its purpose. I watched her turn the sphere over in her hands, slowly releasing her grip. I watched her explode into a million pieces, blood, guts, and body parts raining down on the trees, coating them in viscous syrup. It looked to me like the leaves were bleeding.

I watched my friends laugh and cheer and point at the blood splattered across their faces.

I saw a young boy who'd been taught how to fire a weapon, but not how to keep himself safe from it, hold an armed RPG.

I saw him drop it.

I saw his face contort as he was blown apart.

On another occasion, I watched as a mixed-tribe couple fought over their newborn child. The pair, composed of a Nibolek woman and a Lari man, were splitting up and were arguing over who would keep the child. The father wanted his son to be raised as a Lari warrior, while the mother planned on taking the boy farther south to be raised as a Nibolek.

The battle raged, the voices swelling and crashing against each other. None of us could look away.

The man pushed the woman, who stumbled back, clutching the child to her chest.

He reached out and grabbed the boy from her.

"If you will not give me the child, then we will have to share him," shouted the man, his eyes wide.

He removed his machete from its holster.

He placed the child on the ground.

With a quick motion, he sliced the child in half across the middle and left the head and arms lying in the dust for the mother to take.

"For you," he said, kicking dirt onto the bleeding upper half of his only son.

I turned, vomit filling my mouth, and ran away from the *bouchon*, tears blinding my eyes.

I wanted to quit.

I wanted to go to school and study and become a businessman like my father. I wanted to see my grandparents, my aunts, my mother, but central Brazzaville might as well have been a different country.

I suddenly wished more than anything in the world that my father were home again, that I could speak to him. I racked my brain, trying to remember the last time I'd seen him, but I couldn't even picture his face. All I could see were entrails spilling out, large and clear like the picture on Gervais's television screen.

It wasn't only violence that damaged us during this time.

At age fourteen, I lost my virginity to a woman well over twice my age.

This was not something that I wanted, and I have kept it hidden from everyone in my life until this moment. It cut deeper than the violence because it happened to me, not a nameless body.

I was washing my clothes down at the river when Mama Koudeou, the mother of Oko, approached me. "Tchic," she said, "come pick up this bucket for me and carry it to that tree."

I smiled, grabbed the bucket of water, and pulled it over to an enclosed area, set apart from the river by a natural wall of palm leaves. I thought that maybe she wanted to take a shower in a private space.

She entered the enclave and grabbed my arm.

Slowly, she unwrapped the cloth covering her body and let it fall to the ground. I stared, holding my breath, confused, uncertain what to do.

This was an adult, someone who I was expected to listen to. I watched as she guided my hand down to her vagina and slowly moved it around.

With her other hand, she grabbed me, massaging me until I became erect.

I was still, immobile.

I wanted to run, but didn't know how.

I didn't make eye contact with her the entire time.

It was my first sexual act, and my only thought was that it was with a woman who could have been my mother.

It lasted an instant and an eternity.

She asked me not to tell anyone, told me that it would be our little secret. She promised to bring me candy every time she saw me, and for the next few months, went out of her way to buy me gifts and sweet breads from the market whenever she went.

It happened again and again, causing more and more fear in my life. I became horrified that someone would find out, that my family would discover the secret and kill her.

It was something I couldn't speak about to anyone, not even Gervais.

Sexuality is hidden in Africa, and I didn't know such things were wrong until I came to America. It was shameful and private, and I wished constantly that there was someone, anyone that I could talk to.

The fear and shame of an adult is no match for that of a child.

· · ·

And then, just as quickly as it had started, the war was over. Lissouba and Kolelas signed a cease-fire agreement, and Lissouba agreed to integrate all of the Lari militiamen into the standing military, giving them permanent governmental jobs.

He also reinstituted the gendarmerie, a military body charged with policing the civilian population, and promised to fill it with persons from all areas of the country. Tribal divisions, he said, would be a thing of the past.

The Ninjas saw this as an enormous victory and took to the streets in celebration.

Over two thousand people were killed during this conflict, but that was not the real damage to the Congo. Three militias had been formed: the Cocoyes, the Ninjas, and the guard that had sprung up around Sassou-Nguesso in reaction to our civil war—the Cobras. These militias had learned what a mighty weapon Congolese youth could be in a struggle. This was information that would be ruthlessly exploited in the coming years.

Unaware of our future, we were happy to abandon our checkpoints and prepare ourselves for an equally difficult battle—high school. I had a new enemy to conquer, one whose weapons were powder and lipstick and perfume.

My shower shoes were always with me, but rarely on my feet. Only when I saw girls coming would I take out my shoes and slip them on, nodding confidently. Then I would stop, remove the shoes, brush them off, and return them to my plastic bag.

Shoes were too precious a possession to be dirtied by dust and mud.

They were a symbol of my new life, and I would treat them with the same respect that I felt I deserved.

Plus, all the girls were very impressed by them.

All the girls, that is, except for the one I wanted.

CHAPTER 9

The first time I saw her was under the mango tree.

I went to a school called Lycée de la Liberatión located next to the gendarmerie. Across the street was a private French school called Saint Exupéry, and this creature of beauty would leave the building every day at exactly five o'clock. She would wait for her parents in front of Lycée de la Liberatión so they wouldn't have to turn around on Oua Avenue, one of the busiest streets in Brazzaville.

There was no way around it—I had to walk past her every day, and every day, I fell a little more in love.

She was a *mundelé* with long hair and beautiful, perfect skin. I'd never imagined a creature so perfect. I got in the habit of slipping on my shower shoes as I left school, hoping to attract her attention, but this never worked. She was unimpressed by my extravagant footwear, never pulling her face out of whatever book she was reading at the time. I could never catch her eye as she slid into her parents' midnight-blue 305 Peugeot, could never think of what to say, how to approach.

It drove me crazy.

Every night I would make plans to speak with her and every day I would let fear talk me out of it.

Nothing helped—the comforting weight of my pistol hanging against my back, the resounding flip-flop-flip-flop of my shower shoes, the newfound power I'd obtained from being a minor warlord. In her presence I was worthless, weak, useless.

I loved every second of it.

"She smiled at me today!" I told Gervais, swooning against the side of his house. Since the war had ended, we'd been spending a great deal of time together.

"Are you sure it wasn't a butterfly?" he asked, grinning like the devil.

"It was me. She saw me and looked at me with those beautiful eyes and she smiled."

"And then went back to reading."

"Yes. And then went back to reading. But she recognized me!"

Gervais sighed and picked up the ball we'd been throwing around. "Are you ever going to talk to her?"

"Of course I am."

"It's been weeks. Let's go meet her."

"What?"

"Tomorrow. I'll come to your school and we'll talk to her."

My heart plummeted just imagining the encounter. "I don't think so . . . I'm not ready."

Gervais shook his head, exasperated. "This is the big, bad Congo soldier? Can't even talk to a girl?"

"She's different! She's . . ."

"White?"

"No, it's not that . . ."

"You sure?"

"Well, it's part that, but it's everything else . . . her hair, her eyes, her skin . . ."

"You should talk to her."

"I know, I know. I will."

Gervais stared at me, making up his mind. I hated when he did that. "I'm coming tomorrow, and we're going to talk to her. That's all there is to it."

There was no use arguing.

We spent the rest of the afternoon watching American romance movies so I could study the different lines that the men used. I wrote them all on a piece of paper and committed most to memory.

The next day, Gervais showed up at exactly five o'clock. I was already sweating. My shower shoes glinted in the sun.

"Where is she?"

I squinted. "She'll be here. Some days she's a little late."

"Okay. I better see her."

"You will. Look somewhere else. Don't stare at the tree."

We turned our backs and acted busy for a few minutes. I tried to start conversations about something else, anything else.

Five minutes passed.

Then ten.

She didn't show.

"You sure you didn't dream this girl? Maybe you fell in love with the mango tree," he said.

I was not amused. "Come on. Let's go." I pulled him away from the tree, giving one last look behind me . . .

. . . and there she was.

I clutched Gervais's arm.

"Ow!" he said.

"There," I hissed. "It's her. Don't turn around."

"Go talk to her," said Gervais, his back still facing the mango tree.

"No," I said.

"You memorized all those lines! Go!"

"They're stupid. They'll never work. She'll laugh at me."

Gervais grabbed my shoulders, his eyes boring into my skull. "You taught me to be a man, but can't even talk to a girl? Come on."

He turned around.

I froze.

"Marielle?" he said.

The girl looked up, surprised. "Gervais?"

Gervais laughed and ran over to the tree, hugging the girl as she stood up to greet him. My mouth fell open.

They began giggling and talking, catching up like the oldest of friends. Slowly, I approached them, scuffing my feet in the dirt and waiting for someone to acknowledge me. My shower shoes no longer shone.

I stared at her as she laughed, committing her perfect white teeth to memory, etching the color of her eyes into my brain. But every time she glanced over at me, I would look away.

Finally, after what seemed like hours, Gervais turned to me. "Marielle, this is my best friend, Tchicaya."

Though I couldn't bring my eyes to meet hers, I did manage to eke out a *"salut"* and shake her hand. It was the softest skin I'd ever felt. My mouth went dry and I took two quick steps backward. She smiled and turned again toward Gervais.

As it turned out, Gervais's and Marielle's fathers had done business together some years back and they lived very close to each other. I'd been in plain view of Marielle for years, but had never known it.

As we walked away from the mango tree, Gervais patted me on the back. "See? That wasn't so bad, was it?"

"I didn't say anything!" I exploded, kicking the ground. "I was too scared!"

Gervais put his hand on my arm. "You helped me so much, I will help you get this girl." His voice was serious, his touch firm. "Come on."

We walked to his house and he put in *Octopussy*. "James Bond always has a pickup line," he said. "Watch what he does. This is the way you have to act with Marielle."

We watched the film over and over again until I could recite the lines effortlessly.

I practiced the words the whole way back to my father's house.

The next day after school, I took three deep breaths and walked toward the mango tree. Marielle looked up and smiled. "Tchicaya!"

Dear Lord.

She remembered me.

She was so beautiful, I couldn't even imagine her shitting.

I forced a smile onto my face and instantly forgot anything James Bond had ever said. To be honest, I forgot the name James Bond.

Luckily, she didn't notice. She stood up and walked over, asking me question after question. I didn't say one unprompted thing that entire day, but did manage to satisfactorily answer everything she wanted to know.

"Sit," she said, and I did. I remember every single moment of my first day under the mango tree with Marielle, smelling her perfume, imagining the feel of her skin.

I was in love.

"Hey, Gervais, you think she could be my first wife?"

Gervais shook his head. "She's European, Tchic, she would be your only wife."

I frowned. It was common for men in the Congo to take many wives. My father, for instance, had seven. But for Marielle, I was willing to give up all other women. "Okay. My only wife. What do you think?"

Gervais smiled. "I don't know. I guess you'll have to ask her."

I resolved to do so . . . but first, I had to get her to go on a date.

I learned from Gervais that Marielle loved the outdoors, so I asked her to go fishing with me. Her eyes lit up and she laughed. "I would love to!"

Inside, I cheered. I'd gotten the idea from Tom Sawyer. Marielle, I'd decided, would be my Becky Thatcher.

We walked down to the Djoué, and I scanned the path to avoid having to make eye contact. "That's the *quinkeliba* tree. If you have malaria, the roots can cure you. And these leaves here, they're called *citronelle*. We use this to keep mosquitoes away. It's also good for an upset stomach if you make it into tea. And that there, see that? That's the trail of the *poukoubimde*, a large rat. You can tell because of the shape of the dead leaves. Do you see it?"

"Yes!" she exclaimed, her cheeks flushing. She nodded at everything I said, repeating the strange words, seemingly enthralled. This made me happy, because I had a nearly endless supply of information about the jungle. I felt her staring at me from time to time, but I couldn't bring myself to return her gaze. Maybe I would buy her a present, like a goat or a cooking pan. Dating was difficult.

"If you use something still living, then a fish is more likely to bite," I said, pushing a rusty hook through a wriggling worm I'd dug out of the ground for her. "Jerk the string around like this, to make it seem more alive. When you see it move on its own, you know something's eating your worm, okay?"

"Okay," she said, her nose wrinkling in concentration. It was so cute I nearly fainted. We sat there in silence, watching our lines sway in the current.

Minutes passed, and I began to sweat, struggling to think of something to say.

What would James Bond say?

He probably wouldn't be fishing in the mud, I thought with disgust.

Suddenly, Marielle screamed and jerked her line back. A tiny *carpe* was hanging from the hook. "I caught one!" she said. "My first fish!" And before I could even put my own line down to help her, she leaned over and kissed me on the cheek.

A *mundelé* kissing a black man. I had never heard of such a thing. My heart stopped for an hour as I replayed the soft feel of her lips against my skin. I said nothing to her, but felt the hot rush of blood to my face. I helped unhook the fish and taught her how to keep it fresh for later.

After we parted ways, I didn't say another word for the rest of the day.

I certainly didn't wash my cheek.

• • •

"No way," said Taty.

"Yes!" I said. "*She* kissed *me*."

"On the cheek?"

"Yes, on the cheek," I said. "Here. Smell." The boys took turns smelling the spot where Marielle had pressed her lips.

"I don't smell anything," said Lema.

"Well, she did," I said, exasperated. I didn't understand why they weren't happy for me.

"Do it again," said Taty.

"What?"

"Again, so we can see it. I don't believe that a *mundelé* kissed you."

I stood up straight and stared down at all of them. "Two days from now, we're going fishing again. When she catches another fish, she will kiss me."

"Are you sure?" Taty smiled.

"I'm sure."

"Sure enough to bet twenty fish?"

The other boys were staring now, so I puffed out my chest. "Sure enough to bet twenty fish against your *one* fish!"

The boys nodded and ooohed. Taty stuck his hand out and I shook it.

The bet was on.

Two days later, as I brought Marielle down to the river, I was careful not to acknowledge the group of five boys sitting across from us. As far as we were concerned, they were strangers. But I made sure that Marielle and I were facing them, giving them an excellent view of the proceedings.

We gently tugged our baited hooks and talked about school and about our parents and about Germany, where she'd been born, and about my father's military training in Romania. We talked about the war and about the pistol I carried in my backpack. Marielle didn't understand why it was necessary, and I wasn't sure how to explain it to her. I simply shrugged, watching my line dip and sway. Girls never understood such things.

Time passed, and minutes slipped into hours.

"We should get going," said Marielle, slowly pulling her hook out of the water.

"Why?" I said. "What for?"

"It'll be dark soon. We can always come back a different day." She smiled. "I like fishing with you."

"I like fishing with you, too," I said, scanning the area for some arcane piece of jungle lore to talk about. Anything to keep her there. Anything to get her to kiss me again.

"Come on," she said, and started walking up the path.

I felt my face burn as the giggling of my friends washed over us.

It took me nearly a week to pay Taty his twenty fish.

I went back to the drawing board with Gervais and watched even more James Bond films.

"You have to hold a woman like he does," said Gervais. "Watch." And he would rewind the tape and play the scene again. And again. And again.

"Don't the French kiss differently?"

"She's German," said Gervais.

"But she speaks French."

"So do you."

"Right," I said, thinking. "So I should use my tongue, or no?"

Gervais just shook his head and rewound the tape.

"You want to bet again?" I said casually to Taty in front of the boys.

"You mean do I want some more fish?" he said.

"We're going to the river tomorrow if you want to come and watch me kiss her."

"Twenty fish?" he said.

"Against your one."

"Deal."

I thought for sure this would be the moment. Marielle and I had been spending nearly all our free time together, and I'd even started to look her in the eye when we spoke. We'd held hands a couple of times, and she had recently begun to wait outside for me after school so that we could talk before her father came to pick her up. I knew that if I brought her back to that first spot where she had kissed my cheek, then passion would take its course. Besides, if that failed, I had all my new James Bond techniques that I'd rehearsed with Gervais.

I couldn't fail.

We got to the river, again ignoring the large group of boys staring awkwardly in our direction.

"Sit over here," I said to Marielle, patting the ground beside me. "There's good fish over here."

"Oh, Tchic, I'm not feeling very well. I don't want to get too close."

"Why?"

"Because I don't want to get you sick. I have the flu . . . I should sit at least a meter away."

My hands went clammy. "It's okay, I would rather you catch a fish. Besides . . ." My mind raced furiously. "Besides, I don't ever get sick, so it's probably impossible for you to give me any disease. Nothing you could do would make me sick. Nothing at all."

She sighed. "Well, there's no use in taking chances. I think I'll stay over here." She sniffled and blew her nose into her handkerchief.

The boys giggled and I flashed an angry glare in their direction before sticking my line into the water. Marielle's parents had bought her a nice fishing pole, and she baited the hook before tossing it a few feet upstream from me.

Her coughing was the soundtrack to that day and, after an hour, we gave up and I went home.

This time, it took me nearly two weeks to pay off Taty.

I was humiliated.

The boys, feeling sorry for my numerous failures, tried to comfort me. "Don't worry, Tchic. A white woman will never kiss a black man. You know that's the way things are. It's not you."

And I would sigh and shake my head, feeling the gentle touch of her lips against my cheek. It had happened. And I vowed that it would happen again.

My father's words rang in my head: *A real man is one who takes risks. If you are confident, then risk is nothing.*

I would be the son of the man.

I would be confident.

I would succeed.

We were at her house watching cartoons. She had an extensive collection and had begun inviting me over for viewing parties.

Even her parents had grown accustomed to my visits and seemed to tacitly approve of the growing friendship between Marielle and myself.

I was happy to be around her, but I wanted more.

What would James Bond do?

I racked my brain as the mouse chased the cat around the room with a huge hammer. What should I say? Should I just kiss her? Just about every encounter I'd ever had with Marielle ended with me walking home alone, confused and with very dry lips.

She laughed at something on the screen.

I turned to her.

"Marielle?"

She looked over. "What?"

"Would you be my wife?"

There was no such thing as a "boyfriend" in the Congo, so there was only one place to take our relationship. I scanned her face, searching for a reaction. European girls didn't marry as young as African women, but I was a man now. It was a reasonable request—one I prayed she would understand.

"Tchic . . ." she started.

"Please," I said.

She smiled and leaned toward me. My heart thudded in my chest as if it was going to explode. I willed it to stay in one piece, at least until this moment was over.

Our lips touched, and I felt a more gentle mouth than I'd imagined possible. I'd been sexually active, but had never kissed anyone like this. I certainly had never kissed someone whom I loved.

She pulled away, smiled at me, and ran into her bedroom. Giggles trickled out from underneath the closed door, and I couldn't help but smile in return.

"Wow," I said out loud, gathering my things. "Wow."

For days, I didn't want to wash my face or brush my teeth. I didn't want the feeling of Marielle's lips to ever fade.

I grinned.

"What happened to you?" asked Gervais.

I smiled even wider.

"Did you kiss her?" asked Gervais, standing up and running over to me. He stared at my face. "You did! You kissed her!"

I hugged Gervais, unable to contain the secret any longer. "No, Gervais. She kissed me!"

"Did you use your tongue?"

"No, the lips. Just for a second."

"She just kissed you?"

"No, I asked her to marry me first."

"Are you getting married?"

"Yes, but later. She said she wants to wait until she finishes school."

Gervais shook his head, mouth open. I'd never felt better. "So what do you want to do?" he said.

"I want to watch more James Bond. I need to know what to do next."

He nodded and popped in a tape.

Marielle and I became intertwined in nearly everything we did. I would go over to Gervais's house every day after school, just like when we were young, because that was the only place I could see Marielle without any meddling adult supervision.

I spent countless hours walking through the jungle with Marielle, holding her hand, smelling her hair, kissing her in the bushes beside the palm trees, under the mango trees.

The war was a distant memory. At age fifteen, I started school at University Marien Ngouabi, studying marketing. I began to manage the Oasis hotel, working for my father. I would marry Marielle and begin my life as a businessman.

My heart was filled with hope. I would build a home and start an enormous family. Marielle and I would marry in a huge ceremony in front of my entire tribe and they would cheer.

I became consumed with daydreams of my perfect future.

I truly believed that nothing in the world could stop me.

On my sixteenth birthday, my dad pulled me aside, a serious look on his face. "Tchico," he said.

"Yes, Papa?"

"I have watched you grow. You have become strong."

Pride sent a warm flush throughout my body.

"The second election is coming soon, you know this, yes?"

I nodded.

"The militias are fine for boys, but true respect comes from the gendarmerie. They are the ones who control the country, they are the ones whom the president calls upon. All of my friends have sons in the military, but I do not." He paused. "I know you are a leader, and I know you love weapons."

I nodded, less quickly this time.

"I will not be around forever, Tchico. I need a replacement. Someone to take care of my business. Someone to take care of my family. Someone to be the man of the house in my absence." Here he stopped again, making sure that my eyes were locked on his. "I choose you," he said. "I choose you to carry my name and protect my family."

I held his gaze, aware of what an enormous moment this was in my life. My father trusted me with everything he had fought so hard for.

I truly was the son of the man.

"What do you want me to do, Papa?"

He squeezed my shoulder. "I want you to take the entry test for the gendarmerie. I want you to enroll in the military academy."

"But my university—"

"You can finish your last year of university while enrolled in the gendarmerie," said my father. "They will let you out to take exams, but for nothing else."

I started to offer another excuse, but thought better of it. I didn't know how to tell my father that I was done with fighting. I didn't know how to tell him that I had already seen a lifetime of violence. I didn't know how to tell him that I planned on marrying Marielle and becoming a businessman like him.

Instead, I nodded.

PART 4
THE MARINES OF THE CONGO

*The brave man is not he who does not feel afraid,
but he who conquers that fear.*

—NELSON MANDELA

Brazzaville, Congo
August 21, 2004

Saturday

Wait here for me," I say, and stride toward the ceremony already in progress. I turn my video camera on, adding to the footage I've taken of my family, my home, my old life. I want to share these parts of myself with the new friends I've made in America, so they can truly understand where it is I come from.

I stand up straight in the back row, watching the young students graduate into a world of violence and chain of command. Though sweat pours down my body, I don't fidget. Warriors do not get uncomfortable.

The young soldiers march through a parade deck composed of sand and dirt, the dust coating their shoes with every step. I know from working in the gendarmerie that the general has no doubt received funds for a proper deck of concrete or asphalt, and wonder what the money has been spent on instead.

I feel stares and whispers pointed in my direction, and struggle not to shift from foot to foot.

A man in the second row is glaring at me with anger in his eyes. I recognize him, but don't know his name. I put the camera down and he turns away, whispering to the person sitting in front of him. This person turns toward me, then whispers to a third man—General Bemde.

The general turns and stares, but I do not acknowledge that I have seen him. I nod at the ceremony, holding my body stiff. This man, the sworn lifelong enemy of my father, has risen through the ranks to become the head of the Cobra militia. He speaks to someone else, and I see his figure quivering with rage. Again, his head turns toward me. The ceremony concludes, and I decide that it's time for me to leave.

He glances back again, and I think of an old saying from my youth: *The leopard's stare brings danger.*

I walk away from the ceremony ahead of the rapidly dispersing crowds.

The most dangerous time is not the war, it is after the war. My father's words wander through my brain, and I quicken my step. This man can do me no harm, I know this, but there's never a need for excess risk. The war is over.

In the parking lot, Lieutenant Colonel Okoko and Lieutenant Colonel Nkoyi approach me, smiles painting their faces. They grab my arms and pat my shoulders.

"You are so big!" they say.

"We are glad you came," they say.

"You must come to the celebration at the gendarmerie," they say.

I shake my head and try to smile. "My mother is waiting for me."

They laugh. "Tchic, you must come. It's been too many years. We want to honor you. Your shiny uniform is blinding us in the sun! Come inside."

I decline again, glancing toward my brother.

They persist, and I know that I'm being overly suspicious.

"Okay, I'll come for ten minutes," I say, "to pay my respects to the officers. Then I must go."

"Perfect," they say, showing me their teeth. "We will share drinks with you."

I walk to where Sazouka is waiting with the car.

"We're going to stop by the gendarmerie," I say, not making eye contact with him.

"What? Why? We need to get home."

"Only for a few minutes. I should pay my respects to the officers of the school."

He doesn't argue with me, because he knows better, but I can see that he disagrees.

"Park in the back," I say. "Keep the car running. I'll be right out."

The gendarmerie is cool and loud, crowded with all the officers of the military school. There is drinking and laughing all around, and I force my shoulders to relax.

Okoko and Nkoyi arrive, and we sit and begin talking. They ask questions, as I have to come to expect, about Saddam and bin Laden and the Marines. I tell them shortened versions of the stories I've told to everyone over the last day and a half. Minutes pass, but I don't rush. I will sit with my friends and I will go to my mother and we will share *sakasaka*.

A man approaches me and requests that I come to a separate room. I don't know this man, so I politely decline.

He asks again.

Okoko and Nkoyi smile and gesture for me to go, and I stand, trying to shake the feeling of unease that permeates my skin.

I'm taken into a nearby office and the door is closed behind me. Two men stand in the room. They look like guards, but I know this cannot be.

The door swings open and General Bemde strides in, followed by Captain Mapasa Daye, the cousin of my cousin and the head of the jail facility.

I stand at attention and salute. "*Mes devoirs, Mon Général*," I say, giving him the respect that he desires.

He doesn't return my salute. Instead, he points a finger into my face. "You are the son of Colonel Tchicaya."

"Yes," I say, staring into the face of the man who put my father in prison.

"What are you doing here?"

I begin to answer, but he interrupts.

"You are a deserter, and have come to help your father plan a coup."

"Sir, I do not—"

"Throw him in jail," he says, and turns to leave the room.

"General—" I say, but the door closes with a slam and I feel hands encircling my body.

This must be a joke. The general is playing a prank on me . . . but I can't see the humor in it. I have not stolen anything. I have not killed anyone.

Captain Daye steps toward me, removing handcuffs from his pocket, and I try to fight the rising swells of panic that tighten my throat.

He slips the cuffs around my wrists, averting his eyes.

"Please," I say, but he doesn't acknowledge me. He nods instead to the guards, then steps out of the room.

They grab me roughly, and I think that it's best to go along with their wishes for now because someone will let me out soon. I'm an American. This cannot happen.

I'm pulled outside, away from the party, away from anyone who would recognize me. One of the men leans close to my ear and whispers, "Tonight, we will do to you what we did to your father."

I don't know them, but it's clear that they know me.

I am to be tortured.

I will not get home to my mother.

She will wait with cold food and beating heart as the sun sets and her eldest son does not arrive.

The jail borders the gendarmerie, and we step into the shadows. I scan the hallway, memorizing the route, cataloging the location of each guard. My Marine training kicks in and this time, I don't suppress it. There is no one in this compound who is capable of stopping me. I have received the best military instruction in the world.

I smile at the soldiers and shrug. "Why is the general trying to arrest me?"

They don't answer.

"He is jealous of these ribbons, no? If he asked, I would give them to him."

Again, silence.

I try a few more times with the same result.

Hallway after hallway, deeper into the jail complex.

I am taken into an interrogation room.

"Take off your uniform," says the man waiting there. He removes the handcuffs.

"Why?"

"No questions. Take it off."

"What will you do with it?"

"Hold it for you."

I know that they'll dispose of the uniform, so as to not have American property on the premises in case something happens to me. I shake my head. "My brother is waiting in the parking lot. Bring him here and he'll take it."

They converse quickly, and one leaves the room. I begin to undress, carefully folding each piece of clothing. Every Marine wears shorts and a T-shirt underneath his uniform, and I feel the interrogator sizing me up. I feel loose, athletic, prepared.

My brother enters, his eyes wide. When he sees me, tears spill onto his cheeks. "What's happening?"

I don't have time to comfort him. "I've been arrested."

"Are you joking? I don't understand—"

"There's no time," I say, leaning in close. "Park your car outside, near the north entrance, and wait for me. I'll escape. If you don't see me, go tell Mama what's going on." I pull away from him. "I need tennis shoes. I will not go barefoot." The guards nod as I hand my folded uniform to Sazouka. "I brought shoes to run in after the ceremony. Bring them to me."

I push him toward the exit.

The door slams and I'm alone with the two guards, contemplating what's about to happen.

My brother's face looms in my head, and I discard Plan A. I won't risk Sazouka's life. I can't take two sons from my mother. If I am to die, so be it, but I resolve to die alone.

I quickly come up with a Plan B. I will escape to the outside, jump the surrounding wall, and head for my home. There's no one who can catch me in the open field.

This, I know.

I feel the cell phone in my waistband. If I escape, I can use it to call for help.

The guard comes back with my running shoes and I slip them on, tying the laces extra tight. I stare at the interrogator and smile.

"So the general has become upset, yes?"

I talk to him while running through the escape route in my head. Flashes of the Middle East pop through my mind, and I slow my breathing. I've made it out of worse countries than this. I haven't come all this way to be killed in my hometown.

Tonight, we will do to you what we did to your father.

My appearance is cool, unthreatened. I'm not a danger to these men. I'm unaware what they have planned. Slowly, they relax. They ask me about America, about my life overseas, about the Marine Corps.

I hold the cell phone close to my body.

There are two guards behind me. The guard at the door glances toward me, then at his watch, then at the door.

And again.

The interrogation continues, but the questions are inane, uninteresting.

I see the guard by the door reaching into his pocket.

More questions.

He pulls out a pack of cigarettes.

Questions.

He extracts a cigarette and eases the door open, stepping into the hallway.

I don't have the luxury of debate. I must act on my instinct as I have been trained to do.

I must go now.

This is my opportunity.

Go.

Brazzaville, Congo
1995–96

CHAPTER 10

The gendarmerie is the elite paramilitary force of the Congo. They accept only the best and brightest, so there was no guarantee that I would get in, regardless of the rank or social position of my father.

In the Congo, it's important for every household to have at least one family member in the military. The army and gendarmerie are considered worthy in ways that haphazard militia forces are not. The military can not only police the streets, ask questions of neighbors, and carry weapons, but they have the weight of the government behind them when they do it.

I studied for over two months, readying my brain and body for the exams. My father pushed hard, constantly reminding me that his own reputation was on the line.

"Everyone will be watching you," he said. "They want you to fail."

I trained even harder.

One shot, one kill.

The day of the exam, over a thousand boys filed into the hallways of the École Militaire Général DeClerck in Brazzaville. My father dropped me off only a few minutes before the test began, and I tore down the hallways, finding my room assignment and slipping into the classroom just moments before the French Foreign Legion officer shut the door and locked it. The other officers nodded, recognizing me. I felt the weight on my shoulders grow heavier.

When the results came back, my father approached me with a smile on his face. "Third in the country," he said, eyes gleaming. "Out of all my colleagues at the gendarmerie, no one had a son who scored higher. You have made me very proud, Tchico. The other officers will tire of hearing your name on my lips."

Relief washed over my body like a river.

I was in.

Each passing day brought me closer to my father's goals and farther away from Marielle.

"It's such a long time," she said.

"I'll be nearby. I will visit."

"You can't," she said, her eyes filling with water. "They'll never let you out."

"Only for the first three months. When we return from the field, I'll be the best-behaved recruit in the gendarmerie! They'll have to give me my leave."

"I'll visit you."

"I know," I said, and kissed her. "When I get back, we will be married."

"I know," she said, forcing a smile beneath the veil of tears.

In that moment, I thought my heart would burst.

My father, grinning wildly, thumped the wheel. "You will succeed."

"Yes," I said, watching the sun rise up over the trees. There were few other cars on the road.

"You must be better than everyone around you. They expect much, since you are the top scorer." He paused, rubbing the wheel. "Since you are the son of Tchicaya Missamou."

"Yes," I said again. My bag rested on my lap, packed neatly with clean clothes, soap, razor blades, and a bright new pair of tennis shoes. On top of all this sat a picture of Marielle.

As we pulled up to the headquarters, my father turned to me. "I'm proud of you."

"Thank you," I said, and we nodded at each other.

I took a deep breath and entered the headquarters of the gendarmerie.

The room was nearly empty, as I was over an hour early for the expected call.

"Who goes there?" came the booming echo, and I squinted into the blackness.

I snapped to attention. "Recruit Tchicaya!" I barked.

"Who gave you the right to be called 'recruit'?"

"I . . . am a recruit," I said.

"Wrong! You have to earn that title. Do you understand?"

"Yes, sir!"

"Now you are nothing but an animal. Do you understand?"

"Yes, sir!"

"Get your face on the floor and show me you understand. Twenty push-ups!"

I leaped to the ground as other "animals" trickled in. The drill instructor came close and squinted at me.

"You're the son of Major Tchicaya, is that correct?"

I stood. "Yes, sir."

"You think that makes you better than us?"

"No, sir."

"Are you sure?"

"Yes, sir."

"That's correct. You're not. And to remind you of that, from here on out, your animal name will be *morpion*. Is that understood?"

"Yes, sir."

Morpion, roughly translated, means "pubic lice."

All the new recruits received nicknames from the instructors, ranging from "Hyena Malonga" to "Rhino Samba." For the next three months, I would be "Pubic Lice Tchicaya." I began to wonder what I'd gotten myself into.

We lined up for the bus and I picked up my bag, arms shaking from the sheer number of push-ups I'd already been forced to do.

"*Morpion* Tchicaya, what is that?"

I froze at attention. "My bag, sir!"

"Do you think you are a civilian?"

"No, sir!"

"Then why would you ever imagine you could bring civilian clothes into a military establishment?"

I didn't answer, as there was no acceptable response. The officer, an evil-looking man named Colonel Niama, got into my face and ripped the bag from my hands. He unzipped it and dumped the contents onto the deck. "Soap?" He looked around at the other recruits, feigning disbelief. "*Morpion* Tchicaya thinks he is going to have time for soap!" He picked up a couple of my shirts and my recently purchased pair of tennis shoes. "We will give you everything you need, *morpion*. Don't you trust us?"

"Yes, sir!" I said.

Colonel Niama leaned down. "And what is this?" He stood, holding the picture of Marielle.

"*Mundelé* women in my camp? I don't think so. Everyone, come take a look at this!" The drill instructors stopped their own yelling and came over to ogle Marielle. My jaw clenched. He turned to me again. "The only woman you'll be seeing is named AK-47, do you understand me?"

"Yes, sir."

He pulled the picture close to his mouth and kissed it. "This is my bitch now, my wife. My fourth wife." He slipped it into his pocket. "Is that okay with you, *morpion* Tchicaya?"

I didn't say anything, furious beyond words.

"Well?"

"Yes, sir," I spat through closed teeth.

Colonel Niama smiled and pulled the picture out again, licking it. "I'm going to find her and fuck her tonight." He grinned at me. "Say she's my wife." He kissed the picture again. "Say it."

"Yes, sir. She is your wife."

"Good. She is my wife like your father is my wife." He picked up my things, marched over to the river, and tossed them in. "Everyone onto the bus."

We were blindfolded and laid on top of each other, the drill instructors striding over our squashed bodies for nearly thirty minutes. It felt as if it would never end. My muscles ached, my ego boiled, and my fists clenched as I thought of what he'd done to Marielle's picture.

The shouts melded into a steady wash and the groans of my fellow recruits began to seep into my brain. I wanted to quit, but remembered the promise I'd made to my father.

There was simply no other option.

I would finish what I started, or I would die trying.

CHAPTER 11

The training ground was named Camp Bifouiti and was located about twenty kilometers (twelve miles) outside Brazzaville. It was composed mainly of dust.

We were hurried out of the buses and into the barracks, such as they were, amidst recurring bouts of push-ups and shouting. A handful of us were pulled into a shack to receive our "proper military haircuts." Some of the recruits had been smart enough to shave their heads before arrival, and I wondered why my father hadn't imparted this little piece of information.

A drill instructor stepped forward, raised a bottle over his head, and smashed it against a tree stump. He repeated the motion with a new bottle. And another.

He handed the pieces out and watched with grim delight as we shaved one another's heads with the shards of broken glass. The blood ran down my face, and I distracted myself from the pain by imagining Marielle beside me.

We didn't sleep that night, or for the next two nights. Drill instructors took turns running us through the jungle, making us do push-ups, forcing us to sit in pig shit. It was torture of the worst kind, and within a few hours, every single recruit was stumbling around like a drunkard. Still, the insults came.

"*Morpion* Tchicaya, your father claims you are very strong. You don't look very strong to me."

"No, sir," I gasped, striding up the hill under the glaring eye of the sun.

"You're not strong? Why are you here if you're not strong?"

The lights spotted in front of my eyes, and I struggled to form coherent words. This wasn't what I'd signed on for. This wasn't what I'd expected. It was more aggressive, more brutal.

I wore military-issue shorts, a military-issue shirt, and military-issue shoes. I'd been given no underwear or socks. I carried a water flask and a small metal bowl attached to a thin belt.

Time passed slowly, and I began to learn what it meant to be part of a military unit. As we were the first class to be trained at Camp Bifouiti since the dissolution of the gendarmerie in the 1960s, our drill instructors were old—veterans of the gendarmerie, militias, police forces, republican guards, and on and on. These were experienced men who knew what it took to stay alive in the field—teamwork.

The number-one rule of training was that if one person in your unit screwed up, everyone would pay for it. If one person lagged, everyone would run extra.

Our civilian minds were being crushed.

Breakfast was a vat of water filled with dark coffee grounds. Each "recruit" was given a piece of dry bread and about thirty seconds to eat. However, when the first person finished, everyone was finished. Often, this occurred before I even received my food. The drill instructors watched to see who was aware of their fellow soldiers and who was selfish.

"We will give you everything," they shouted. "We will give you food, knowledge, weapons, and clothing, but we won't give you time. That, you must learn to make for yourself."

And we did.

A recruit named Mbemba became my object of study. He was a monster. Every morning, he would shove his bread into the coffee cup, let it soak up the thick liquid, then swallow it whole. The entire process took less than ten seconds. I challenged myself to finish before him, vowed to learn his techniques. In this way, I slowly climbed through the ranks of recruits, observing the best of the best in each area and modeling myself after them. The military has no place for ego, only for results.

We were awakened three or four times every night by the banging of metal cans, and would be put through a series of physical exercises and continuous roll calls. In theory, this was to ensure that no one had escaped, but I couldn't imagine anyone having enough energy to even dream of freedom, much less take steps toward achieving it.

The cans clanged and I sprang out of my bed, leaping to attention. The drill instructor headed straight for me. The scent of his breath wrapped around my nostrils and I tried not to gag.

"Everyone, I had a dream about *morpion* Tchicaya. I dreamed that he wanted to kill me. Is that right?" he shouted.

"No, sir!" I responded, my voice cracking.

"Well, in case you're lying, we're not going to sleep tonight. Everyone, line up!"

As we ran, the other recruits tossed me angry glances as if I was somehow responsible for infiltrating the dreams of the drill instructor. I didn't understand how we could simultaneously be taught the value of teamwork while learning to hate each other.

The gendarmerie was composed of representatives from all three militias. The French Foreign Legion, which was the driving force behind the reinstitution of the paramilitary unit, didn't care where you came from, as long as you were one of the best and the brightest. We were repeatedly told that if any fighting or discrimination was witnessed, the responsible party would be immediately expelled from the camp.

This happened only once.

A Cocoyes recruit named Wando was being harassed by a Cobra drill instructor. It was nothing personal—the role of "designated target" seemed to be on permanent rotation. Honestly, I was relieved that it was someone else's turn, anyone else's turn.

It was Wando's impression, however, that he was being treated unfairly.

"I'll kill you," he said to the drill instructor. "I've killed more Cobras than you can imagine. It's nothing to me."

The drill instructor stared at him, then backed away.

The next day, Wando was gone.

We learned to act civilly toward one another, but did not mix with different tribes during meals. We were all gendarmerie, yes, but the memories of the first civil war were fresh, and hatred does not disappear because someone commands it.

Lunch was a dry fish called *mosseka* that was tossed into a pot of boiling oil, then poured onto the ground. Recruits would scramble to get their fish and a piece of cassava before the thirty seconds was up.

"Do not taste the fish," the drill instructors would shout. "Eat it now and enjoy it later."

I would swallow the fish whole, followed by the requisite two cups of water for hydration and digestion. Then, I would smile at Mbemba.

After lunch, we would run.

And run.

We learned that the limits of exhaustion are not limits, but merely suggested guidelines. We learned that exercise can beat any disease. We learned that discomfort is not an obstacle.

"Showers" were long sprinklers that we were herded through like cattle, usually for no longer than thirty seconds. Since there was no toilet paper in the wilderness, we learned to prioritize, washing only our armpits and asses, trying to avoid getting what we called "monkey butt."

We learned to march in the classic Russian style, arms swinging high, legs jutted out nearly parallel to the ground.

We learned to make our beds.

We learned to crawl through mosquito-infested waters.

We learned to rely on a partner.

The last five years of my life, I had grown up with Gervais by my side, and for the previous two years, I'd rarely been without Marielle. Now I found myself alone. The drill instructors paired me with another sixteen-year-old boy, named Kosi, whom I grew to trust with my life. He saw that I was a target because of my father, and saved my ass more times than I would care to count. I could rely on him to fix my bed if I was running late, to share his water, to share his food, to carry me if I collapsed.

Oftentimes during those three months, when I thought I was going to die, Kosi was the one who kept me focused and alive.

"Come on," he would say to me, out of sight of the drill instructors. "You can't let them beat you. You are stronger than this. You can't let them win. You have to keep going."

And I would.

I did the same for him, and day after day, we grew close through the shared torture. In boot camp, a few weeks can easily equal a year in the outside world, and I found that I trusted him without thought or hesitation.

Soon, we were able to communicate by simple glances or murmured words. I learned that in combat situations, friendship becomes more important than clothing, shelter, or water.

"Tchic, when we get out of here, we will do great things. We're better than the gendarmerie, stronger than the Congo. Promise me we will do great things."

"I promise," I said, meaning it with every ounce of my being.

Still, as much as Kosi and I talked, notions of individuality inevitably began to blur. Those three months at Camp Bifouiti could have been an entirely separate life, and I struggled to remember Marielle's smell, lay awake at night trying to recall the rules of the games Gervais and I had played. I noticed that as one became part of a collective, personal memories could not help but fade.

CHAPTER 12

Get up! Out of bed!"

We sprang to our feet and I straightened my cot, still half-asleep.

"Grab your weapons. We're going to teach you how to kill."

We were driven out to the firing range, about sixty kilometers (forty miles) north of Brazzaville.

No one could keep his eyes open. The previous night, we'd been awakened over and over again by a succession of maniacal drill instructors, each more aggressive than the last. My arms and legs ached, my chest burned, and my eyes had more red in them than white. I nodded off again and again, clutching my AK-47 to my chest.

The truck was filled with over thirty recruits, most sitting back to back on benches in the center of the cab. The repetitive jostling lured many of us toward sleep, only to be shaken awake by a particularly vicious rock or divot.

The driver was an instructor known for his habitual drinking, and it was clear that he'd been up even later than us. The constant swerving brought grim smiles to dirt-covered faces.

We were wearing full battle gear, complete with packs, helmets, weapons, and boots. The weight added to the dreamy feel of the ride, and I struggled to keep my eyes open. I didn't want to be the one caught sleeping while holding a live weapon.

The boys on either side of me talked about nonsense, letting their tongues wag, hoping to stay awake themselves.

A loud squealing jolted my eyes open and I grabbed the bench, letting my weapon fall to the floor. The truck tilted wildly to the right. I lost my grip, falling against other recruits, pinning them to the wall. The sound of shearing metal erupted, and the world exploded into movement and light. Someone screamed as the truck flipped over and over, but I gritted my teeth, fighting to find purchase somewhere amidst the rolling blackness.

I saw legs and arms and splatters of blood as I fell against the roof of the truck, then the other side. I braced myself for each fall, thankful that my helmet was firmly secured.

The truck stopped, groaning and settling, quiet now beneath the howls of pain.

I oriented myself, staring back at where I'd been sitting. The two men on either side of me were crumpled, their necks contorted at strange angles.

They were the only fatalities.

I was the only one who escaped without injury.

No one said anything as we exited the truck, carrying the wounded, passing them to safety. The drill instructors patted us on the backs and made genuine eye contact for the first time. They wanted to bring us helpful pain, not tragedy. They wanted us to suffer, not die.

The driver of the truck received only a few scratches.

At the funeral, we watched as the two trucks carrying our comrades followed each other down a long dusty road. As the road ended, one truck turned left, heading north. The other turned right, heading south.

For some reason, this image burned itself into my memory, and I don't doubt that it had a similar effect on the others.

No matter how much we'd been through as recruits, no matter how much we'd learned to trust and rely on each other, I was still a Lari. Mbemba was still an M'Bochi. Kosi was still a Nibolek. There were some things that training couldn't teach, that education couldn't cure.

· · ·

Shortly thereafter, we returned from the field to the main base of the gendarmerie. Our three months were over and we were to be considered Élève Gendarme. We could now use the title of "recruit" without fear of retribution.

The drill instructors, who had spent three months haunting our every waking moment and most of our sleeping ones, suddenly became friendly, helpful, human.

We had all lost weight and gotten three shades darker.

We showered, put on new clothes, and genuinely felt something had changed.

Our civilian minds had been destroyed.

We were soldiers.

I ran to the phone, grinning as Marielle's voice exploded into my ear. I instantly got both chills and an erection.

"Tchic!" she said, the happiness spilling through the phone lines.

"I'm back," I said. "I want to see you."

"When?"

"Every Saturday, if I don't have any demerits, they let me off until 5:00 NK . Sunday night."

"And if you have demerits?"

"My leave is suspended."

"If your leave is suspended, you'll get demerits from me."

I smiled. "I'll be the best-behaved soldier in the history of the gendarmerie."

And I was, attending classes on Congolese politics, military maneuvers, fighting techniques, criminology. The last three months in the field, every single instructor had been a black soldier from the Congo. Now every instructor was French *mundelé*. The black drill instructors still had sway over us, but their goal was no longer to break us down. Their goal was to build us up.

Our favorite was Sergeant Mabiala, known as Quinze because every time he saw a recruit he would say "Quinze" and expect fifteen push-ups, rain or shine, inside or out. He was a tough man whom I never saw tired or down. He was by far the hardest drill instructor, but also by far the most loved. The more we hated him, the more we adored him. It was an odd exchange, but one I took note of.

Even though we were back in civilization, the same basic rules applied. If one person was late to class, we were all punished. If one person failed a test, we would all pay for it. Slowly, I began to notice the results this produced. We helped each other study, examined each other before inspections. We developed a vested interest in the well-being of our fellow soldiers. We realized that we were all connected physically, mentally, and spiritually.

That first Saturday, I spent more time on my appearance than ever before. My shoes were like crystal, my uniform, flawless. I stood still as the drill instructor scraped a piece of paper along my cheek, listening for a single sound to indicate that I wasn't perfectly shaven. He examined my shirt, my pants, my canoe-shaped hat. My heart thudded in anticipation of his reaction—I'd dressed perfectly that day, but it wasn't for him.

I walked outside the base to find Marielle waiting for me. She threw her head back and laughed, her teeth gleaming white in the sun. In that moment, she was beautiful, perfect. I ran to her, squeezing her body, kissing her over and over again.

"I missed you," she said, staring into my eyes.

"I missed you, too," I said, my hands finding familiar spots along her body, my skin trembling as her fingers traced the creases of my blue gendarmerie uniform.

"You look amazing," she said.

Marielle was my past and my future rolled into one. I couldn't disguise the roaring emotions she stirred inside me.

We made love all night and all day, and I barely made it back to the base before the 5:00 ₦ₖ . deadline. I was exhausted, but happy. Three months is a long time to be away from the woman you love, and there were no words to describe my happiness. Before we parted, we made plans to meet the following night inside the walls of the base. It was a risky move, but I believed the damage caused by not seeing her would have been worse.

I snuck out of the barracks, something that would have been impossible during the field training, and waited by the wall. Soon, I heard the scratching of someone climbing, then watched as one beautiful leg swung over. I caught her and we ducked behind some bushes next to the obstacle course.

She giggled, and I covered her mouth. There were regular patrols in the area and I couldn't risk being spotted. I would be discharged immediately. I pushed thoughts of my father out of my mind and made love to Marielle there on the grounds of the gendarmerie.

Two nights later, she snuck in again. Then again. Three or four nights a week I saw her, and every weekend. She would bring me gifts each night—chocolate, milk, sugar, lotion, soap—all the extravagances I could imagine. We became bolder, always going to the same bush, sometimes for hours at a time.

Our signal was simple. Around 2000 hours, she would throw three rocks onto the roof of the barracks, then wait. I would slip out and whistle a special tune. She would whistle back, then scale the wall. It became commonplace. We grew overconfident and careless.

One night our whispering giggles must have alerted someone, because the sound of quickly approaching footsteps made me freeze. I pushed my hand over her mouth and held my breath. Her eyes grew wide, as she knew the potential repercussions. She was still in university, as was I, and neither of us could afford the public shame of exposure.

The footsteps came close, and a flashlight shone around our area. Someone muttered a few words, walked around the bush, then slowly retreated.

We didn't move for at least five minutes, then relaxed. The bush had saved us, but we both realized how lucky we'd been. I was an adult now, not a child. I couldn't risk my future on such actions. Still, Marielle continued to sneak in, and I continued to see her. Love was more powerful than any rationality could ever be.

Besides, that night we had the best sex of our lives.

CHAPTER 13

She showed up one night, upset and anxious.

"What's the matter?" I asked.

"Gervais," she said.

"What?"

"He's being sent away to the Ivory Coast for school."

"What? When?"

"Soon. Less than a week. He told me to let you know in case he wasn't able to see you before he left."

"Not see me? He has to see me!"

"Not if his parents put him on a plane before he has a chance. They might, you know. They don't think about things like saying good-bye."

"Tell him I have to see him."

"I will," she said, then kissed me.

My chest hurt. My brain began recycling the countless thousands of memories that I'd shared with Gervais, the things we'd done and the things we'd planned on doing. In that moment, I realized that Gervais and I had grown apart, that his loss was inevitable, that somehow, Marielle had . . . not replaced him, exactly, but filled a similar place in my heart.

I felt like part of me was disappearing.

I pulled Marielle closer, trying to feel that completeness.

"I need to see him again," I murmured into her ear.

"I know," she said.

But I didn't.

His parents put him on a plane a few days later, before we had a chance to talk, before I even got a chance to say good-bye, to tell him what he meant to me.

I never saw him again.

Even without fighting, the military had managed to take something dear from me.

It was my first taste of the true pain of solitude, and I thanked the gods that I had Marielle by my side.

One afternoon, the recruits were piled into a room with a large screen set up against the far wall. One of the French instructors turned on a projector and we watched a movie called *Full Metal Jacket*. I'd never seen a film like this, and it spurred flashbacks to the Marines I'd met on the golf course. Finally, I was training to be like them, undergoing an experience similar to theirs.

I was mesmerized by this American film that somehow diagrammed what I was going through, excited that my hardship connected me to people so far away.

The word "Marine" flashed through my mind again and again, and somehow, I felt that I was creating my own destiny.

I began to take special pride in my uniform, shining my boots for hours at a time, staring at my reflection in their glassy surfaces. I vowed that no one would have more impressive boots than I did. Contests began, rivalries sprang up, but no one worked harder than me. I began storing them in plastic bags on Friday, the day before inspection, so that no one could compare theirs to mine. I carried a sponge with me to inspection for the dust that always seemed to accumulate on the walk to the parade grounds. My uniform was pressed, the creases were sharp, and the brass was shined.

I was becoming more like my father every day.

Saturday inspection was one of the key things that allowed us to leave the base every week, and I wasn't about to risk my time with Marielle on a uniform error. I was almost always perfect, but others weren't as lucky. I became a leader in the group, helping others prepare for inspection, knowing that their laziness could affect my leave.

This was a powerful, continuing lesson. The collective was both stronger and more important than the individual. Without the happiness and support of my peers, I could not achieve my goals. Without Kosi by my side, I could never have gotten through the three months in the field. Without Marielle, those nine long months inside the gendarmerie would have made me go insane.

People need people.

By yourself, you cannot do anything.

The whistle was strange, delayed, stuttering.

I stood waiting by the bushes, anxious to see her.

She dropped down, her eyes red and swollen from crying.

I grabbed her, whispering furiously.

"Marielle, what is it? What's wrong?"

She shook her head, her lower lip trembling. "My parents. Th-they're getting a divorce."

I took a second to collect my thoughts, rubbing her shoulders softly. "I'm sorry, Marielle. But it's okay. Things happen. My parents are separated, too. It'll be okay."

"No," she said, beginning to sob, "I have to go with my mother."

"Go?"

"She's moving to Germany. They say I have to go with her."

"But—but, what about school?"

"They say I'll finish in Europe. She's leaving on Friday. And I'm going with her."

Pain blasted through my heart like a bullet, and I blinked the confusion away. "Friday? This Friday? But—"

"There's nothing anyone can do, Tchicaya. I told her I wanted to stay here, to be with you, but they wouldn't listen."

"You could stay with your father—"

"They won't have it. I'm going, Tchic. I'm going." I held her as she broke down, pressing her against my body, struggling to contain my own tears.

"It will be better for you. The school—"

"I want to be with you."

"You can come and visit when I'm out of the gendarmerie. Or I'll move to Germany. I'll find you, Marielle. I'll come to you. I promise."

We were being loud and reckless, but I didn't care.

"You can't promise that, Tchic, you can't. I'm leaving. Moving away. For good."

"I promise. I promise you, Marielle."

She shook her head. "I don't know. I—"

Tears obscured the rest of her sentence and I bowed my head, defeated. I didn't know what to do. "My father—" I started.

"There's nothing he can do," she said.

I fell silent.

She was right.

Sometimes, other people's mistakes could bring misery to everyone. Sometimes, pain wasn't limited to the victims.

I held her until the rays of the sun touched our skin, then helped her back over the wall, crawling into my bed empty, feeling exhausted. It couldn't be true, I thought. It was so sudden, so unexpected.

That Friday, I *courviaté* (went AWOL), leaping the wall of the gendarmerie by moonlight and running to Marielle's house. I had to see her one last time, had to tell her how I felt, had to make her remember it forever.

I arrived at the house, panting and sweating in the summer heat. Her room was dark. The house was empty, lifeless.

She'd been telling the truth.

She was gone.

I stared at the house, circling it again and again, eventually crumpling onto the front porch. I sat there, feeling the ghost of

Marielle around me, and I cried until I thought my heart would break.

The months passed quickly after that, and I devoted myself 150 percent to the military lifestyle.

Graduation arrived and I wore my uniform out to the parade deck, forcing my grin into a scowl as we marched past the spectators who had come to share in our happiness. We were the first class to graduate from the gendarmerie in over thirty years and represented a return to tradition, a celebration of Congolese history. The turnout was enormous.

My father, as commandant of the regiment, led the parade. I, as one of the top graduates, was near the front of the troops.

We watched the television later that day, and I don't think I've ever seen my father as happy as I did at that moment. He stared at himself marching past the camera, arms swinging high, uniform perfect . . . and there, not ten steps behind him, was me. His son. Marching in unison with him. Wearing the same uniform. Arms swinging high.

He laughed out loud and clapped me on the back. I grinned, proud.

I'd lost Marielle, but I had discovered myself.

Even then, I understood that this was a fair trade.

Marielle, I could learn to live without, at least temporarily.

My training, I was to learn very soon, I could not.

PART 5
WAR AND BUSINESS

The greatest glory in living lies not in never falling,
but in rising every time we fall.

—NELSON MANDELA

Brazzaville, Congo
August 21, 2004

saturday

G o.

Now.

I leap to my feet and run.

I feel hands on my arms and push them away without looking. I throw the door open and head down the hallway, knocking over the smoking guard.

Behind me, I hear *"Bosimba yé!"* and the clatter of feet, but I force myself to stay calm. I'm in no danger here. I am a Marine. There's nothing I'm not equipped to handle.

I head down the hallway as I rehearsed it, my shorts and T-shirt flapping, my tennis shoes squealing against the concrete floor. I am a leopard stalking his prey. I focus on my freedom and pursue it with every ounce of my being.

The front of the building approaches and I lower my head, powering through the lobby. A body crushes against mine, and I glance up to see the eyes of Captain Mapasa Daye widening against my arm. I push him to the ground and slam against the door. I am outside.

The muggy air stops my lungs and I take a deep breath, forcing oxygen to my muscles. I head for the corner of the yard.

The wall is getting closer . . . closer . . .

I leap up, throwing one foot against the seven-foot barrier, propelling myself to the top. As I throw my hands down, I feel the cell phone smashing against brick. I toss the pieces down and land on the other side, directly in the middle of midday traffic on one of the busiest streets in Brazzaville. I take in my surroundings and turn right, where two police officers are standing. I charge forward, slamming into them with all the force I can muster, feeling their muscles seize up as they fall. I run, not knowing who is behind me, not knowing what I will find in front of me.

I must get away. I must get to my mother. Only among my people will I be safe.

I churn my legs, only vaguely aware of the direction I'm heading, my ears tuned to the slightest sounds.

In the distance, I see the wall of the Lycée de la Liberatión and run toward it. I know the grounds better than I know my own house and quickly sort through potential hiding places. My mind begins scanning them, cataloging them, prioritizing them. The wall is one hundred yards away, then eighty, then fifty . . .

Gunshots splatter against the brick, throwing chips of red and brown onto the dull grass of the lawn.

AK-47, says my brain. *Not very accurate.*

You, it says a second later, *they're shooting at you.*

Another burst of gunfire erupts, and I hear bullets whizzing past my head.

Screams from all around me.

Women covering their children.

Crowds running and ducking behind buildings.

Gunfire.

Chaos erupts on the streets, and I slow down.

I would rather be shot in the chest than the back.

If I'm to die, I'll die facing my attackers, not running from them.

I stop.

I turn around.

My hands stretch toward the sky.

"Don't shoot!" I scream, showing them my palms.

"Don't shoot!" I shout with every ounce of my being, willing my voice to carry over the gunshots. My lungs crack with the effort.

Another burst of gunfire, and I collapse, crippling pain lancing through my right shin. I hear the cry of my own voice, but it comes from hundreds of miles away.

The guards are upon me. Heavy boots, fists, buttstocks of AK-47s are pounded over and over against my chest, head, and arms. I curl myself tightly on the ground, noting that it's now slippery and red, noting that my body is numb, noting that I feel bulletproof in this moment.

The beating goes on and on and on, new guards arriving to replace the tiring ones. Everyone wants a piece of the American Marine. Everybody wants to take his shot. The boots stomp and the gunshots seem like distant memories. I feel myself floating, calm, waiting.

My cheek opens up, and blood streams into my mouth and nose.

Someone steps on my leg. And again. And again.

My head is pressed farther and farther into the concrete, until I feel that I might break through, burying myself in the earth.

This goes on for minutes, hours, days, a lifetime.

All the guards are exhausted, and the blows begin to dwindle. I force myself toward consciousness. I don't want to slip away, for fear that I may never come back. My eyes are swollen shut, but I feel hands beneath my arms, feel the concrete grating against my legs as I am dragged. I'm surprised to find handcuffs around my wrists. I can't recall when they were put on.

The kicks resume. I feel them against my ribs and chin. A group surrounds me now, shouting, spitting on my face, screaming into my ears. As we walk, the numbers grow, the wall of sound encircles me.

Concrete turns to grass turns to pavement.

They're dragging me back to the jail, I think, unable to comprehend the notion of surviving for another three hundred yards.

Then, like everything else, the pain from the boots dies down and I'm left focusing on my brain, nurturing it, keeping it alive.

Pain is what lets you know that you're not dead.

Yes. I must focus on the pain, for it will keep me on this Earth.

I see the *Ndoki* in front of me, holding a live mamba, but then he is gone.

Somehow, in the distance, I hear the sound of the *bôda* and feel the cool hand of my father on my arm.

I feel myself floating higher and higher above the clouds.

I force my thoughts to the Marines, reciting the manual in my mind like a mantra. I think of my father, alone in France, unaware that his son is about to re-enact his darkest day. I picture the phone call when he hears the news, watching as he clutches his chest, staring as he crumples to the ground. I think of my mother, hovering over the stove, adding thick cassava leaves to the *saka-saka*, wanting to make sure that her son lacks nothing. I see her sinking to her knees. I see tears pouring into her wailing mouth. I see her heart breaking.

I force air into my lungs.

Stay alive.

Focus.

I've trained my whole life for moments like this.

The tugging continues, and my arms feel as if they're separating from the rest of my body. The pain comes and goes, but when it's here, it's unbearable. Blood pours from my mouth. I've nearly forgotten about my leg.

I'm a dead man. I know this.

It's only a matter of time and agony.

The group surrounding me has become immense, their shouts and spittle covering my body like a monsoon. I drop my head as low as I can, trying to focus on anything but their raspy cries.

The temperature changes and the sound dips and I know we're in the lobby of the jail. The soldiers don't even break stride, and my legs bounce against the gritty sand of the hallway.

I try to speak, not because I have something to say, but to reassure myself that I am still capable of making a sound, still able to influence the world around me. Nothing comes out, and I let my head drop.

Stay alive.

The sand slips away and I feel my body battering against cement stairs.

The sounds taper and the darkness comes, but it is not my mind fading. I'm in a jail cell. The inner door shuts with a clang, and I hear a grate sliding into place behind it. Rustles of movement crowd the room, and I lean back into a sitting position. I squeeze my eyes into a squint, blinking away droplets of blood.

I see only blackness.

A fist slams against my face and I fall, my head bouncing against the floor.

Another fist, this time against my chest.

A foot strikes my lower back.

Then they're upon me, the only sounds in the room the thumping of bone against bone, the moans seeping from my bloodied lips.

My hands pull against the cuffs, tearing my skin. My face grinds into the piss and shit and sweat on the floor and I grit my teeth against the pain. It is fresh. It is real.

I am no longer numb.

Ten, twenty, a hundred, a million hands strike my battered body, and the darkness is so complete that I can't tell if my eyes are open or closed.

The beating continues.

I'm helpless, here in the dark, on the floor.

I am helpless.

I want to scream, but can't make a sound.

I want to run, but can't stand.

I want to live, but can't bear the pain.

Blow after blow after blow, and time loses all meaning.

Then, a voice, floating through the air. *"Bo tika yé."*

And again.

This voice, it has power here, for the beatings slow and then stop.

My body quivers and shakes, and I feel that I've forgotten how to control it.

I'm surrounded by the sounds of the jungle. Fierce, heavy breathing, the scratch of skin against skin, the grunt of the forgotten.

Tears well up, but I don't let them fall.

I try to speak, but words don't come out.

My mind refuses to process the silent screams of my body. In my head, I am a free man. In my head, I am a Marine.

These things are still true, I remind myself, as the blackness rises, engulfing me.

Nothing has changed.

Brazzaville, Congo
1996–97

CHAPTER 14

I barely had time to sleep.

Like many of my fellow gendarmerie graduates, I'd been assigned to Lissouba's Republican Guard, a mostly superficial designation. The president's real protection was provided by the Aubeville, a group of Israeli-trained Niboleks from the south. His inner circle of bodyguards were all from Tchigidi, his birthplace. In fact, all the key positions in the Lissouba administration were manned by members of his own tribe—a fact that would prove to be his undoing.

My father had been transferred to Pointe-Noire, the economic center and second-largest city in the Congo, located about 510 kilometers (320 miles) southwest of Brazzaville. In his absence, I was in charge of feeding five of his sons and daughters, paying and feeding the workers, running the hotel, and protecting his house. Luckily for me, Lissouba considered it bad taste to live in Sassou-Nguesso's old headquarters, and built his own palace not far from my father's house.

To save time, I moved into the Oasis and spent most of my nights there, occasionally sleeping over at the house with my brothers and sisters. Even when we shared a roof, I spent little time with my siblings, who were all pursuing their own goals, their own missions. They had little time for my dreams, and sadly, I had little time for theirs.

Business was good. My father was becoming a wealthy man and, even though I was barely seventeen years old, I was quickly making a name for myself with the *mundelé* tourists.

Life was busy, but quiet.

Bang.

Bang.

"Sous off! Sous off!"

My eyes slammed open and I looked at the clock: 2:00 ? ,к ,

I leaped out of bed and threw open the window, naked.

A man stood there, dripping and shivering, his body covered in grass and mud. "You must help us," said the man, whom I now recognized as a bodyguard for Mr. Alard DeVos, the Belgian *mundelé* who lived beside my father's property. "My boss is being robbed."

"Now?" I said, my heart pounding.

"Now. They tied us up and threw us into the river. My partner, I don't know where he is, maybe dead. I managed to get to the bank and free myself. You must come quickly."

I threw on a pair of shorts and grabbed my AK-47 from its usual position beside my bed. I ran out the door and over to Mr. DeVos's compound, firing several rounds into the air. As I had hoped, the shots scared off the intruders, and I watched as members of the Ninja militia leaped the wall and disappeared into the jungle.

Slowly, gun raised, I entered the compound and approached the front door. Mr. DeVos's wife was standing there, shaking, her shirt ripped, her breasts exposed. Beside her, head in his hands, was Mr. DeVos. Their daughter was sitting on the couch, stone-faced, stunned.

"Are you okay?" I asked, suddenly aware that I was half-naked and holding an AK-47.

Mr. DeVos looked up. "Yes, yes, thank you for coming. You, you saved us. They were going to—"

Mrs. DeVos began to cry and ran out of the room. His daughter didn't move.

He cleared his throat. "They got away with some jewelry and money, nothing serious. At least everyone is okay."

"That's the important thing." I lowered my weapon and clicked the safety.

"Thank you," he said again. "You saved us."

"No problem," I said, turning to leave.

"Wait." I stopped. He walked over to me. "What if they come back?"

I thought it over. It wasn't likely, but stranger things had happened. "Come sleep in the hotel tonight. I'll make sure you're safe."

"But what about our house?"

The security guard stepped forward, still dripping brown water all over the rugs. "I will stay and protect the house."

Mr. DeVos nodded. "Let me get some things and alert my wife. We'll stay with you tonight."

I shivered in the night air and waited for them to gather their belongings.

The next morning, I found Mr. DeVos sitting on the steps of the hotel, smoking a cigarette. It was clear he hadn't slept.

I smiled. "How are you?"

He shook his head, exhaling a large cloud of smoke. "Couldn't sleep. My wife took a few pills, so she's out, but I couldn't stop thinking." He took another drag. "Thank you for saving us."

"It's no problem," I said, recalling what my father had told me about his neighbor. Mr. DeVos had escaped Congo-Kinshasa, the country bordering us on the east, during its civil war in 1991. A lot of *mundelé* had fled the country during that time and moved to Brazzaville. He was a well-respected engineer at the nearby plant and was very wealthy.

He put out his cigarette and stood up. "Would you be my personal bodyguard?"

I blinked, but didn't change position.

"I'll pay you," he said. "I'll pay you well."

Slowly, I nodded. "Because of my gendarmerie schedule, I can't be with you full-time, but I have friends who can guard your house when I'm not available."

"I need protection, Tchicaya. My wife—she'll leave me if this happens again. We came here to get away from the violence, do you understand?"

I nodded again.

"I just got this job . . . I can't leave now. I need to stay."

I stared at his thinning hair and slowly wrinkling skin. He wasn't a small man, but he was frightened and confused, and this made him appear much smaller.

"Let me talk to my friends," I said, and nodded one last time before walking off.

He lit another cigarette and continued to sit.

"A *mundelé*?"

"Yes."

"Protection from what?" asked Kosi.

"Robbers, Ninjas coming in at night. He's scared."

"Right. How much?"

"Thirty thousand francs a month per person." Kosi's eyes lit up. This was about fifty dollars—a huge amount in the Congo at that time.

"Let's do it. Who else should we get?"

I smiled. "I got the best already, who else do we need?"

He laughed, then helped me pick two others.

Boukoulou and Bamona both joined the group once they heard the amount of money involved. The gendarmerie didn't pay well, and any opportunity to make good, legal income was a godsend.

We showed up the next day at Mr. DeVos's house in full gendarmerie attire. I inspected my men as if I were the drill instructor, then led them into the foyer and stood them at attention. From my father, I'd learned that the first impression is the most important. I watched Mr. DeVos carefully as he scanned my men, smiling.

He pulled me aside. "I love the men you've brought, but I want to make sure that you are here at all times. You're the one I trust."

I thought for a second. "I can't work all day and be here all night. I've got many responsibilities to my father, and I have to sleep at some point. But I have a solution." I paused and he leaned in even closer. "I'll carry a radio at all times. If things go wrong, I'll leave what I'm doing immediately, day or night. At least one of my men will always be here. Is this satisfactory?"

He thought for a second, eyes flicking nervously, imagining all the things that could go wrong, all the faceless intruders he'd learned to fear over the last few days. Finally, he extended his hand.

"Deal," he said.

I smiled.

I was the chief of security for a wealthy *mundelé*, a position I'd earned through my own actions. Mr. DeVos would pay me, and I would distribute the wages to my men, instilling respect, earning their trust. It was my first business. They were my first employees.

The next few months were fantastic. The group, which we nicknamed "Kiavou" (Brothers), loved both the work and the constant influx of free food. I loved the money—seventy-five dollars a month for me and fifty a month for each of my men. As money was sporadic at best from the gendarmerie, this couldn't have come at a better time. I developed a close relationship with Mr. DeVos, eventually becoming his chauffeur and driving him to business meetings in his blue Range Rover, which I affectionately nicknamed "Marguerite."

For the first time in many years, life was good.

But like all things in the Congo, it couldn't last.

CHAPTER 15

The constant travel allowed me a unique perspective on Brazzaville, and I began to notice signs of tension. The vast majority of people appeared displeased, upset, even angry—and the dark cloud hanging over the city seemed to grow larger every day.

During his tenure, Sassou-Nguesso had helped ensure payment for all government employees through his network of contacts. Through his negotiations, many of these employees were allegedly paid directly from the coffers of the French oil company ELF—the primary recipient of Congolese oil. When Sassou-Nguesso was voted out of office, payments to hundreds of workers ceased. Lissouba, lacking both the extensive network of contacts and the support of ELF, was unable to balance the budget. Salaries were not getting paid, except to the Niboleks in high governmental positions. In response to criticism, these government employees created a slogan: *"Ya ba colere vé"* or "Don't be mad." They'd suffered for fifteen years under Sassou-Nguesso's M'Bochi rule and now considered it their time to live off the fat of the land. *"Bakouté,"* they would say with a smile—"It's my turn to eat."

Lissouba further jeopardized his situation by opening negotiations with American oil companies, apparently believing they could offer better profit margins and less political baggage. However, with thousands of unpaid salaries and growing civilian discontent, Lissouba couldn't risk stopping even that meager flow of money into the country.

In 1995, enormous amounts of oil were discovered at a new site called N'Kossa. As the oil companies moved in, Lissouba immediately promised that all back salaries would be paid. A cautious optimism was felt around the country. I was more skeptical, wondering what would happen in the upcoming 1997 elections. I resolved to keep an eye on the movements of Bernard Kolelas, now the mayor of Brazzaville, and Denis Sassou-Nguesso.

The threat of war always hung heavy over the Congo, and I didn't want to return to the life of a militia soldier. I was a businessman now, not merely a fighter. I did my best to think as my father would think, act as he would act. I tried to anticipate the actions of the politicians, predict how they would influence my business.

Sassou-Nguesso made me the most nervous. Following his defeat in 1992, he'd gone into voluntary exile in France, making contacts and biding his time. It was unknown if he would return to run again for president, but with this new oil discovery, it seemed increasingly likely. ELF had helped put Sassou-Nguesso in power, and they certainly had a vested interest in returning him to that position. It was rumored that he was meeting with them daily in France, laying the groundwork for his return. Furthermore, in his absence, he'd married his daughter to the president of Gabon—a man old enough to be her grandfather—in order to strengthen that country's allegiance to him. His alliances were growing, and that made him dangerous.

I did my best to stay out of the fray. My priorities were extremely clear: my family and my pocketbook.

Pre-election polls showed that Sassou-Nguesso held a substantial lead, and banners began showing up all over Brazzaville reading *"L'Espoir Revien"* or "The Hope Is Back."

Finally, he did come back.

The Mayamaya airport was a mob scene as thousands of people crammed onto the airfield hoping for a glimpse of the former leader. Men climbed trees, women held up their babies—it was like the videos we'd seen of Michael Jackson concerts. Even his old ally Bernard Kolelas showed up to greet him. The Cobra militia provided security, whisking him away from the adoring mob and up to his old living quarters in the northern section of Brazzaville.

For twenty miles, the public followed his motorcade on foot, gathering outside his palace and cheering.

Lissouba's palace, where I was that day, was ominously silent.

It wasn't long before tension flared.

History was catching up to the Congo.

In 1968, Sassou-Nguesso was part of a coup that overthrew then-president Massamba-Débat and his prime minister, a man named Pascal Lissouba. In appreciation of this, Sassou-Nguesso was named minister of defense in charge of intelligence under the new president—Marien Ngouabi. Ngouabi's main contribution to the Congo was aligning the country with Russia's ideal of Marxist governmental structures. As this was not considered good for business, France (particularly ELF) began grooming their chosen replacement—Sassou-Nguesso.

On March 18, 1977, President Ngouabi was assassinated. Everyone associated with Ngouabi slowly disappeared and the investigation was eventually dropped. Sassou-Nguesso, as minister of defense, appointed an interim president who was not part of the labor party and thus could never be considered a permanent contender for the position. This man, Joachim Yhombi-Opango, was overthrown less than two years later and replaced by Denis Sassou-Nguesso on February 5, 1979.

He ruled unchallenged for nearly fourteen years.

Lissouba, in one of his first acts of hopeful reconciliation, appointed Yhombi-Opango as his prime minister. This proved to be an enormous mistake that would soon lead to uncontainable violence.

On May 10, 1997, a few days after Sassou-Nguesso arrived in the Congo, he made a trip to campaign in Owando, the stronghold of Yhombi-Opango. There, he was received like a king. He was carried through the streets on a *tipoyé*, praised, and venerated. Yhombi-Opango, now the prime minister, took this as a personal insult and alerted his followers, who came out to observe the commotion and protest the intrusion.

A skirmish broke out. Two of Sassou-Nguesso's Cobras fired on the supporters of Yhombi-Opango at point-blank range, killing them instantly. Sassou-Nguesso's entourage then returned to his palace in northern Brazzaville.

Lissouba was outraged at the violence and the perceived insult to his prime minister, and called for the immediate arrest of the two guilty soldiers. Sassou-Nguesso refused and began fortifying his palace, daring Lissouba to come and get them.

For nearly a week, the tension in the Congo grew as the political rhetoric became increasingly threatening. News anchors began reporting exclusively on this issue, predicting an inevitable decline into violence. It appeared that both politicians were seeking a reason to enter into battle, but neither wanted to take the first step.

On the night of June 4, 1997, Lissouba's patience expired and he mobilized his personal guard, the heavily armed Aubeville, intending to take over Sassou-Nguesso's palace and convict the guilty parties. They approached Mpila with the full weight of the government forces behind them, expecting an easy victory. Instead, they encountered heavy gunfire from the Cobras, and a whole battery of tanks and RPGs. Sassou-Nguesso had been biding his time for a reason.

Blood spilled into the streets of downtown Brazzaville. Sassou-Nguesso, not content to be trapped in his palace, began pushing the Niboleks and the Lari south, toward Lissouba's palace. The battleground was the streets, and casualties immediately climbed into the hundreds.

Once again, the Congo was at war.

CHAPTER 16

Unaware of the exploding chaos in the northern part of the city, I tucked my little sisters into bed. The next morning, they would be taking the most important test of their lives—the Congo baccalaureate exam. This would determine their college potential and, more important, their eligibility to apply for a foreign visa. Everyone my age wanted to study abroad, to leave the Congo, to have at least the possibility of a bright future.

Witch doctors were working overtime, parents were praying to the gods, and children's bloodshot eyes were cramming in facts, figures, and diagrams. To prevent cheating, the test was issued everywhere in the country at the same exact time. The gendarmerie was mobilized to proctor the exams, so I'd agreed to escort my sisters Francine and Carole to their testing location.

As I put them to bed, the phone rang.

"Tchic."

"Kosi, I was just—"

"Something's happening. Tonight."

"What?"

"I don't know. But there are lots of people loading trucks. Guns, ammo—"

"Where are you?"

"The presidential palace. Everyone's excited, but no one knows why."

"What do you think it is?"

"I think you're lucky you're not on duty."

"Are they sending you?"

"I don't know. Probably just the Aubeville, but there are rumors flying around that we all might go. There are ministers and secretaries going in and out constantly."

My mind churned. The elections were still a few months away . . . it didn't make sense for fighting to break out before there was a result to contest.

"Call me when you hear something else," I said.

A few minutes later, the phone rang again. I jumped.

"Hello?"

"Tchico, how are you?"

"Good, Papa." My heart clenched up in my chest. My father never called.

"Good. Is there plenty of food and water in the house?"

"I think so, yes."

There was a short pause. "I want you to buy a fifty-kilogram bag of rice, some milk, sugar, batteries, and flashlights. Pull some cash out of the bank."

"Why?"

"It is best to be prepared."

"Prepared for what?" My mind was racing now, frightened. "You think there will be war?"

"For everything," said my father. "I'll call you tomorrow to let you know how much cash you should withdraw."

And then he hung up. I stood there, holding the receiver, feeling unsteady on my feet.

The house was quiet as I tiptoed to my sisters' room and watched the rise and fall of their chests.

Their lives were my responsibility.

I awoke to find my brother Zabatou shaking me. "Wake up, Tchico, wake up."

I was standing before he even finished speaking. "What is it?"

"We're at war," he said. He was nineteen—older than me by two years—but I was the one who'd been left in charge.

"War?"

"Listen."

We both cocked our heads, wincing at the sound of machine-gun fire coming from the north. An explosion rocked the ground, and a series of screams echoed through the house. My sisters ran into the living room, nearly bowling me over.

"It's okay," I said. My sisters stared at me, eyes wide. They didn't remember the first war the way that I did. "Turn off all the lights."

Zabatou shot me a questioning glance. I knew what he was asking. The exams were so important . . . we couldn't risk missing them, couldn't risk jeopardizing Francine and Carole's future. I took a depth breath. "Get dressed, girls. Everything will be okay. Get ready to go to school. I'll take you."

We left the house cautiously, alert for the slightest hint of danger, taking back roads all the way to the Lycée de la Liberatión. "It's going to be okay," I said into the silence, watching as my sisters rubbed their hands together, blinking again and again. "It's going to be okay."

I dropped them off and headed next door to the gendarmerie to get some news.

No one seemed to know anything, and this made me even more nervous. I shook my head in disgust and walked over to the presidential palace.

Brazzaville was empty, the streets inhabited only by stray dogs and the occasional monkey rummaging through the heaps of trash beside the roads.

The guard waved me through the gates of the palace.

The first person I saw was Kosi, armed from head to toe with guns, ammunition, and grenades. "What are you doing?" I asked.

"The Republican Guard is invading Sassou's place," he said. "We're trying to get the soldiers who killed Opango's men. There's fighting all over Mpila, Potopoto, and the downtown area. Civilians are joining in. On both sides."

My head started to spin and I felt my stomach clench. The country was once again tearing itself into pieces, the tribal distinctions merely suppressed, not forgotten. In the Congo, the tribes and political parties were one and the same. Not only that, but the militias had no reservations about slaughtering civilians. This created more fear, which only worked to their advantage. "Come with me," I said. "I need to get cash out of the bank."

"We'll take my jeep," he said, clearly relieved to have something else, anything else, to do. We jumped in, listening as the sound of gunfire echoed down from Mpila. He turned the car toward the violence, took a deep breath, and pressed the gas pedal.

As we drove north, the streets faded into chaos. Men and women were running, screaming, carrying belongings and children on their backs. Kosi kept his eyes on the road, avoiding the bodies dotting the cracked asphalt. Though most of the corpses were clad in military gear, I couldn't help but notice the numerous civilian casualties—spillovers from untamed tribal violence, Lari killed by M'Bochi, M'Bochi killed by Nibolek. Cabs passed by with government soldiers hanging out of the windows, brandishing AK-47s. Trucks, loaded down with pistol-waving villagers, took corners on two wheels. Gunshots surrounded us, but I couldn't tell where they were coming from or who they were aimed at.

"Shit," said Kosi. I licked my lips with a dry tongue.

It was awful.

I wanted out.

We arrived at the bank, not surprised to find it closed, surrounded by government guards. One was a boy holding an RPG, and I couldn't stop staring at him, couldn't stop flashing back to my own past.

"Come on!" said Kosi, flinching as a woman approached us.

Her eyes were blank and nearly half of her white dress had been stained red.

"I've been shot," she said in a listless monotone. "They shot me in the back." She turned around to show us where she'd been hit, and I bit my lip so hard I tasted iron. There, in a piece of cloth around the woman's body, was a baby. A bullet had destroyed most of its face, and blood poured from the wound like a faucet. I stared at the perfect little hands dangling from the makeshift cradle. They twitched.

"I've been shot," said the woman again, turning back around. "I've been shot. I've been shot."

I ran over and held her shoulders, staring into dull eyes. I moved behind her and put my hands on the child. Its jaw was separated from the rest of its face, and I could hear the gurgles emanating from its chest as it tried to get air into crushed lungs. I lifted the tiny jaw and tried to hold it against the rest of the mouth, feeling how futile my gesture was, knowing that there was nothing I could do, but needing to do something. The blood spilled over my hands and onto the ground. I looked to Kosi, but he could only shake his head. I tried to apply pressure to the wound, gritting my teeth as I felt the child's fingers feebly grasping at my own. The child worked what was left of its mouth, trying to scream, to cry, to shout, but no sounds came out, just this strange whistling whimper. Time slowed and sound stopped as I pulled the tiny body out of its mother's sling. The baby stared at me with wide, scared eyes, begging me to save its life, asking me to help. There was nothing I could do. I could feel the child spasming, jerking, quietly choking on its own blood.

I looked up, seeing bits of flesh and bone on the mother and, not thinking, leaned in and brushed them off. The woman turned around, slowly staring at the messy bundle I held in my hands. I shook my head, wishing I knew how to make all of this better. In a dull haze, I remembered that the mother had been shot as well, but it appeared she'd forgotten about this. She stared at the child openmouthed, a thick cord of saliva connecting her top and bottom lip. A scream erupted from her body, forcing me backward. She screamed again, a cry so deep and so full of pain that chills ripped across my body like bullet wounds.

"No!" she cried, then turned her face to the sky. "God!" she howled, "Where are you?"

The sound of machine guns erupted again, closer this time.

Bombs.

"Where are you?" she cried.

Kosi pushed me, and time suddenly slammed into gear. Bullets rained down around us, and my body jolted into action. We were caught between the two opposing forces, and no one on either side would care if we lived or died.

"Run," I said. "You must run. Run for your life. Go."

She turned to face me. Women screamed and kids fell to the ground with pieces missing from their bodies. Blood covered the streets. Red gushed onto my hands and feet from the child I held in my arms.

"The Cobras are coming," said Kosi.

I turned and saw two schoolchildren lying dead at the side of the road, backpacks still clutched in their hands.

"Come on," he said. "We have to leave!"

I grabbed the woman and pushed her into the back of the jeep. "We'll take you to the hospital," I shouted, leaping into the passenger seat, still holding the dying child.

Kosi peeled out, swerving around the piles of bodies, instinctively ducking every time he heard a burst of gunfire. The wailing of the mother filled the car like a siren.

"That way," I shouted, pointing toward a back road. "The Cobras will set up checkpoints. If they see us, we're dead."

He spun the wheel, spraying a cloud of dust onto the bodies of two women lying beside the road. I watched as windows were broken and the looting began. Downtown Brazzaville was in utter disarray.

My stomach churned.

We headed south, back toward the hospital and the high school.

The child stared at me, naked, a cloud rising across its eyes. The silent screams and spasming twitches slowed, then ceased.

It was a boy.

He died in my arms.

The Makelekele hospital was already filled beyond capacity, but we dropped off the woman and her child at the front door amidst the piles of bodies. She was silent. I wished there was something I could do for her, but I needed to get to my sisters.

As we pulled away, I tried to wipe the blood from my clothes, but couldn't.

The Lycée de la Liberatión was in a panic. Explosions rattled in the distance, and children poured out of the doors, screaming and crying.

I leaped out of the jeep and pushed my way into the school, remembering where I'd dropped each of my sisters off. I took the stairs three at a time and maneuvered around the fleeing hordes, releasing my breath as I saw Francine standing against the wall. She screamed and pointed. "You're shot!"

"No!" I said, "I'm okay. It's not my blood." I picked her up and headed for the first floor, where Carole had been scheduled to take her test. Carole was four months pregnant, and I worried about her ability to negotiate the crowds.

Fortunately, I spotted her quickly. "We have to leave!" I shouted. "Come on!"

"What about the exams?" she said. Carole wanted to leave the country more than anyone.

"There is no exam. We're at war. The Cobras are coming and they're going to kill everyone."

We began running toward the jeep. "Where are we going?" shouted Carole.

"We're grabbing clothes from the house, then going to the hotel," I said. "Farther south will be safer."

Kosi tried to merge into the rising swells of traffic, shaking his head as car after car drove by with bodies hanging out of the trunks, out of the windows, lifeless arms spilling out of open doors.

People were fleeing either north or south. No one was heading east or west. With the fear had come an immediate memory of tribal affiliations, and my heart filled with incredible sadness. I watched the M'Bochis running toward the fighting, toward the north. We passed them, making eye contact, nodding sadly to each other. Yesterday, we could have been friends. Now we were enemies.

The bombs were getting closer.

"Wait," I said to Kosi as he drove onto Oua Avenue. "Pull over." He squealed into the parking lot of the gendarmerie. I told my sisters to wait in the car while the two of us ran to get supplies.

I'd been there not three hours before, but nothing looked familiar. Not a single person was visible, and huge stacks of papers floated across the yard in strange whirlwind patterns. I ran inside. Even the prisoners were gone, and worse, the armory had been emptied.

"This happened too fast," I said. "Everything's gone."

"They knew," said Kosi, and I agreed as we ran back to the jeep.

Kolelas had mobilized the Ninja militia to set up checkpoints preventing the intrusion of Cobra forces into the south, and we crawled our way through the streets, answering questions about names and about *fou-fou* and keeping our heads down.

I realized that Kolelas was in an awkward situation—he'd positioned himself as a mediator between the two camps, but he was also the leader of the Ninjas and a former ally of Sassou-Nguesso. Many of my friends were still members of Kolelas's militia, and I nodded to them as we rolled through yet another series of check-points.

My mission was twofold: protect my brothers and sisters and protect my father's property. Nothing else mattered at this point. I was done with politics, done with the militias.

I tried to imagine what was happening farther north. By now, the gendarmerie would have split into Cocoyes, Ninja, and Cobra. All the bonding, the training, all the dissolution of tribal boundaries had been for nothing. Once again, the country would be carved into three sections, and there was little doubt in my mind that the electricity and water would soon be cut off. As much as I didn't want to side with any one group, I had to go where I was safe. Déjà vu struck as I rushed my sisters to the Ninja-controlled region of the city. I knew that as of that moment, there was no such thing as a civilian.

At the Oasis hotel, I reunited with my family. We'd raided the place for whatever we could grab quickly, then reassembled farther south at the Djoué. We gathered around a radio, as all the television stations were out. Lissouba was advancing hard against the Cobras, still confident that he could overpower Sassou-Nguesso and invade his palace. I had my doubts. Lissouba didn't seem to realize the strength of the Cobra forces, didn't seem to realize that money and power could get you only so far in a war.

Days passed without any drop in the level of violence.

After a week, we received word that a temporary cease-fire had been negotiated by the French Foreign Legion in order to ferry out all the French *mundelé* trapped amidst the fighting.

Foreign troops flooded the streets and began escorting French citizens to the Mayamaya airport for airlifting to either Gabon or Pointe-Noire. Meanwhile, the cease-fire was falling apart. It was rumored that the French were using the cessation of violence as a chance to get weapons to Sassou-Nguesso and were going to give him the airport after they vacated it. In reality, both sides were ferrying in weapons from neighboring countries. Russian helicopters, tanks, guns, and ammo flooded the Congo from parts as distant as South Africa.

Brazzaville was a time bomb.

I returned to work, beginning a daily commute from my father's hotel to the presidential palace, to his house, then back again. The fighting hadn't reached that far south yet, so it was relatively quiet work, but the travel was always an adventure.

The checkpoints had grown in intensity from the previous civil war. Kids and adults alike stood guard, wearing anything that looked tough. Cutoff sleeves, shower shoes, bandanas, machetes tied to their legs, machine guns . . . many wore rank insignia that weren't theirs, resulting in a lot of captains and generals under the age of sixteen.

I recognized a number of them from my own days in the militia, and one in particular caught my eye. We had called him *Colonel Sans Pitie*—Colonel No Mercy—and he certainly worked hard to live up to the name. His regular uniform was military pants, a civilian suit jacket, flip-flops, a machete, a machine gun, and a pirate hat. Red bandanas covered both biceps.

Daily, I would watch as civilians ran toward the checkpoints carrying mattresses, refrigerators, and wheelbarrows full of personal items, hoping to make it far enough south to escape the fighting. I watched with familiar dread as they were questioned and required to show ID, living or dying on the first letters of their names, or the dialect that spilled out of their mouths. I watched a family heading south, all Nibolek except for the father. The family was allowed in, but the father was turned back. I have no reason to believe he survived the trip.

Rape became a common weapon among all militias, north and

south. Whispers reached our ears that even the French Foreign Legion had begun forced prostitution, using the airport as a staging ground. Congolese women would have sex with the French soldiers in exchange for money or food, or in the vague hope of escaping the country. Rumors also abounded that they were robbing the businesses surrounding the airport and were leaving the country with bags of gold watches, diamonds, and silver jewelry. I began to see men in the streets carrying refrigerators on their backs, televisions, air conditioners, computers. Looting became the norm across the whole of Brazzaville, as no one was getting paid—civilian or government. Food became scarce, electricity was nonexistent. Prices in the markets doubled, then tripled. Starvation set in quickly among the poorer population.

I couldn't stop the sinking feeling in my stomach.

It was happening again.

Kolelas found out about the escalating violence at the checkpoints and ordered that all civilians be allowed entry into the south. The only people turned away, he declared, would be those carrying weapons. Though a noble effort, this lasted only a few days before violence reigned again.

The hospital was filled, unable even to provide pain medication for the horribly wounded. Churches and schools became makeshift hospitals, residences, and orphanages.

I saw Kosi daily at the presidential palace. We were both still technically gendarme and both had responsibilities. Our sworn duty was to protect the president and guard his premises. As the fighting intensified, our nervousness grew.

"This isn't our fight," I said one day.

He nodded. "But it's become that way, hasn't it?"

I didn't answer.

He showed up the next day driving a Mercedes and carrying a bag of watches. "The French were looting, so we did, too," he said, not making eye contact with me. "All the cars at the airport are gone."

Shortly thereafter, the French withdrew from the country and the militias began battling for control of the airport. Whoever controlled the only landing area in Brazzaville would be able to ferry in virtually unlimited amounts of weapons and ammunition from neighboring countries.

The gunfire intensified.

My mother had moved out of my grandparents' house where we all grew up and now lived in the Moungali area, about twenty minutes west of where the main fighting was occurring.

"Come to the hotel," I said to her. "We have room."

"No, Tchic, I'm fine. I don't want to leave the house. There are many of us here. We're safe."

"For now."

She made a *tsk* sound. "They are fighting over each other's palaces, why would they come west?"

I sighed. "Politics control the tribes, Mama, and tribes control the politics. They are one and the same. If the Cobras and the Ninjas go to war, then the M'Bochi and the Lari go to war. You know this. Violence will spill into the streets. There is no such thing as civilians."

"I will stay here. It is my home."

"Fine, then I'll come and visit you every day."

And that became my daily routine. I would rise in the morning, ensure the safety of the hotel, then go to the presidential palace. I would pass both Ninja and Cocoyes checkpoints, but because I was dressed as a Republican Guard and a member of the gendarmerie, I was allowed access to the roads. I would check my father's property, then journey to my mother's house to make sure she was safe.

Amidst the chaos and the violence, I discovered the value of routine.

Horrible sights became the backdrop to my daily existence. Rape, carnage, murder, theft—these things became expected, normal. My life was my responsibilities—my family, my business, my father's business.

Nothing else mattered.

But with all the stress, all the people depending on me, a mistake was bound to happen eventually.

CHAPTER 17

After a long day of travel, I arrived back at the Oasis. Two of the employees ran up to me, breathless. "The *mundelé* is looking for you!"

My senses jumped to attention. "What?"

"All day, he's been calling, searching for you. You must go over there."

I realized I'd forgotten to bring my radio with me that day. I turned and ran out the front door, leaping hedges, trying to coax my body into moving faster. If something had happened to Mr. DeVos or his family because of my negligence . . . I couldn't even allow myself to think such thoughts.

I found him on the back porch, staring at the Djoué and smoking a cigarette.

"Tchicaya!" he said, turning around.

"Are you all right?"

"Everything is okay . . . but not really."

"Your family, are they safe?" He nodded and I relaxed slightly. "If you and your family are safe, then I'm not worried," I said.

"Come," he said. "Sit." He led me into the living room and got me a soda. We sat beside each other on the couch. I wondered if any of my men had turned against me, stolen, showed up drunk. I couldn't imagine that would ever happen.

He sighed, then began speaking. "A few days ago, I received a phone call from some friends in Congo-Kinshasa about a man named Tom Thibaut. He's gone missing, and my friends were worried that he'd been injured in the attacks. His house, you see, is located directly in the middle of the fighting, just west of Potopoto." I nodded as he took a sip. "I assumed that he'd been evacuated by the French along with everyone else, but no one has heard from him. They gave me his emergency radio frequency and asked me to listen. For three days, I tuned in and heard nothing. But today, I heard his voice. He's still in Brazzaville."

"What?" This was absurd. A *mundelé* in the middle of that type of fighting didn't stand a chance. The militias wouldn't think twice about assassinating him and stealing his undoubtedly substantial stockpile of money. "Why didn't he leave?"

Mr. DeVos shook his head. "The French couldn't get to him. His house is directly beside Cobra headquarters. Even during the cease-fire, this wasn't safe territory. Cobra soldiers live beside him and above him."

"Do they know he's there?"

"No. He's in hiding with his bodyguard, his four-year-old daughter, and his wife."

I shook my head, chills springing up on my arms.

"He's been living off his reserves and is running out of food and water. There's no electricity. He can't leave the house for fear of being seen. He assumed, wrongly, that the war would be over by now. His family is hungry, and he's been sending out radio distress signals for thirty minutes every day, attempting to conserve batteries."

"You've spoken with him?"

"Yes. I told him not to leave the house under any circumstances."

"You told him the right thing."

"I can only imagine what would happen if the Cobras found out he was there." He paused again and we stared at each other. I waited for him to ask the question that I knew was coming. My muscles tensed as I thought of the danger involved. I couldn't risk my life for a white man. I had too many responsibilities, too many people dependent on me. Money was worthless if I was dead.

"His wife—she's Nigerian." He paused. "And she's pregnant."

I shook my head, feeling the pain in my chest that those words caused.

A Nigerian wife. Pregnant. Four-year-old daughter. These were people who had no options beyond me.

One of my sisters was in danger, and needed rescue.

"I want you to save him and his family," said Mr. DeVos. "I realize the danger involved here, but you will be paid handsomely. This war won't be ending any time soon." He proceeded to give me more details about this Tom Thibaut, stopping only when I held up my hand and stood up.

"I'll have to ask my people. I can't do this alone, and they would need to agree before we can go any further. We'd need a foolproof plan."

He stood and shook my hand. "I understand. Please, go quickly."

I called my men and asked them to assemble at the hotel immediately. They filed in, looking curious, but said nothing.

"Thank you for your work over the last two months. Mr. DeVos is very happy with the security of his house. His family feels safe." I nodded to each of my men in turn. "He has asked me to take on another mission. I can't do this without you. There is a *mundelé* trapped in the center of downtown. His house is beside Cobra headquarters. They don't know he is there."

I watched the faces of Boukoulou and Bamona fall as they realized what I was asking. No doubt they were having the same internal struggle that I'd gone through. *Why should I? Why would I risk my life for a* mundelé, *when they're the reason the war is here in the first place? Without their desire for oil, without their desire for wealth, we would still be living in peace. They take our money and leave us in poverty. Let the white man die. It's of no concern to me.*

I continued. "His wife is Nigerian. She's pregnant. They also have a young daughter."

I paused, watching their reactions. This was information that truly changed everything. One of our sisters, pregnant, stuck in the middle of this horrific fighting. We had a duty, a responsibility. It also meant that Tom Thibaut was not a racist like many of the *mundelés* we encountered. "This needs to happen fast."

"Does he have money?" Kosi asked.

"He's *mundelé*," I said. "Of course he has money."

The others nodded, deep in thought. I had to give them some information, but not too much. "This Tom Thibaut, he's Dutch. He's the owner of ———."

More slow nods, along with a few raised eyebrows. ——— was one of the largest, most recognized businesses in the Congo.

What wasn't being discussed was the fact that Kosi and Boukoulou were both Nibolek. They risked more by entering Cobra territory. As Laris, Bamona and I were both technically neutral in the war, though allied slightly with the Nibolek/Cocoyes militia.

"Why is he still there?" asked Kosi. "Why didn't he leave with everyone else?"

"It doesn't matter at this point," I said. "We're here to find a solution. Are you in, or are you out?"

The room was silent. Kosi stood up. "I'm in. Let's do it."

Boukoulou stood beside him, then Bamona.

"Good," I said. "We need more people."

We drove straight to the presidential palace and recruited two high-ranking lieutenants and four of their best men. I was careful not to mention the amount of danger involved, but only the potential monetary reward. The original four musketeers had quickly become ten. We were a fighting force to be reckoned with . . . and I was the leader.

We made plans to leave the following day. The Cobra forces traditionally fought and drank all night, sleeping as the sun came up. At sunset, they would rise and begin the cycle again. This meant that we had to extract Tom Thibaut before dusk. We'd have to leave early, as it was not a short drive to the center of the fighting. I returned to Mr. DeVos and told him that we would accept the mission.

"Thank God," he said, releasing a long, smoky breath.

"I need to speak to Mr. Tom Thibaut," I said, and he went to get his radio. He tuned it carefully and began speaking Flemish into the transmitter. He did this for a few minutes, and I paced nervously, wondering what would happen if the Cobras got there first. Finally, a voice crackled through, deep and scratchy. A few more words were exchanged, then Mr. DeVos gestured for me to speak.

"Mr. Tom Thibaut?" I said in French.

"Tchicaya," came the voice, jittery and heavily accented.

"Are you okay?"

"I am, but we are out of food and water. My family is scared."

"How many people are in your house?"

"Myself, my wife, my daughter, and our bodyguard."

"Four total."

"Four and a half."

"Your wife is pregnant."

"Yes."

I looked to Mr. DeVos as I spoke into the radio. "What's the situation out there?"

"Bad. Bullet holes in the walls, fighting every night. The front lines are visible from our windows. I don't know what to do. We have run out of everything, Tchicaya. I need your help."

I shook my head. A *mundelé* said he needed me. That was an incredible thing. My whole life, I'd been told that the white man was superior, and here he was asking for *my* help. The world truly was a strange place.

"We'll help you. Do you have a vehicle?"

"God bless you. Yes, yes, I have a white pickup truck. Four doors."

"Which way is it facing?"

"Facing? Oh. Toward the road. There is a gate blocking it."

"But it's ready to go?"

"Yes, yes, plenty of gas. I haven't used it in almost two months, but it should be fine."

My mind churned. "Good. I want you to pack light and be ready to go tomorrow morning. Keep your radio on. I'll contact you when we're close. I'll knock on the gate three times. You must respond with two knocks on your front door. This is how we can be sure of each other's identity. Do you understand?"

"Yes, yes, I understand. We'll pack now."

"In the morning, we go. Bring only what you need."

"Yes, I will. Thank you, Tchicaya. Thank you."

"I'll contact you tomorrow when we're close."

Mr. DeVos clicked off the radio and shook my hand. "Be careful," he said.

"I will. I'll let you know when we have him," I said, turning toward the door. "Now excuse me. I have to prepare."

CHAPTER 18

We assembled in the presidential palace with an incredible array of weapons. The beauty of inviting lieutenants onto the team was that we had access to vehicles, guns, ammo, RPGs. For our transportation, we chose a lightly armored French vehicle called a Sovamag. This would carry ten of us there, but after picking up the four new passengers, we'd need to convoy back with the pickup truck.

We spent the evening loading weapons and poring over maps.

The next morning, we gathered, each decked out with a strange mixture of bandanas, weapons, and military gear. It was an army of Rambos and Schwarzeneggers, and I smiled grimly. "If we succeed here," I said to my men, "you will all be rich."

They nodded, because they trusted me. I had a reputation as a friend of the *mundelé* and I'd already proven that I could set up and deliver transactions with them. To this day, Mr. DeVos does not know the power he provided to me as a teenager.

We loaded into the Sovamag, four soldiers hanging off the sides, weapons raised, looking like a scene from some war movie. The ranking officer drove, while I took the A-driver position in the passenger seat and helped navigate. The plan was to stay off the main roads as much as possible, to avoid potential combat. This meant more checkpoints.

At least twelve times we had the same conversation as we rolled up to the makeshift barricades and were greeted by children carrying oversized weaponry.

"Where are you going?"

I would lean out the window. "Who's in charge here?"

The boy would straighten up and hold his gun high. "I'm in charge."

Another boy would come out and stand beside him, serious as death. "No, I'm in charge. What do you want?" Other men would trickle over to the truck, many of them claiming authority.

Finally, I would raise my hands and voice. "It doesn't matter. We're going on a mission and when we return, we'll pay you cash, each of you. Let us pass safely, and you'll be rewarded."

"How much?" the first boy would ask.

"Five thousand francs," I would say, "each." They would step back, nodding, satisfied with the roughly ten dollars I had promised them.

And we would drive on.

Checkpoint after checkpoint, we promised incredible sums of money to strangers in exchange for our supposed safety.

But I knew this was nothing to the *mundelé*. Mr. Tom Thibaut would not blink at such prices.

The front line of the battle was drawn at the Mbamou Palace Hotel, a high-end resort designed for visiting dignitaries and the überwealthy. Now it was abandoned, bullet-ridden, worthless. The Sovamag idled in the back parking lot. I let Kosi speak to his Nibolek friends stationed there and pulled out my radio. My men waited nervously, stretching their tired limbs and smoking cigarettes.

"We're coming," I said. "Thirty minutes."

"We're ready," said Tom Thibaut.

"Slow day," said the front-line soldiers. "Not much gunfire, haven't seen too many Cobras out and about."

Everything was going according to plan. The weather was good. The area was quiet. The gendarme lieutenant lent us credibility, so no one asked too many questions. We didn't tell anyone what we were doing, but gave the impression that we were up from the south to scout the area for reconnaissance on the Cobras.

I gathered my men behind the hotel. "Kosi, Boukoulou, Bamona, and Lieutenant Mpassi will come with me to extract the target. The other five will be placed around the house to provide covering fire once we have the target in our possession. That will keep the Cobras from getting a clear shot at us. Do you understand?" They nodded. I pulled out a map. "Here, here, here, and here will be station points with solid views of Mr. Tom Thibaut's house. This, here, is the Cobra headquarters. They will return fire. Be prepared." I thanked the gods for the gendarmerie training we'd all received.

In order to avoid attention, we left the Sovamag parked behind the Mbamou Palace Hotel and took off on foot, running from house to house, one at a time, covering one another as we went. There was no movement from the Cobra side.

A wide field separated us from Tom Thibaut's house and, as we approached it, I felt my heart sink. The smell was overwhelming. Bodies were strewn about like branches after a storm. Packs of wild dogs were feasting on the human remains, and I couldn't tell if the bodies were Cocoyes or Cobra. I watched as a crow flew down and began pecking at the eyeball of a woman in a torn sundress. Nearby, two dogs fought over what had probably been her child. It was a cemetery of decomposing bodies and carrion predators. The air was heavy, thick, hard to suck into my lungs. I began to realize how hot the day was.

The silence horrified me, and the enormity of what we were attempting began to set in. One misstep and we were dead. Behind enemy lines, no one would come to our rescue. I could hear my men murmuring and straightened up. I could not show fear. I was the leader. Even though doubt surged through my heart like a river after the rains, I could not allow myself to exhibit anything but confidence. I took a step into the field, slowly, setting my heel down, then rolling onto my toe.

And again.

Heel.

Toe.

Heel.

Toe.

My men and I crept through this field of death, and I felt that I had entered the worst place in the world. The stench was truly overpowering. Even the breeze seemed afraid to blow. It was one of the quietest places I'd ever been. Occasionally, the silence was broken by the snarling of dogs or the ripping of flesh, but I don't think I heard a single breath from any of my men.

Within minutes, we were across the field and approaching Tom Thibaut's house. I adjusted the guns on my belt and my grip on the AK-47. My vest suddenly felt very heavy. Sweat dropped into my eyes. I gave the signal for the five gunmen to take their positions and watched as they did so, spreading in a rough semicircle across the field.

Ducking low, I ran over to the gate and knocked three times.

Nothing.

I counted to thirty, then knocked again, three times.

Nothing.

The silence was deafening and I wondered if the Cobra scouts could hear the strange thumping coming from outside the supposedly abandoned house. Maybe I was knocking too softly, afraid of who might be alerted. I realized I could no longer judge the quietness of actions or events. Fear was the only sense that remained.

I knocked again, loudly.

Then I heard it.

Knock.

Knock.

He was there.

I knocked again, three times.

And again, the response.

Knock.

Knock.

The gate began to swing back, squealing horribly on its rusted hinges. I gritted my teeth as the sound echoed through the empty streets. If the Cobras didn't know we were here before, they certainly knew now. I took a brief look at the battered white pickup truck in the driveway. Thanks to a backseat, it could comfortably seat four, but we would be many more than that. It promised to be an uncomfortable ride back to the hotel, even without the threat of grenades, RPGs, and gunfire.

We ran in, and I greeted Tom Thibaut face-to-face. He looked as if he hadn't slept in a decade. His cheeks hung low, quivering with every step he took. There was crust in the corners of his eyes, which were supported by enormous dark circles. His clothes were wrinkled and dirty.

"Thank you," he said, gripping my hand. His voice was gruff and worn, but there was strength behind it, confidence. This impressed me.

"No time," I said. "Grab your bags and throw them in the back of the truck. Get in the backseat. Your wife can sit on your lap. Keep your daughter on the floorboards. Kosi, you sit on their left, Boukoulou, on their right. Try and keep their heads down. I'll drive. Lieutenant, you sit in A-position."

Tom Thibaut ran inside and came out a few seconds later, gently escorting his wife. In that moment, that snapshot, it was easy to see how much he loved her. A white man, caring for our sister, even in the most dire of circumstances. A wave of guilt swept over me for the silent judgments I'd made of this man.

His daughter, standing alone in the shuffle of weapons and boots, appeared to be on the verge of tears. Doing my best to conceal my fear, I scanned the floor and spotted a stuffed teddy bear. I picked it up and handed it to her. "How are you doing?"

She didn't say anything.

Her tears would mean our death. I tried again.

"It's okay. We're here to take you somewhere safe, okay?"

She nodded, wiping away the silent drops of water that had formed beneath her eyes. I held out my arms, and she let me carry her to the truck. Tom Thibaut passed me, returning to the house.

I ran back and found him with his back to the door. I watched as he removed a pair of silver handcuffs from his pocket, picked up a briefcase, and attached it to his wrist. I grabbed his arm, pulling him out of sight of the others.

"Mr. Tom Thibaut, take the briefcase off." His eyes got wide. "Pack it in your suitcase, and put the suitcase under your feet. Everyone will know there's money in that case if you attach yourself to it. You're only asking for trouble. Give me some cash to bribe the checkpoints with. I don't want to open the briefcase in front of my men."

I held out my hand and watched as he opened the golden clasps. My mouth dropped open. The briefcase was *full* of money—and not just Congolese money, but currency from every country in the world. Dollars, francs, lira, yen—all in enormous amounts. He handed me a stack of ten-thousand-franc notes (roughly the same as U.S. twenty-dollar bills). An enormous stack. I took it and shoved it into my pocket.

"Come on," I said, and pushed him toward the door.

We approached the truck and I realized that the gate had closed behind us. "I need someone to stay behind and open the gate," I said, understanding that I was suggesting a potential suicide mission.

I looked around, not seeing anyone whom I could spare. I needed my men to sit at the windows, to provide firepower. The security guard stared at me, then walked over to the gate controls.

I nodded at him, closed the door to the pickup truck, then leaned my head out the window. "Don't open the gate before I start the engine," I said. "I won't have time to stop. Make sure you jump into the back before we go."

He readied himself.

I acquainted myself with the controls, took a deep breath, then turned the key.

Rrrr-rrrr-rrrr.

Nothing. The sound was deafening. Kosi flipped the safety off his AK-47 and stuck it through the window.

Rrr-rrrrr-rrrr.

My heart was pounding even louder than the scratching of the engine.

Again, nothing.

I stared into the rearview mirror.

"It's a diesel engine that hasn't been started in months," whispered Tom Thibaut frantically. "Try it again."

Suddenly, I heard shouts from the next house over.

Cobras.

They'd heard us.

I turned the key again, holding my breath against the momentary silence that I knew was about to erupt into explosions and machine-gun fire. My hand was shaking so hard I could barely grip the steering wheel. In my head, I could hear the Cobra forces waking up, could hear them stepping outside, could hear them loading their weapons. I prayed to every god on earth.

Rrr-rrrr-rrr-rrr-rrrrr-rrrr.

The truck sprang to life, black smoke pouring from the exhaust pipe. The guard opened the gate, the horrific squealing now obscured by the roaring of the diesel engine.

I heard footsteps running toward the house and pictured the hordes of drowsy Cobra soldiers staggering to their feet, grabbing their weapons.

I floored the gas, listening as the wheels spun uselessly against the gravel driveway. "Come on," I whispered, releasing my breath as the wheels caught and the truck leaped forward through the gate.

I spun the wheel to the left, the back of the truck following in a counterclockwise movement. An RPG exploded, directly where the rear of the truck would have been if it hadn't spun out. I whipped the wheel back to the right in a maneuver I couldn't repeat if I tried. The truck lurched forward in a series of awkward jumps. Another RPG exploded, and I knew the bodyguard was dead.

Machine-gun fire erupted and we all ducked. My men returned fire as I floored the gas, heading for the main road. We had to get back behind Cocoyes lines.

The main thoroughfare was dotted with potholes from previous explosions, and machine guns sang as the diesel engine revved to its limits. I wove from side to side, hoping to confuse the just-awakened Cobra militia. Every few seconds, a thud would rock the truck as I ran over a body that had been left in the middle of the road.

I glanced in my rearview mirror, breaking into a grin as I saw Tom Thibaut's bodyguard hanging on to the back of the truck. I nearly laughed out loud as we locked eyes and he gave me a tiny thumbs-up and a huge smile.

We spun into the hotel parking lot and squealed to a stop, hands on our weapons, waiting for all five men who had provided gunfire cover to sprint back to the Sovamag from their assigned positions. It felt like an eternity, but finally we saw them running toward us, heads down. "Get in, quick! We need to go!" They ran even faster, leaping into the jeep and starting it up with a roar. I spun the wheel of the pickup truck around and headed back for the main road. Thanks to our incursion, a full-blown firefight had broken out, and we passed Nibolek soldiers running for the front lines, strapping on their weapons.

Mr. Tom Thibaut and his family kept their heads down as I drove. They didn't move a muscle or make a sound.

As the gunfire began to fade, I pulled back and let the Sovamag take the lead. We had the *mundelés* with us and couldn't afford to stop at the checkpoints. If they saw what we were carrying, there would be a lot more questions asked and a lot more money paid.

"Stay down," I said, and gestured for Kosi to cover them as best he could.

I readied a stack of money as we approached the first checkpoint. The soldiers recognized the Sovamag and raised their hands in greeting as it rolled forward. The driver, not stopping, gestured behind him to the pickup truck. Looks of suspicion were quickly eliminated as I shoved a stack of bills into the hands of one of the children. They began to fight over the money and we squealed away, never coming to a full stop.

And again.

And again.

Back through all of the original checkpoints, feeling better and better as we got closer to the presidential palace. We weren't safe yet, but the worst was certainly over.

We pulled into the parking lot and began to cheer, hugging each other, singing.

Mr. Tom Thibaut got out of the car and pulled me aside. "We can't stop now," he said. "Please, we aren't safe here."

I approached my men. "Let's escort him all the way to Mr. DeVos's house. *Mundelés* don't feel safe until they see other *mundelés*."

They piled back into the trucks and we convoyed out to Mr. DeVos's house.

As we rolled up the driveway, Mr. DeVos ran out, eyes wide.

Mr. Tom Thibaut got out and the two men ran to each other and hugged. They began to cry.

I was worried. In Africa, men cry only if they are sad or hurt.

"Are you injured?" I asked Tom Thibaut, watching his skin change from white to bright red.

He shook his head.

"Why are you crying?"

He released Mr. DeVos and grabbed me by both shoulders. "I am crying because I am happy, Tchicaya. You have saved my life."

I nodded, still confused, and stepped backward, joining my men. We watched the men celebrate for a few minutes until some of the soldiers began asking about payment. I stepped forward, tapping Mr. Tom Thibaut on the arm. I gestured to my men.

"Yes!" he said. "Of course!"

He ran to his suitcase and opened the briefcase still nestled inside. He pulled out another stack of ten-thousand-franc notes and handed it to me. "Count that," he said.

My hands trembled. I'd never held so much money.

I distributed the money to my men, thanking them for their bravery, thanking the gods that we hadn't suffered a single casualty.

They smiled, satisfied with their cut. Kosi gripped my arm tightly. We'd come a long way from having our faces in the mud at military school.

I was only eighteen years old, but had developed credibility among the leaders of the gendarmerie. I had credibility with the *mundelé*.

My life was changing faster than I could understand.

A few days later, I escorted Mr. DeVos, Mr. Thibaut, and their families out to a nearby golf course where they had arranged for a helicopter to pick them up and fly them to Congo-Kinshasa, where they could then catch a plane to Pointe-Noire.

Mr. Thibaut smiled at me and pulled out a stack of cash. "Tchicaya, I owe you my life. How much money do you want?"

I shook my head. "As long as you take care of my men, I'm happy."

Mr. Thibaut took my hand and placed a cell phone into it. "If you are ever in need of anything, you contact me. I will not let you down." And then he shoved over a million francs into my hand— nearly two thousand dollars.

I stared at the helicopter as it took off, gripping over a year's salary tightly in my fist.

I was a warlord.

The Congo was falling apart, but I was rich.

And I was about to get a great deal richer.

PART 6
DAYLIGHT

For every dark night, there's a brighter day.

— *TUPAC SHAKUR*

Brazzaville, Congo
August 21, 2004

saturday

The grate slides back and the door opens with a stuttering clang. Everyone cowers and squints. I do not.

Two guards hold my arms and undo my handcuffs. They grab the man next to me, a lanky, light-skinned boy no more than twenty years of age, his face ashy in the sudden glow of the fluorescent lights. They thread my arm through his and then recuff me. I am joined to this man now, this man whom I do not know. We are one in our captivity, united in our isolation.

I hear a voice . . . and slowly it takes shape as my aunt.

"What do I do?" she whispers through the bars of the inner cell door, a glimpse of home amidst the glowering eyes of the guards. It is standard practice to allow family members supervised visits with prisoners during daylight hours, but I am still surprised they have brought my aunt to me. This gives me a strange sort of hope. *They are frightened of the uniform*, I think.

I clear my throat, wincing with the pain. "Mama Nicole, you have to tell the consulate what has happened. You must—"

She steps forward, closer, and sees my face. She brings a hand to her mouth. Her eyes scan my body, stopping with a jolting shock.

"Your leg . . ." she says.

"A rock," says a guard, and pushes her backward.

"That's what happens when you mess with the Cobra," says another, stepping toward the cell.

"Tchic, do not leave this cell. Don't let them take you to the hospital. You're safe here. Don't let them bring you—"

And the grate begins to slide shut, compressing her voice to a muffled moan. She is frantic, hopeless. Never before have I seen my aunt like this, and it's worse than any bullet could be.

Darkness returns.

In the ceiling, a small hole allows a single beam of light into the cell, creating hulking shadows in the center of the room.

The only sound is the rustle of skin against concrete. The floor is gritty, sticky, wet with sweat and blood and urine.

"Who are you?" asks a deep voice, and others murmur in assent.

I close my eyes, hoping to adjust them more quickly to the pitch that engulfs me.

I open my mouth, but no sound comes out.

I stop, breathe, and try again.

"I am Tchicaya," I say. "Son of Colonel Tchicaya Missamou. I am an American. I am a United States Marine."

Silence falls across the room and I feel the creeping tension of disbelief. The man who is chained to me moves uneasily, creeping as far away as the handcuffs will allow.

I open my mouth to repeat the words, but am stopped by another question.

"You escaped across the ocean? Why did you come back?" says an elderly voice.

"Yes," says another. "If you left here, why did you return?"

Their words are coated with sarcasm, with anger, with suspicion.

"My mother," I say to the darkness. "I came for my mother."

"Where is she?"

I can't answer, for fear of a quivering voice. Instead, I shake my head and hope that they can see, pray that they can understand.

• • •

Hours pass. I don't speak. Instead, I focus on my body, willing my blood to clot, forcing my bones to knit.

A rising wave echoes in the distance, and conversation in the room dies down.

"What's that?"

I close my eyes as I comprehend the sounds.

Voices, raised together in desperate harmonies, seeping in through the prison walls. Singing, stomping, clapping, drumming.

"Zoto é coma mboda."

Your body is a drum.

People can beat you from the sunrise to the sunset.

They will get tired, but you will not feel pain.

We are here to support you.

The voices, I recognize.

I feel the rustling around me as I stand, pulling my partner to his feet, and face in the direction of the song. I let the distant voices wash over my wounds. My friends will heal me. My family will save me.

They've come, and their numbers are large.

They've come to let me know that I'm not alone.

I will not die in this room.

I will not die in the Congo.

I am an American.

The voices waft through the air like a rainshower, and I fight not to open my mouth, fight to keep from drinking it in.

Brazzaville, Congo
1997

CHAPTER 19

The cell phone rang.

I stared at it, suddenly breaking into a sweat.

"Hello?"

"Tchicaya, it's Tom. How are you?"

"Good, sir, thank you."

"You taking care of Alard's house?"

"Yes, sir. All safe. I would not let Mr. DeVos down."

There was a pause. Mr. Tom Thibaut would not call without good reason.

"Tchicaya, I'm wondering if you'd like to take on another mission."

"What kind of mission?"

"Well, I've been bragging about you to some of my friends out here in Pointe-Noire, and many of them seem to think that you could be of some service."

"How can I help them? They're already out of Brazzaville."

"They are, that's true. But many of their belongings aren't." I now understood the phone call. "The pay is good, Tchicaya, but the risk is high. I won't continue if you think this isn't for you, but I have talked you up quite a bit over here."

The implication was clear. I didn't have to do it . . . but a black man in the Congo would never turn down a request from a white man. It was unthinkable.

"Yes, sir," I said.

"If it's all right, I'll put you in touch with a friend of mine, Mrs. Fumier. She's got some money and jewelry stashed away in her house in downtown Brazzaville that she wasn't able to take with her. Is that something you think you could do?"

"I'll have to hire more men."

"That would be fine. Everyone will be compensated for their efforts. This is a win-win situation, Tchicaya. My friends get their belongings back, you and your men make a nice profit. Don't you agree?"

"Yes, sir. Thank you for calling, sir."

"Of course," said Mr. Tom Thibaut. "I told you I would look out for you. I'll give this number to Mrs. Fumier."

"Yes, sir."

"Call if you need anything."

"Yes, sir."

I held the phone against my ear until it began to beep. I was very aware that I was entering a whole new economy, an entirely new lifestyle. Smuggling the belongings of the *mundelé* would get me killed instantly if the militias were to discover what I was doing. But I was tired of fighting, tired of running scared, tired of scrounging for scraps to feed my family. This type of steady income could change everything—it was more than I had ever dreamed possible.

I decided to try one mission. If it was a success, I would contemplate more. If it was a failure, there wouldn't be anything left to think about anyway.

When the time came, Kosi and I chose three other men and set off for downtown Brazzaville. This time, the house was far away from the front lines and was relatively quiet. We entered the burned-out building, weapons drawn, found three boxes of jewels carefully hidden in a secret safe, and headed back toward the hotel.

Not a single shot was fired.

We were hooked.

The phone began ringing almost every day with requests from the *mundelé* friends of Mr. Tom Thibaut. We could barely keep up with the demand.

For every mission completed, I was given two thousand dollars for myself and another two thousand to be split among my men.

The country was falling apart, but I was growing wealthier than I'd ever dreamed possible. I had gendarme, militiamen, civilians, everyone coming to me looking for work. My reputation was spotless—I paid my men well, I didn't steal, I didn't cheat anyone. It was a perfect business, and not a single man had been injured while working for me. It was dangerous work, but it was paying off handsomely. I was known at every checkpoint, recognized everywhere I went. Money was flowing from the *mundelé* back to the people of the Congo where it belonged. In many ways, I felt that I was doing a public service and convinced myself that the work was noble.

More money passed through my hands during that month than I had ever imagined existed in the Congo. Gold, silver, diamonds, jewelry, stacks of cash, computers, we salvaged it all. I would drive huge boxes of goods to the Mayamaya airport, which was now under Nibolek control, and meet with a Russian pilot and a Lebanese man named Ali. They would check the goods, stow them away, then fly them to Pointe-Noire for delivery. I was initially suspicious of these men, especially Ali with his big belly and unwashed face, but I never had any complaints about missing goods. It was a chain of trustworthy people, and the phone rang more and more and more.

"Tchico."

"Yes, Papa?"

"I'm glad you are successful with your business, but I want you to be careful."

"Yes, I know. I am."

"I don't believe you do know, son. Do not have an appetite for money. People will begin to envy you, do you understand?"

I thought back to the whispers around town when my father had built his hotel. "Yes," I said. "I understand."

"I hear your name in Pointe-Noire. People know who you are. They know what you do. This is dangerous."

"I understand."

"I want you to be careful."

"I will."

"Good," he said, and hung up.

I considered my father's fears. I was the one taking the risk. It was my name that the militias were hearing, my name the *mundelé* were using. I knew this couldn't last forever.

"Go to my house, make a right down the first hallway, and find the bathroom. The wall behind the toilet isn't a real wall. Break through it and bring me what you find there."

"Yes, sir," I said, writing down all the details.

I called up Kosi and four others and we headed off to the mansion of Mr. Bourge, a Frenchman.

The house was quiet and exactly as he'd described. Like nearly all the properties we'd been hired to infiltrate, this one had been looted many times over and was a mess of broken glass, shattered furniture, and scorched ceilings. I punched through the fake wall and stepped around the toilet into an extravagant back room. Bags of money, jewels, gold, and silver were piled against every wall. Art, statues, computers—the room was filled with more treasure than any of us had ever seen.

We stared, eyes and mouths wide-open.

"Where did this money come from?" murmured Boukoulou.

"Us," said Kosi. "It came from us."

"Let's go," I said, suddenly nervous. "Grab the jewels first and get them to the car. Hurry."

"Why should we?" said Kosi suddenly, holding his hand in the air.

"What?"

"Why should we? Why should we risk our lives to get all this back to the *mundelé* when it was ours in the first place? Our oil makes the white man rich while we starve. He buys mansions while we live in shacks. They throw food away and we raid their garbage. Why should we give this back? Shouldn't we keep it? Don't we deserve it?"

The slow nods of the others made me nervous. My name was at stake here. I hadn't gotten where I was by lying or stealing from my clients. "We gave our word, come on. Load up the truck."

"Load up the truck, but not for the white man," said Kosi.

I grabbed his arm and pulled him aside while the others began loading the jewels. "What are you doing?"

"I'm tired of risking my own life for other people to get rich," he said, and spat.

"But we're getting rich as well!"

"Not like this," he said, gesturing to the bags of cash. "This is different. And it could be ours, but we're giving it to the white man just like we always do. Don't you see that?"

"I made a promise to these men. And I will not let you break my promise. Do you understand?" I stared him down until he looked away. "What are you going to do with diamonds, Kosi? We're at war! Where will you sell them? And for what price?"

"We'll talk about this later," he said, and walked over to a computer.

The grumbling of the men made me uncomfortable, and I pried open two jewel cases on the ride home, distributing a handful of diamonds equally among them. There was no way the *mundelé* would miss something so small, and the guilt I felt was easily suppressed as I knew my gesture had salvaged the rest of the mission. Still, I began to understand that I could no longer continue this line of work. Money was of no use if you were dead, and my name was growing at a faster rate than I could contain it.

I began refusing missions from Mr. Tom Thibaut, citing my need for safety. In his defense, he never badgered or coerced me, but simply continued calling and offering new opportunities. My men were angry at me for cutting off their supply of money, but I had no other choice.

I'd seen enough. I'd done enough.

I began searching for a way out.

CHAPTER 20

Meanwhile, the war continued to intensify. Lissouba, in hopes of gaining more support for his cause, named Kolelas his wartime prime minister. When Kolelas accepted, the Congo became locked in a true civil war—south versus north, Ninja and Cocoyes versus Cobra. This union made Sassou-Nguesso nervous, and he realized that his only hope was an all-out offensive against the entire southern region. It didn't matter what he hit or who he killed, as long as they were Lari or Nibolek. If they lived in the south, they were the enemy.

I was the enemy.

Even markets were not safe from the Cobra air strikes. I remember buying food one afternoon for my brothers and sisters. I remember the low whistle of an incoming bomb filling the air. I remember hitting the ground, squinting as the market exploded into screams and a red shower of body parts. Hundreds died around me, and I saw headless bodies on top of single arms, ragged chunks of human flesh, endless puddles of blood and entrails.

Checkpoints sprang up at every intersection, manned by younger and younger children. I winced at the eight-year-olds carrying the AK-47s, shut my eyes as they killed women old enough to be their grandmothers, shut my ears as I heard them taking bets on which of them could kill the most people each day. Still, more guns and drugs arrived daily to supply the new recruits.

Houses were being raided by militiamen looking for able-bodied soldiers. If you were between the ages of ten and twenty and were not supporting the war effort for your tribe, you were considered a traitor. Even my own friends began pushing me to fight.

"Why should I kill my own people?" I would say to them.

"We're all from the Congo—why should I fight Lissouba's battle for him? Let the politicians get in the ring and fight. Then we'll see who wins. I never see Lissouba's sons fighting in the streets. I don't see Kolelas's children manning the checkpoints. I see them leaving the Congo to study in the West. If this fight isn't for them, it isn't for me." But my friends didn't listen.

I put down my gun and resolved to help my mother evacuate the area. I would convince her to leave the Moungali region ahead of the Cobra expansion and come farther south where it was safe.

"Listen to the radio," I said to her. "This war is never going to end. It's going to get worse. It will come here and it will swallow you."

She shook her head. "I will not leave my home. Your grandmothers are not well—Mama Ntsiangani is too sick to walk, and Mama Loukoula isn't much better. We will stay here and care for them. The militias will not bother us. Your brother Sazouka isn't even old enough to fight."

"He's old enough."

"Well, he doesn't look old enough," she said, dismissing me with a wave. "Do not worry so much."

"We need to get out of Brazzaville. Sassou-Nguesso will take over and he'll have us all killed, Mama. Pointe-Noire is the only safe place. Let me take you. I have money. The militias are dangerous. Even the people I work with don't like me."

My mother sighed, and I could tell that what I was saying made sense to her. She could hear the bullets at night, could see the explosions. The war wasn't distant, it was in her backyard. And she knew exactly how much money I had at my disposal, as I'd asked her to bury it underneath her bed.

"What will we do?" she asked.

I took advantage of her hesitation. "I have Mr. DeVos's Range Rover outside. You must pack your bag and get everyone else to do the same. We can leave tomorrow for the Oasis, then talk about heading down to Pointe-Noire."

"I don't know, Tchic . . ."

"We have to, Mama. We can't be here when the Cobras break through." I didn't tell her that I was just as frightened of my own tribe.

She sighed again, then straightened up. "I'll tell Mama Loukoula to pack."

"Thank you, Mama."

She patted my arm, then walked out of the room, yelling to her sister, my aunt Julice.

The six of us packed our bags and both grandmothers went to sleep early in anticipation of the big trip south. Mama Ntsiangani was very ill with diabetes and hypertension, and I secretly worried about the toll that the trip would take on her body. But, I convinced myself, anything was better than murder at the hands of the Cobras.

Around 6:00 ɴᴋ., as the sun was falling, there was a cluster of sharp knocks on the door.

I was listening to the radio, searching for the latest war report, and was startled by the sounds. They were harsh, angry, almost like a series of gunshots.

"*Jubula moelo!*" shouted a man from outside. *Open the door.* He was speaking Lari.

Ninjas.

I picked up the oil lamp and walked to the door. They were my own militia, and I hoped that I could talk some sense into them.

Again, the banging.

"*Jubula moelo! Jubula moelo!*"

I'd barely managed to unlock the door before it exploded toward me, hitting me in the chest and knocking the lamp out of my hands. Droplets of fire and oil scattered across the room, landing on a nearby curtain.

"Hey!" I said, putting my hands in front of me. "What are you doing?"

Seven men holding machetes and AK-47s pushed their way into the house. The first of the men got into my face, his breath reeking of old meat. "We're here to take you!"

"What? Where?"

He got even closer. "You're saving *mundelé* instead of fighting the Cobras!"

My muscles tightened up. "What are you talking about?" I said.

The fist struck me before I even saw it, knocking me to the ground. I leaped back to my feet.

From the corner of my eye, I saw my mama run out from her room. "What's going on?" she shouted.

"Give us the money!" shouted another man, circling me like a leopard.

I heard Mama Loukoula cry out from the back bedroom. *"A la wo!" Who's there?*

"Give it to us now!" yelled a third man. They were all armed, rabid, muscular. I could smell the alcohol on their breath, the marijuana on their clothes.

I struggled to keep my voice calm. "I don't know what you're talking about," I started, before being slapped across the face.

They turned to my mother. "Your son isn't fighting for his own people. He's stealing from them instead. Give us the money or we'll kill all of you."

"Get out of my house!" shouted my mother, backing against the far wall.

They began listing dates, numbers, specifics, and I realized suddenly that one of my friends must have alerted the militias. These men knew too much, knew too many particulars about my operation. They had an informant.

I'd been sold out.

Three men grabbed me. The leader scanned the room, his eyes

landing on my quickly swelling face. "Take him to *le petit matin*," he said, and I shook my head. I'd worked the checkpoints. I knew that this was the signal for death.

I began to struggle against my captors, pushing them with all my strength.

"Traitor!" yelled one, spitting in my face.

I could hear my mother yelling in the background, fighting against the men.

"Give us the money," shouted a soldier.

"We don't have any money!" she said.

I turned my head, following one of the men as he strode over to my mother and slapped her across the face, knocking her to the ground.

I felt a surge of energy flood my veins like liquid metal, and I was suddenly unable to control myself. I threw the hands off me and leaped onto the man who had hit my mother. In seconds, I was on top of him, pounding his face over and over again with my clenched fists. For that flash of time, this man became the object of my rage for every bad thing that had happened to me in my life—the war, the atrocities, the militias—he was the manifestation of pure evil, and I smashed my hands against his face until I felt blood running freely.

A horrible pain shot through my body, and I felt my muscles contract.

I fell off the man, holding my back.

I couldn't tell if I had been burned, shot, or stabbed—my kidneys, my stomach, my buttocks, they were all screaming. Awful sounds spilled out of my mouth as I landed beside my mother, staring in horror as her eyes slid back in her head.

I rolled over to find one of the soldiers holding a blood-covered bayonet. My butt was bleeding from a deep wound. Two men had grabbed my legs and were tying them together. Two others had my arms behind my back and were straining to bind them.

I screamed.

Smoke was filling the house now, as the lamp had ignited the curtains and the roof.

They tied me like a goat, my face pressing against the floor.

I leaned my head to the right, back toward my mother.

It was then that I saw something no man should ever have to see. I stared, numb, as two soldiers held my mother's legs apart. A third approached her and began to rape her. There was nothing I could do.

The fire crackled behind me and I felt that I had plunged into the deepest depths of hell.

I couldn't look away. My eyes saw it, but my mind could not process it. It was real and it was unreal, all balled into one horrific rush of sight and sound.

They were holding me down, taking turns raping my mother in front of me. The nightmare would not end.

The fire grew, but the room was strangely quiet. The men were no longer shouting, my mother was nearly unconscious, I was unable to speak.

Sometimes, pain is so great that even screams cannot come.

The fire snapped and growled, licking the ceiling, filling the room with a thick black smoke. I wanted it to move faster, to burn me, to melt my eyes so that this horrific image would disappear.

A gun went off and my mother howled. One of the soldiers had shot her in the foot. I couldn't tell if this was an act of aggression, a mistake, or some sort of punishment. I couldn't tell if it mattered. I watched my mother's face contort into the most awful grimace of pain and hopelessness. She didn't look at me.

A few of the soldiers ran toward the back of the house, and I watched from my vantage point on the floor, unable to move, unable to help.

They returned with Mama Loukoula, Sazouka, and Aunt Julice. Their screams joined the strange pops of the inferno, and I felt that my body would break with anguish. Sazouka they hung upside down from the rafters, his lanky body swaying in the sizzling air, just ahead of the slowly creeping flames. Mama Loukoula they stuck in the corner, facing her toward the room so she could watch. Aunt Julice, they began to rape. Two men held her legs down, while a third pressed himself against her chest. Her arms were tied together. "Help me, God! Help me!" she shouted over and over again.

I noticed that Mama Ntsiangani was missing.

Aunt Julice was twisting, spitting, biting, shouting, fighting her attackers with every thing she had.

I was helpless, tied, bleeding.

One of the militiamen took out his machete as he thrust into Aunt Julice and stabbed her thigh, dragging the blade toward himself. He was going to cut off her leg—a traditional method of female mutilation following a sexual assault.

I listened to the attackers speaking Lari and wondered how this was happening at the hands of our own people. The war had turned husband against wife, military against civilian. Now it had turned brother against brother.

The fire crept even closer.

Mama Loukoula blacked out, slumping onto the floor.

Aunt Julice screamed, her voice breaking into tearful shouts as the soldiers held her down.

Still, I could do nothing.

"Come on," shouted the leader, and everyone climbed to their feet. Blood was everywhere. Aunt Julice's leg was deeply wounded, but still attached.

They left the house without looking back, and I groaned as I heard the sound of the Range Rover roaring to life, then driving away. All our bags, gone. Our transportation, gone.

I strained against my bonds, shouting, watching in horror as the fire crawled toward my little brother's writhing body.

My wrists grew raw as I pulled and twisted. If I couldn't break the rope that held my arms, not only would I perish in the growing fire, but my family would as well.

An eternity passed. My muscles ached with the effort, straining beyond their limits.

Blood poured from the bayonet wound, but I didn't notice.

Finally, the rope snapped with a hiss and I extracted my arms. There wasn't much time. I untied my legs and slid over to my mother.

"*Voumbouka*," I said into her ear. "*Voumbouka*, Mama. The house is burning. Come on."

She didn't answer, but a moan escaped her lips.

Blood spouted from the gunshot wound in her foot.

I stood up, wincing, and held Sazouka with one arm while I cut him loose with the other. I set him on the ground, squinting against the smoke and the echoes of his screams.

Mama Loukoula was shaking now, convulsing. I had to get them outside, away from the heat, away from the danger. Every sound I heard was more soldiers, every fiery crackle was a gunshot. Aunt Julice was screaming, bleeding to death on the floor. Her right leg was floating on a sea of red.

I ran to Mama Loukoula and forced her eyes open, yelling into her ear. Her skin was so fragile beneath my hands, her bones so frail. "Mama Loukoula! Listen to me! Where is Mama Ntsiangani? Where is she?"

Her eyes fluttered open and a strange, brief smile appeared on her face before being replaced by an expression of utter terror. "Dead," she whispered. "Her heart—she is dead."

I leaped up and ran to the back room, where Mama Ntsiangani lay on the floor. She had no pulse. She wasn't breathing. I held back my tears and ran to the front door, throwing it open. I needed help. I didn't care if the soldiers saw me. I didn't care if they shot me. I was dead anyway. My soul had perished in that room.

"Help!" I shouted, but the street was in chaos. The war had finally migrated to my mother's neighborhood. The Cobras were coming. Families were fleeing toward the south carrying their belongings on their heads. Children were crying and the faces of the mothers looked like masks.

I turned and saw a wheelbarrow full of garbage. Beside it was a *pouspous*, a larger version of a wheelbarrow, also filled with trash. I emptied them both and wheeled them to the door.

I ran to my mother, slipped my arms underneath her, and lifted her onto the wheelbarrow. She was silent, her glazed eyes watching me. The house was an inferno now, and I knew that I couldn't save the body of Mama Ntsiangani. I would have to leave it behind to be burned. I didn't want to do this, I didn't want to dishonor her in this way, but there was no room. There was no time. I lifted Mama Loukoula onto the *pouspous*, then went over to Aunt Julice. She was no longer screaming, but her eyes were wide with pain and terror. She clutched her leg, cut to the bone, between both hands, watching as the blood gushed through her fingers. I lifted her up and placed her beside Mama Loukoula.

"Sazouka!" I shouted, placing him behind the wheelbarrow. "You must help me push!"

We rolled the women away from the house, coughing from the smoke in our lungs. Blood trickled down my legs. A layer of red was slowly rising in the *pouspous*, and I realized that Aunt Julice would never make it if I didn't stop her bleeding. I ripped a piece of cloth from my mother's wrap and tied it tightly around my aunt's leg. Fortunately, she passed out from the pain a few moments later.

I tore off some more cloth and wrapped my mother's wound as well.

We began the twenty-kilometer (twelve-mile) journey to the hospital.

It seemed the whole of Brazzaville was running down Avenue Mayamaya, pushing against each other, struggling against the quickly fading light. Women were screaming, and spots of red dotted the landscape like drops of paint. The fighting grew louder and louder in the distance until suddenly, it overtook us.

Gunfire sprayed the crowd, dropping two, three, four people at a time. We were Lari, they were M'Bochi. No questions needed to be asked. I didn't duck. I didn't slow. My life was over already, and it didn't matter if I was shot.

I pushed the *pouspous* over fallen bodies, over dismembered limbs, over headless corpses. Sazouka panted, struggling to keep up, his ankles bleeding and raw from the ropes.

Bombs exploded alongside the road as we reached the first checkpoint. Boys raised their AK-47s, then saw what we were pushing. They waved us on, ready to terrorize the next batch of fleeing citizens.

I passed a woman kneeling beside her son. His leg was a few feet from his body, but he wasn't dead. She was screaming, holding his head in her arms. Ninja soldiers came up to her, pulled her from the body, and told her to run. She knelt back down, still screaming.

"Get out of here," said the soldier. "Your son is already dead."

The woman turned her tear-streaked face to the soldier, raised her blood-covered hands, then stood and stumbled away from the body. The soldier took a step backward and put a bullet through the head of the boy, either out of incongruous sympathy or unnecessary cruelty.

The journey took hours, but passed in an instant. My mind wasn't functioning, but my body marched automatically.

The Makelekele hospital was a human depot. It was surrounded by hordes of people, many simply depositing bodies of their loved ones for proper burial. I fought my way to the front of the crowd, splashing through pools of blood on the linoleum of the hospital floor. There wasn't enough medicine, doctors, or space.

Aunt Julice was still unconscious and was losing an incredible amount of blood. I needed to locate help for her immediately.

I left the women with Sazouka and took off down the hall, searching for help. I stumbled over bodies, fell onto the dying, avoided rivulets of blood and gore. I found myself in a surgery room and stole a handful of supplies off the wall. A nurse ran by and I grabbed her.

"You have to help me," I said. "My mother and my aunt are bleeding to death. You can save them. You must save them."

"I'm sorry," she said. "I'm busy."

I shook my head and dragged her down the hallway toward my mother and aunt. She protested at first, but then fell silent, brushing my hand away and walking on her own. One life was as good as another to her, I thought, and it probably didn't matter who she saved. I just needed her to save the people who were important to *me*.

She looked at the gash on Aunt Julice's leg and chewed her bottom lip. "I can't help her. The injuries are too bad. She needs surgery and we have no doctors."

"You have to," I said. "She'll die without your help. Please. You can save her."

The nurse stared at the wound, then at me. "Wait here," she said, "I'll be right back." She left before I could respond, and I held my breath, praying that no one else would grab her before she returned.

A few minutes ticked by, and I saw her hurrying back toward us carrying a small metal tray. It had needles, thread, knives, and a few other medical devices on top of it.

"I'll need your help," she said, picking up a needle.

I nodded.

"Push the skin together," said the nurse, removing the make-shift bandage I'd applied. I reached down and wiped away some of the blood until I could see the edges of the wound. Using both hands, I squeezed the gash together until the two edges touched. The nurse began to sew.

I gritted my teeth, watching the needle enter the flesh over and over again. After about fifteen stitches, I felt the muscle twitch.

Aunt Julice suddenly sprang back to consciousness. She screamed and sat up on the *pouspous*.

"Hold her down!" shouted the nurse.

"What's happening?" shouted Aunt Julice, her eyes wide, her fists pounding against my arm. She screamed again, a strange com-bination of fear and pain. Two men came over and held her down. I looked at them with appreciation as Aunt Julice howled. The nurse was fast, finishing the second half of the wound in only a few minutes. Then she was gone, disappearing into the crowd to help someone else.

I smoothed back the hair from Aunt Julice's face, whispering to her, calming her down. "It's going to be okay," I said. "We're at the hospital. You're going to survive. We're going south."

She nodded, gritting her teeth with pain, and let her head fall against the hard metal of the *pouspous*. I walked to a nearby shelf and grabbed a roll of toilet paper. I unwrapped my mother's leg, wound the entire roll of toilet paper around it, and rebandaged it with more material from her clothing.

I pushed the two wheelbarrows against the wall and slumped down, staring at the ground. We were safe, temporarily out of the war zone, but surrounded by more pain and suffering than I had ever seen. Screams echoed through the halls of the hospital, and the smell of blood permeated every breath. Everyone was look-ing for loved ones, babies were crawling alone across red-puddled tiles, crowds were moaning. There were no doctors or nurses to be found.

I must have drifted off for a second, because I was startled when Mama Loukoula touched my arm. It was the middle of the night. "Tchic," she whispered, showing me the inside of her wrap. "I have money."

She had sewed a long pocket into the lining of her dress, and she told me that it contained a decent sum of money. "We need to go somewhere safe. We will not survive here in this crowd. The fighting will reach us."

"Where do we go?" I asked, my brain nothing but a pile of wilted grass.

"We cannot walk, but maybe we can find transportation. You must find someone to take us south."

I stood, wavering in the glaring hospital lights. My wound was aching now, hampering my movement.

The crowd was thick and full of wailing pain. I pushed my way toward the road and spotted a cab in the distance. I ran over, jumping in front of it. The driver was a small, nervous man who had his wife and child with him in the front seat.

"You must take me and my family south," I said.

"I have to take my own family," he said. "I'm sorry."

"You have room."

"How much money do you have?"

I shook my head. "Not enough. But my aunt is injured, my grandmother cannot walk, and my mother has been shot in the foot. Without your help, we will die. You have the chance tonight to save our lives."

The man wavered and I pounced on his indecision. "Wait here," I said, then spun around, plowing my way through the crowd to get to my family. I woke them and began pushing the *pouspous* and wheelbarrow toward the cab. The man was still there, staring at the swarming masses.

"Look at these women," I said. "You must help us."

The man opened the back door. I lifted Mama Loukoula in

first, followed by Mama and Aunt Julice, who winced with every movement. Sazouka and I climbed into the trunk. We had no luggage.

The car pulled away, and I was happy to be off my feet and heading south.

It was a drive that should have taken thirty minutes, but lasted over five hours. The streets were clogged with the dead and the dying, the fleeing and the mourning. The cab driver was quiet, and I drifted in and out of sleep as we inched forward.

I was aware that the Congo wasn't safe for me anymore. The Cobra wanted me dead because I was a Lari. The Lari wanted me dead because they considered me a traitor. My luck had run out. My father had been right.

The distance between the checkpoints grew greater and greater, until there were hardly any at all. Our ID cards identified us as Lari, but we still had to answer batteries of trick questions in the Lari tongue, ensuring beyond a doubt that we weren't from the north. The cab pulled up at Mama Loukoula's old house in Matsimou, where I had grown up. I handed the driver all the money we had and thanked him. "You have saved our lives," I said.

He took the money and pulled away.

The house was filled with families, some of which we didn't even recognize. Everyone needed a safe place to sleep, and this house had become a refuge. More than twenty-five people were crammed into that two-bedroom house, hoping for shelter against the onslaught of the Cobra militia. The men and women nodded as we entered, but few said anything.

We joined them, sitting in silence.

I felt defeat begin to settle in.

"Mama," I said. "We have to do something. We can't just wait here. We must get food. We must get medicine."

"How, Tchic? You see the conditions. The country is falling apart."

"The money I gave you to store. Where is it?"

She shook her head. "Buried beneath my bed."

"So it's safe."

"It may be safe, but the house is not. Forget about that money. It is gone. It is not worth your life."

We were interrupted by the sounds of a woman giving birth. She howled, quieting the entire house. Three women gathered around her, holding out a bunch of banana leaves to catch the child. My heart grew heavy as I thought about the world this child was coming into.

He didn't stand a chance.

CHAPTER 21

The next day, I went out to hunt, but found the jungles empty. Even animals know when there is a war on, and I didn't see a single bird, monkey, or snake. After many hours, I returned empty-handed and met with Sazouka outside the house.

"We need to get the money," I said.

"But how?"

"I can get it, but there is much risk."

"Without it, we may starve."

"Yes," I said. "We've come this far. I don't want to die now."

"Is it burned?"

"I don't think so. It was buried deep and dirt doesn't burn."

He nodded, saying nothing.

Another day passed. My mother grew terrifyingly weak. Aunt Julice moaned as a strong fever took her. I had to do something. Any action was better than watching your family die a slow death. If I had to die, then I had to die.

There was a chance that my mother's house was still in contested territory. I had a better chance with the Ninjas, whom I could fool, than the Cobras, whom I could not. The longer I waited, the farther behind enemy lines I would have to go.

I got up the next morning and dressed myself like a Ninja. I tied a red bandana around my head and cut the sleeves off my gendarmerie shirt. My jeans were faded and dirty. I was taking a huge risk, assuming none of the Ninja militia would recognize me, and I vowed to stay away from anyone in a leadership position.

I snuck out of the house and began walking north.

Almost an hour into the journey, I heard the sound of an approaching vehicle and jumped behind a tree.

My mouth fell open as I saw Mr. DeVos's blue Range Rover barreling down the road, loaded with weapons and soldiers. There was nothing I could do besides shake my head and continue walking.

I hitched a ride on a tractor trailer with some other refugees, but didn't pay them anything, because I was in character. I harassed the civilians around me and hung my legs off the back of the trailer. A strange self-loathing swept through me as I watched the ground rolling under my feet.

"Hey!" said a group of Ninjas as the tractor stopped, and I leaped down.

"What?" I said.

"Where you going?"

I snorted. "Heading to the front lines. Where you going?"

They nodded. "Same."

I walked over to them. "Let's go kill us some motherfucking Cobras, huh?"

They laughed and handed me an AK-47. I smiled and joined their group. This was much safer than traveling alone, as long as I remained incognito.

We arrived at a checkpoint and were given instructions to guard it while the previous group was called up to the front lines. We grumbled, but I could tell that many of the boys were secretly relieved.

"Hey," I said, as the soldiers and commanding officers walked away. "I'm gonna take a shit."

I stepped into the jungle, breaking into a run the second I was out of sight. I covered the three miles to my mother's house in a matter of minutes and crouched behind a clump of bushes. The house was in ruins, the concrete charred and crumbling, the front door missing.

This was the most dangerous part of my mission. If I was recognized here, I would be shot, no questions asked. I approached the door, then ran to my mother's room. Her bed was a pile of ashes, and I pushed them to the side, digging furiously with the barrel of my AK-47. I didn't know where the money was, but the ground looked untouched. It was here somewhere, and I wasn't going to leave until I found it.

The thought of Mama Ntsiangani lying charred not twenty feet away made me gag, and I pushed the thought from my mind. I didn't want to see her body. It wasn't the way I wanted to remember her. I dug and dug and dug, blisters springing up along the palms of my hands, the bayonet wound on my backside throbbing with every movement.

Finally, I hit something solid and pulled out a bag full of wet, moldy cash. I smiled and tucked the stacks of money, nearly ten thousand dollars, into my pants and underwear.

I took a deep breath and headed for the door.

Voices.

I dropped to my stomach.

The sounds grew louder, and I crawled toward a huge pile of trash beside the door, covering myself in it. The voices were not speaking Lari or Koutouba, they were speaking Lingala.

Cobras.

My blood grew cold and I bit my lip to keep it from shaking.

The soldiers walked past me and entered the house.

"Nothing here," said one.

"Yeah," said another.

They explored for a few minutes, then left, nearly stepping on my legs as they went. I lay in the trash heap for twenty minutes before slowly extricating myself and looking around. I was alone. I stood and ran back to the checkpoint.

As I arrived, sweating and breathing heavily, the other Ninjas trained their weapons on me. I held up my hands. "Cobras!" I hissed. "Cobras are coming! I saw them. They chased me." Every single one of the Ninjas turned and ran. Within twenty seconds, I was alone at the checkpoint.

I took a deep breath, then ran after them. Better the enemy you know than the enemy you don't, and I needed to be with other soldiers to make my way back south to safety.

"Why did you do that?" asked my mother, but I shrugged off the question.

"I'm going to Pointe-Noire to get medicine for you and Aunt Julice," I said. "You won't survive without it."

"Tchic—"

"I have money now. I'm going south. I'll get antibiotics and come right back. The journey is too dangerous for anyone else to risk it."

Her expression softened and she cradled my face in her hands. "I love you, Tchicaya."

"I love you, too, Mama. I'll get medicine for you. I promise."

She nodded and let me go.

I found Sazouka and pulled him outside the house, behind a large tree. I shoved a stack of money into the front of his shirt, and pressed it firmly against his chest. "Buy food. Don't let anyone see you. You're in charge of the family until I get back. Do you understand?"

He nodded, scared, and I squeezed his shoulder, realizing that I was putting an incredible amount of pressure on him. "You'll be fine," I said. "Just be careful, and don't show that money to anyone."

He nodded again, biting his lip, and I headed into the jungle. There would be too many questions if I tried to say good-bye to Aunt Julice or the others. I would explain when I returned.

I took a bus from Matsimou to Kinkala, then another bus to Mindouli, where I caught the train to Pointe-Noire. This train traveled only once a week, but I was lucky enough to arrive at the station only a few hours before it was scheduled to depart. The station was swarmed with people and the train cars filled up in a matter of minutes. I, and the others not lucky enough to get seats inside, climbed to the top of the train and settled in for the two-day journey.

I sat and watched the countryside pass by, feeling the comforting weight of money inside both of my shoes. The war hadn't reached this far south, and I stared into the jungle, feeling its tranquility and age.

This is what the Congo should always be, I thought.

The train didn't make any stops. Occasionally, I'd see a body sailing out of the cars—an unlucky man or woman who'd passed away during the journey. Asphyxiation was common on these trips due to the extremely cramped spaces and the relentless heat.

At Pointe-Noire, I watched as they carried even more bodies off the train.

I couldn't help but think that maybe they were the lucky ones.

CHAPTER 22

I hid outside the main headquarters of ——, watching as car after car pulled out of the parking lot. I'd already been asked to leave the premises by two security guards who didn't believe that I'd been invited by the owner himself.

I was dirty, bleeding, sick, unsure that I could go on. I watched the gate for hours until lunchtime arrived and a white pickup truck pulled out. The driver was black, but his passenger was unmistakable.

Holding up my hand, I ran in front of the truck and stared into the eyes of Mr. Tom Thibaut. Confusion mottled his face before being replaced by a fast smile. He jumped out and ran over, opening his arms and sweeping me into them. The mouths of the security guards dropped open. A *mundelé* was hugging a black man.

Mr. Tom Thibaut brought me into the truck and asked what was going on. He noticed my torn clothes, the blood streaking my pants, the fear in my eyes.

"You've lost weight," he said. "I barely recognized you, Tchicaya."

"The Cobras are taking Brazzaville," I said. "The M'Bochi are fleeing north, everyone else is heading south. The city is emptying out. They're shooting everything that moves."

"What can I do for you?"

"I need medicine. Antibiotics for my mother and aunt."

He nodded. "Of course. I have an apartment close by."

We arrived at his apartment and he took me inside. It was sparse, but luxurious. He grinned at me, stroking his beard. "Take a shower. You need to sleep. The apartment is yours as long as you need it. My family is in a house outside the city."

"No," I said. "There's no time."

He shook his head. "The train doesn't leave again for another five days. Take a shower. I'll prepare a bed for you."

Within minutes, I was passed out in the bedroom, lying on fresh sheets and pillows.

I didn't wake up until the next morning.

"Antibiotics," I said as we walked the back halls of ————. "Then I need to leave the country. Soon, it will not be safe for me anywhere. I don't know how much time I have."

"I can help you," Tom Thibaut said. "It will be difficult and it will be dangerous, but I can help you."

"It's more dangerous for me to stay."

He opened a heavy wooden door and led me into the infirmary, walking across the room and gesturing for me to follow him through another doorway. I found myself in a small storage area, lined with shelves that supported bottles, boxes, and stacks of bandages. Mr. Thibaut handed me an empty briefcase. "Hold this," he said, then swept his arm along the second shelf, knocking its contents into the case. "Take this back to your family. Here." He reached into his pocket and pulled out two million francs, about four thousand dollars. He shoved the money into my hands. "Go to your family and make sure they are safe. Then, you return to Pointe-Noire. We will get you out of the Congo."

I knew he wasn't lying, and a strange tightness filled my chest. This white man was going to help me. He would save my life from the fighting, from the militias, from the men who wanted to attack me and my family. I nodded, saying nothing, nervous that my voice would betray my emotions.

I imagined Marielle's face in front of my own, smelled her perfume in my nostrils.

He smiled and snapped the latches on the briefcase.

"When you get back here," he said, "I will take care of everything."

I decided not to alert my father to my presence until I returned for good. There was too much to explain, too many questions to ask, and I needed to remain focused on my mission.

I spent much of the next three days in bed, recuperating and dreaming of my mother as she had been years ago—not as I had left her.

The ride back wasn't as crowded, as few people were foolish enough to head into a war zone. I clutched the briefcase nervously. It was full of medicine, and that was worth more than gold in a city like Brazzaville. Briefcases were carried only by *mundelé*, so I tried to exude an air of toughness, of militant anger. I spoke to no one, brushing off every friendly overture I received.

The closer we got to Brazzaville, the worse things looked. The Cobras were advancing quickly now and would soon begin shutting down the railroads to prevent reinforcements from arriving. I snuck into the animal car where grass was grown to feed the transported cattle and goats. I hid my briefcase under a pile of feed and cut grass.

I walked back to my seat and slowly tied on a red bandana.

At the Mindouli station, hordes of Ninja and Cocoyes stormed the train. I stood up and disappeared into the crowd, harassing passengers, shouting questions into scared eyes. I couldn't show the faintest sign of weakness, couldn't give any indication that I'd been anywhere but Brazzaville.

I exited the train with the Ninja militia, then stopped suddenly. "I'll be right back," I said, then ran to the train and retrieved my briefcase. My heart felt as if it was going to leap out of my chest. All it would take was one observant soldier . . .

But I was careful.

I was smart.

I snuck out the rear of the train and marched through the station, appearing as official and confident as possible. Once I'd made it beyond the gaze of my fellow Ninjas, I took back roads all the way to the house, running on bleeding feet, ignoring screaming muscles and biting stomach pains.

I opened the briefcase to show my mother what I'd done. Her mouth dropped and she crushed my body against her own. "I am so happy to see you alive, Tchicaya. I was so worried. Sazouka has been bringing us food, but—"

I squeezed her tightly, cutting her off, painfully aware how thin and weak she'd gotten in the days that I'd been gone. "I promised you I'd come back. I brought money as well. You can buy food and you can take the medicines. They're antibiotics. They'll make you healthy. Mr. Tom Thibaut helped me," I said. "He's going to help me escape the country."

She pushed me away, confusion etching her face. "Tchic, you know we are not allowed to leave the Congo." By "we," she meant "black people."

"Mr. Tom Thibaut will help me. He's a powerful *mundelé*, Mama. He promised me his help. I will escape."

Slowly, she nodded. Her hand traced its way down my cheek. "It's not safe for you here," she said sadly.

"I'll come back for you, Mama," I said. "I will not leave you alone."

She nodded again.

"I promise," I said.

"I love you, son."

I pulled her close. "I love you, too, Mama. Everything will be okay. I'll make everything okay."

A week later, I stuffed nearly two million francs into my mother's hand, said my good-byes to my family, and snuck out of the house before the sun came up.

Atop the crowded train, I stared at Brazzaville as it faded into the distance. I did my best to memorize every line, every curve.

I said good-bye to the city where I was born.

But as it disappeared, I realized that that city had died many years before. I was saying good-bye to a specter, a ghost, a memory.

I turned around to face the front of the train.

The fight wasn't over.

My father's apartment building, where I spent much of my youth.
Ours was the top floor, third from the left. This picture was taken when
I returned in 2004 before I was arrested.

The first time I met my father and sisters, 1982. From left to right:
me, Mireille, Linda, Francine, and Michele. The baby is Magalie.

At the opening of my father's hotel. From left to right: my sister Linda,
my brother Jurity, my father, me, and my sister Francine, 1987.

My mother tasting smoked monkey stew, 1989.

The infamous "Nestor," 1989.

Mama Loukoula, 1990.

Crossing the Djoué River, 1995.

In front of my father's hotel, 1996.

In front of the congressional palace at the gendarmerie school graduation, May 1996.

Me and Marielle, 1996.

Guarding Mr. DeVos's property in my
gendarmerie uniform, 1996.

My father in his military uniform, just before the 1997 war.

Mama Loukoula re-bandaging my mother's leg after the assault on her, 1997.

Halloween at Master Thompson's gym, 1999, Roseville, California.

My mother's house after the fire, 2002.

Scout sniper in training, Bridgeport, California, 2002.

Iraq, 2003. Third Squad Machine Gun, Golf Company,
Second Battalion, Eighth Marines.

Me and Corporal Lopez on our final day in Iraq, 2003.

My father and I in France, just after his release from prison in 2003. He had been severely beaten, and his left eye and arm had been left paralyzed.

Mama Loukoula and Pépé Nsienta, 2004. This picture was taken only a few hours before I was arrested.

The last picture I took before leaving the Congo after being released from prison. Upper row from left to right: Pépé Nsienta, my mother, Sazouka, Mama Nicole, Mama Loukoula, my cousin, Uncle Serge. Middle row: Kinata, my two cousins, Mama Julice. Bottom row: my three cousins, and my sister Mabakani, August 2004.

My father, second from right, and uncles in France, where he remains in exile, 2006.

My new family—The Warrior Fitness Camp, 2008.

My wife, Ana, my mother, and my daughters, Marie Vangasi and Yana Simbasi, 2009.

Tchicaya with his son, Tchicaya Jr., aka "The Legend," aged two months, 2009.

CHAPTER 23

It would take a combination of black and white magic to free me from the Congo.

I lived with Tom Thibaut for a few days while he secured a French passport. The picture looked nothing like me, and the name read "Yven Mahonza," but it was a real document. "I will stay here in Pointe-Noire as long as I can," said Tom Thibaut, "but you must be ready to go when it is time. I can't promise you a plane ticket, but I will do my best."

"That is more than I could ask for," I said, staring at the picture of the man I would have to pretend to be.

Political tensions were incredibly high, and the border guards were strictly enforcing the retention of all natives in the country. I was unsure how I would manage to overcome the color of my skin, but it seemed there was nothing Mr. Tom Thibaut couldn't do. If he said he would do his best to get me a plane ticket, I truly believed that I would have a plane ticket.

I spoke almost daily with Mr. DeVos, who was now living in Belgium with his family. He was excited about my escape, and offered me a place to stay once I arrived in Europe.

When I had made all the preparations that I could on my own, I walked to my father's house and knocked on the door. He stared at me, a slight grin on his face, then invited me in. He was living alone, focusing on his various private businesses as well as his rapidly advancing rank within the police force.

I took a deep breath. It was important that he knew I had behaved honorably, that I had done everything in my power to take care of my family and myself. "I want to leave the Congo, Papa. Mr. Tom Thibaut is going to help get me out."

"And you want my permission."

"No," I said. "I want your blessing."

He nodded and pursed his lips. It was important for him to approve of what I was doing. I'd already gotten my mother's blessing, and this was the last step I needed to take. I wanted to come to him as a man seeking understanding, not as a child seeking permission. "It was meant to be," he said finally. "If my son has to leave, then he has to leave. I will help if I can."

We stood and shook hands as if sealing a business deal. And, in a way, it was—a transaction completed, a training done, a life ended.

"Be careful," he said. "The war is moving south."

The Cobras had pushed forward, securing nearly all of downtown Brazzaville. The Cocoyes militia from the south, though still allied with the Ninjas, was in disarray, and was fleeing in droves. Meanwhile, to further ensure his hold on the country, Sassou-Nguesso had forged an alliance with Angola, using its military in his strikes against the centrally located Ninjas. Pointe-Noire sat along the Angolan border, and was no longer considered safe territory. Whoever controlled Brazzaville controlled the influx of money from the oil industry. Whoever controlled Pointe-Noire controlled the oil wells.

The city slipped into full evacuation mode. All the whites were packing their belongings, shipping their jewels, selling their land. The blacks were scrambling for shelter, food, water. The country was falling apart, and no one wanted to be there when it collapsed.

Finally, a few days later, the time came.

"If you're going to leave," said Mr. Tom Thibaut, "you must do it with me now."

I nodded. "Mr. Tom Thibaut, wherever you go, I will go with you."

He looked at me, then reached into his back pocket and re-

moved a small envelope. "Good," he said. "We're leaving tomorrow."

I opened the envelope to find a plane ticket from Pointe-Noire
to Congo-Kinshasa, a ticket from Congo-Kinshasa to Switzerland,
and a ticket from Switzerland to Belgium. Together, they were
worth over two thousand dollars. My chest caved in on itself, and
I felt my heart thudding against my rib cage. My eyes burned as
water obscured my vision. These, I thought to myself, are what
tears of joy feel like.

"The hard part," said Mr. Tom Thibaut, "will be getting you on
that first plane and out of Pointe-Noire. That, I'm still working on.
Give me all the money you have left and I'll wire it through for
you. I don't want you getting searched."

"I'll meet you at the airport tomorrow. Thank you."

The white magic had come through.

It was time for a dose of black magic.

I showed up at my father's house early the next morning.
"Help me," I said. "I have a ticket to Congo-Kinshasa, but Mr. Tom
Thibaut is not sure I will be allowed on the plane."

My father looked at me, his expression serious. "You are going
to leave this country today, no matter what I have to do. I promise
you this." He walked to his room, put on his full police uniform,
strapped on his pistol, and grabbed his AK-47.

He sat me down and stared into my eyes. I could feel that this
moment had a weight, an importance. I listened with every fiber
of my being. "Tchicaya, a father should never bury his son." Here,
he stopped, cleared his throat, and started again. "Today, you are
leaving the country with the blessing of all the gods. You are *le fils
de l'homme*. If the white man wants to take you, you are blessed
and no one will stop you. If I have to give my life for you to leave,
then I will do that. I will do that gladly."

Here, he stopped speaking, but continued to stare. I didn't
look away. My father was giving me the greatest gift he could.

"Everywhere you go, never forget where you came from. The people who made you will always need you. You don't have a future here, not yet, but you have a future out there."

He took my hand in his and squeezed it.

I understood what he was trying to say.

"No matter where I go, Papa, you will not be disappointed. You've taught me everything I know today. You've taught me to be a man, how to handle problems. You've shown me that when times are bad, the solution is always next to me. I won't be alone, because of what you have given me."

He nodded, looked at his watch, and stood. "Let's go. You have a plane to catch."

And with that, everything was said.

The cab dropped us off at the Agostinho Neto International Airport. It was overflowing with frantic *mundelé*.

There was only one flight a day into Congo-Kinshasa.

My heart beat furiously, and I pulled at the collar of the European-styled shirt my father had given me for the trip.

I had to get onto a plane full of white people, at a time when it was illegal for a black man, a Congolese native, to leave the country.

Inside, I watched Tom Thibaut approach the immigration line and hand over his passport. He spotted me and nodded. This part of the operation was up to me.

I walked away from my father and handed the agent my passport. I'd dressed like a Frenchman and was affecting as natural a French accent as I could manage. The agent glanced at it once, looked at me, then put it to the side. He called his superior over and waved the next person forward.

I felt as if I might pass out. This was my very last chance to escape. As a Lari, I would have no chance in a Cobra-controlled

Congo. There were no other people to help me. If this plane left and I wasn't on it, my life would be over.

My hands shook.

I struggled to keep my expression neutral.

The head of customs arrived and picked up my passport. He glanced at it, whispered to the agent, then approached me. "We know this isn't you in the picture. Why do you want to leave the Congo?"

My mouth was dry, my lips hard, my tongue heavy. I let my mind wander over possible responses, finding nothing of use.

At that moment, my father stepped forward, sending both customs agents snapping to attention. As chief of police, he had jurisdiction over airport security. "What's going on?" he said.

"Sir, we have discovered a man attempting to leave the country with a fake passport."

My father let his gaze trace over me as if he were seeing me for the first time. "I see," he said slowly, then turned back to the agents. "Let him go."

"What? But sir, this is illegal—"

"The country is at war," snapped my father. "You are going to tell me what is legal at a time like this? You will let him through because he is my son."

The customs officials averted their eyes, and handed me my passport. My father walked toward the tarmac and I followed him, carrying my bag.

At the base of the plane was another checkpoint, this one composed of military police, set up to confirm the work of the Congolese customs agents. The plane was full of *mundelé*. I would be the last one to board.

Word had spread that I'd been held up at customs, and the white pilot barely even looked at my passport. "This isn't you," he said.

I straightened up. "It is."

"No, it's not." He handed it back to me.

"Can you prove that it's not me?" I said, trying to keep the whine out of my voice, the desperation from seeping through.

"Who are you to stop my son from boarding this plane when he has purchased a ticket?"

The pilot made an expression somewhere between a grin and a sneer. "Sir—"

My father took a step forward. "Listen to me. If my son is not on that plane when it takes off, I swear that I will shoot it down."

The two men stared at each other, and even I couldn't tell if my father was bluffing.

The captain scuffed his feet on the asphalt.

Above him, the curious faces of the other passengers began to press against the small circular windows of the plane. I knew that the longer we stood there, the more pressure the pilot would feel to take off.

My father took another step forward, nearly touching the pilot. "You people are the reason this country is at war. If you don't take my son with you, I will shoot your plane down. It is your decision."

The pilot stepped back. "Hold on," he said, and climbed the stairs to the plane.

My father and I stood silently, waiting for the decision. He didn't look at me.

I didn't breathe.

My entire future rested on this one moment.

After a few minutes, the pilot stuck his head out of the door and waved me onto the plane.

I exhaled.

My father turned me around and pulled my head toward his, touching our foreheads together, then our temples, then our foreheads again. He put his hand on my scalp and blessed me. He spun me around, then said his final words to me. "When you start walking, do not turn around."

That climb took forever, but I followed my father's wishes, finally stepping into the cool air of an airplane cabin for the first time in my life. I scanned the scared faces of the *mundelé*, then took the last remaining seat on the plane, beside Mr. Tom Thibaut. He smiled and touched my shoulder.

I was the only black man on that flight.

It dawned on me that I had accomplished the impossible.

I'd escaped from the Congo.

PART 7
THE PRICE OF FREEDOM

After climbing a great hill, one only finds that there are many more hills to climb.

—*NELSON MANDELA*

Brazzaville, Congo

August 21, 2004

Saturday

The hour is late, and most of the men around me snore gently.
   I cannot sleep.

Screeching of metal on metal.

The grate slides open.

I squint against the light, ready to face my captors, and am surprised to find a tall white man with a cowboy hat. The men around me draw back, but I pull my tethered cellmate toward the door.

"Tchicaya Missamou?" says the man, staring at me.

I nod, defiant, bloody, proud. "My name is Sergeant Tchicaya Missamou, 0331 Infantry, Second Battalion, Twenty-third Marine. Encino, California. Social 555-12-1221."

He nods back, slowly. "I'm Tim Morano with the American embassy in Kinshasa. I just wanted to see you, make sure you're okay."

"I am."

He shakes his head. "They told me you're refusing medical treatment."

"Yes."

"Why?"

"This is how they attacked my father. They tortured him, then treated him with HIV. Now he's infected. Here, at least I'm safe."

He lowers his voice and moves closer. I watch the guards glaring at me from behind him. My cell mates stare at this white man who has come to see me. The murmurs rumble as they hear me speaking with him in English. I can't shake the creeping feeling of pride welling among my cuts and bruises. Now they believe me. Now they will listen to my story. The guards stare, unable to understand our dialogue, but unwilling to interfere with a white diplomat. Anything this Tim Morano asks the guards to do, short of releasing me, they will do. In the Congo, he is respected, powerful.

He whispers to me, and I smell cigarettes on his breath. "Don't try anything stupid, all right? We'll get you out of here."

"What will you do?"

"I tried to meet with the general, but he's gone for the weekend—should be back Monday morning. I'll be here waiting for him. They say you violated military law. They plan on keeping you at least forty-five days, with an option for extension via augmentation demands."

"I'll escape," I say.

He shakes his head. "It's not worth the risk. Just sit tight. I'll get you out of here."

I lower my voice even further. "The longer I wait, the weaker I'll become. I need to leave soon."

"I understand. I'm asking you to trust me. Can you do that?" He takes his hat off, and I squint, my eyes adjusting to the comparatively bright lights of the hallway.

I stare at this white man who has come a great distance to see me. His face is deeply lined, his eyes warm and gentle. Patches of white are scattered through his hair, matching his shirt and hat. His suit is dark, and it's difficult to see where he ends and the captivity begins.

The sounds of singing crash through the back wall of the cell, hiding our words from the prying ears of the guards. I know that Tim Morano hears these voices. I know he realizes they are for me.

"I won't last forty-five days," I say.

"You won't have to," he says. "I'll be back on Monday to meet with the general. I'll use tomorrow to get all the paperwork in order. Hang in there." He pauses. "You're a Marine. If this continues, we might have an international incident on our hands." He steps back, and I nod as the grate slides closed, separating me once again from the light.

Silence.

Darkness.

A voice then, strong. "You are a Marine like we see on the TV?"

Someone shakes my hand, rattling the cuffs.

"*Makoundzi*, the white man comes for you."

Another voice. "You are the boss of *mundelé*. They will come to rescue you."

More voices begin chiming in, pressing against me, hopeful, excited, animated.

"We will follow you."

"We will protect you."

"We will be your bodyguards."

Voiced assent.

"You must escape to tell the white man of our troubles. You can help us."

"Yes, you can help us."

"We will protect you."

I allow myself to be ferried to the rear of the room, where, through the thick stone wall of the prison, the voices of my family are louder. I place my hands against the rough rock, pulling my chained arms close to my face, dragging my cell mate.

These are my people.

I will not die here.

The song swells as if in agreement. My body bleeds and the bullet fragments in my leg pulse like drops of fire. But a smile begins on my face, here in the dark.

None of us are tired anymore, and I open my mouth to speak of my capture, of my betrayal, of my need for escape.

I speak of freedom, of democracy, of a world where everyone is given the chance to make a difference. Where every man is allowed to live life as he chooses.

The nods of the men bob in counterpoint to the voices of my family and friends singing outside, and still I talk, power swelling my chest, pride filling my voice.

It is for me as much as it is for them. I remind myself who I am and how I got here.

I remind myself that I will not die in a dark cell in my hometown.

I cannot.

I have a story that must be told.

Democratic Republic of Congo
Switzerland
Bruges, Belgium
1997–98

CHAPTER 24

As the plane touched down in Congo-Kinshasa, Mr. Tom Thibaut patted my arm. "Here, I can take care of you."

I smiled at him, heart pounding from the short plane ride.

I held his hand as we walked through the terminal toward our next flight.

My flight to Europe.

My flight to Marielle.

My palms felt like rivers.

We strode across the tarmac to an airplane as large as a city. It had two levels and was called an "airbus." I didn't see how it could possibly be light enough to fly, but I'd committed to trusting this *mundelé*. If he said this plane was my path to safety, then I would be on it.

We climbed the ladder, then turned left toward first class. A white stewardess with blond hair smiled at me. "Good evening, sir," she said.

Sir.

A white woman called me "sir."

In the Congo, no black person would ever dream of speaking

to a *mundelé* without first saying "Mr." or "Mrs." and here, a white woman had called me "sir."

I didn't respond, because I didn't know how.

Mr. Thibaut pulled me into one of the most luxurious seats I'd ever seen, and I sank into the soft leather cushions, sighing contentedly. Out of the corner of my eye, I saw Mr. Thibaut taking his shoes off, so I did the same.

He tugged on his beard, then reached over to the seat in front of him and pulled out a television.

My mouth must have been a mile wide. The white man truly was a magician if he could give everyone his own television! Nervously, I reached for the seat ahead of me and slowly extracted a tiny screen.

I began pushing buttons, watching as the perfect picture changed from station to station. It was incredible.

Mr. Thibaut smiled at me as the plane took off. I tried not to let my nervousness show as steam streamed from the wings of the plane and a dull roar filled my ears. He leaned over and adjusted my armrest. I felt the seat beginning to fall away from me, and I leaned forward, frightened.

He laughed. "No, it's okay. Lean back. Watch." And he lowered my seat even farther. Slowly, I laid my head against the pillow and felt my muscles relax. I hadn't rested in weeks, and my body began aching with comfort.

I looked up to see another beautiful white woman wearing a black uniform. I inhaled deeply, smelling her sweet perfume. She smiled. "What would you like to drink, sir?"

I shook my head. First, she called me sir, and now she was asking me what I wanted to drink? It was nearly unbelievable.

"Water," I said, feeling like a king.

I turned to Mr. Tom Thibaut, trying to say something, anything, attempting to express my feelings, my gratitude.

He smiled. I smiled back. That seemed to be enough.

The stewardess brought my water. I took a sip and felt it work its way down into my stomach. It was the clearest, coldest, most perfect water I had ever tasted. I shivered with joy.

When she passed by again, I inhaled deeply, then asked for a second glass.

Once again, she smiled.

A white woman *happy* to serve a black man.

It was a dream, but not one that I would have been capable of imagining.

She was the perfect woman. Beautiful, caring, attentive. I fell in love five times on that flight.

The speakers crackled and a voice came on, identifying itself as the pilot. He welcomed me onto the plane, told me how long my journey was going to take, then announced the menu for the flight.

White people would be cooking for me.

The mystery continued to deepen.

"Fish or chicken?" asked the stewardess.

I smiled. "Chicken."

She put down a tray containing salad, a steaming-hot chicken breast, and a slice of cake.

I immediately picked up the cake and took a bite.

This was comfort.

This was freedom.

"What would you like to drink with dinner, sir?" asked yet another stewardess.

"Red wine," said Mr. Thibaut, gesturing to both of us.

"It's a celebration," I said, catching on.

Two glasses were brought over, and I took a sip of the dark liquid. It warmed my throat as it went down, and I could feel it merging with the chicken and cake that lined my stomach. My body began to tingle, and I felt a strange relaxation flooding through my veins.

I began to drift off, but sat up, realizing I hadn't put my tray away. I gathered the containers and my empty wineglass, looking around for a place to stow them. Mr. Thibaut was snoring beside me, so I couldn't ask him.

The first stewardess, the one with the blue eyes, walked up to me. "I'll take that for you, sir."

And she did.

My head nearly exploded.

I settled back into my seat, attempting to reconcile this flight with the last five years of my life. The world was much different than I'd imagined, and I hadn't even arrived in Europe.

For the first time that I could remember, I was excited about my future.

I wanted to stay awake, to appreciate every tiny thing about the journey, to make sure that I wasn't dreaming, that I wouldn't wake up back in the Congo, but the TV lured me toward slumber and the seat enveloped me and the wine made my head spin . . .

I woke to a warm napkin being placed in my hands.

I unwrapped it carefully, expecting to find more food, but there was nothing.

I sat up, watching as Mr. Thibaut wiped his face and hands with his own cloth. I did the same, enjoying the steam against my skin, the faint scent of lemon in my nostrils. Hot water is unheard of in the Congo, except for the wealthiest of citizens.

I wanted to ask the stewardesses for a stack of the napkins so I could rub them under my armpits and over my body, but I resisted. I wouldn't do anything that Mr. Thibaut didn't do. This was a new place, a new life, and I would have to be observant. I would have to fit in.

They served us three meals on that flight, and I ate every morsel.

"We will be landing shortly at Geneva International Airport," said the speaker. "Please return your seats to their upright position."

I took a deep breath, craning my head to see the rapidly approaching ground. It was bright outside, and I could see the earth screaming toward me like a bullet. My body tensed up and my ears ached as we plummeted toward the runway.

The plane touched down with the barest of bumps, and I released the breath I'd been holding.

Mr. Thibaut leaned over. "Alard will be waiting for you in Belgium. He's promised to take care of you once you arrive," he said.

"Thank you," I said.

"I won't be traveling to Belgium with you, but I'll get you to your flight. Come on."

We stood up to exit the plane, only this time we walked toward the front. The stewardesses said good-bye to me, and I smiled broadly, thanking each of them individually. After a few steps, I found myself in a long tunnel.

How big is this plane? I thought. This was an entirely new section I didn't remember seeing from the outside. We walked and walked, and I kept searching for the stairs that would take us down to the tarmac.

We turned a corner and stepped into the terminal. I stopped abruptly, attempting to figure out exactly when we had left the plane. Mr. Thibaut walked on, and I hurried to catch up with him.

We arrived in front of my departure gate and Mr. Thibaut placed his hand on my shoulder. "I'll call Alard to come and pick you up." He handed me a piece of paper. "If you get lost, call this number. Okay?"

"Yes, sir."

"I'll wire your money over to Alard so he can give it to you. I don't expect you'll be searched, but it's better to be safe."

"I understand."

"Good luck, Tchicaya. I'll talk to you soon."

"Thank you, sir."

He smiled. "No, thank you."

And then he turned, disappearing into the swirling crowds.

I never saw him again.

CHAPTER 25

The customs official in Belgium took my passport and scanned it under a tiny blue light. I held my breath, staring at his thin mustache, his dark blue shirt, his pistol. This *mundelé* held my life in his hands.

He didn't even look at the picture. He just nodded at me, stamped the passport, and waved me on.

I couldn't believe it.

I was in.

I'd made it to Europe.

The airport was overwhelming. I'd never seen so many white people in one place before.

I took a deep breath and began searching for a pay phone to call Mr. DeVos. For nearly forty-five minutes, I wandered the terminal looking for anything that even remotely resembled a phone, but was woefully unsuccessful.

Nervousness and fear crept in as I avoided yet another horde of *mundelé* travelers. Finally, I approached an information desk and found a woman who spoke French instead of Flemish. She pointed me to some strange boxes that I'd walked past easily thirty times. Apparently, even the telephones looked different in Europe.

I tried to find a place to insert my coins, but had no luck. There was only a space for a card, and I hadn't been given one of those. I flagged down a passerby, gave her a few coins, and asked her in French if I could borrow her card.

Finally, the phone began to ring and Sofie, Mr. DeVos's wife, picked up.

"It's Tchicaya. I'm here. I'm at the airport."

"Tchicaya! Tom just called us! I'm on my way to come get you now. I'll be there as soon as I can. Don't move."

She sounded genuinely happy to hear from me. My headache began to dissipate, but my tension did not. I still felt that everything could be stripped away from me at any moment, that this was all some horrible joke that was about to collapse.

Three hours passed.

That feeling grew.

I fought the urge to call Marielle right then and there. I'd planned to wait until I was settled, until I knew where I would be. The anticipation was killing me, and despite my exhaustion and fear, a smile traced its way onto my lips.

I could almost hear her reaction, could almost see the color of her eyes.

I watched hundreds of people walk by in their European clothes, talking on their mobile phones, hurrying through the airport. People moved differently here, gestured differently, walked at a different pace. The air smelled sweeter, the ground looked cleaner.

Finally, Sofie showed up, and hugged me tightly. "I'm sorry that took so long. We live pretty far north."

"I would have waited a week," I said. "I'm happy to be here."

She smiled. "That's good. We're happy to have you." She paused, taking in my new French-styled clothing. "You look like a businessman!"

"I *am* a businessman," I said.

I put my suitcase in the trunk and we piled into her Saab convertible. I smiled as we left the airport and merged onto the freeway. The scenery streamed by at incredible speeds, and I did my best to absorb the sights of bridges, farms, houses, and forests. It was September, so the weather in Bruges was beginning to get very cold, but I relished the brisk feel of European air whipping against my skin.

"We live by the ocean," she said. "It's a tiny place, but I bet you'll love it."

"I already do," I said, then fell into silence as the wind assailed my face and the strange smells assaulted my nostrils. My mind was racing faster than the car, and I struggled to keep up with it.

They lived in a small suburb of Bruges, in the Flemish section of Belgium. As promised, it was right next to the ocean.

She pulled up to the apartment building and pressed a small button attached to the car visor, causing the gate to open. I shook my head. In the Congo, there would be two black men standing there, waiting for the boss to arrive. Here, their job had been replaced by a tiny button.

We took the elevator to the second floor and entered a tiny but immaculate three-bedroom apartment. It couldn't have been more than one thousand square feet. Mr. DeVos was cooking when we walked in and he turned, smiling. His daughter, Stephanie, now almost fourteen years old, got up from the couch and gave me a hug.

"Tchicaya!" said Mr. DeVos, shaking my hand. "I can't believe you made it!"

"Neither can I," I said truthfully.

"Come on, let me show you where you'll be staying. It isn't much, but you have a place to sleep."

"That's more than enough," I said.

The hallway led to three bedrooms, and Mr. DeVos directed me into the middle one. I carefully put my suitcase down and stared around the room. I was in Europe and I had my own bed. It was incredible. I wished my mother could have been with me.

A small box in the corner of the room was labeled "heater," and I unsuccessfully fiddled with it while unpacking, shivering in the strange, dry air.

. . .

We ate dinner together that night, and I did my best to follow the conversation. Unless they were addressing me directly, they spoke Flemish, a language I had little experience with. They smiled at me as I shoveled food into my mouth.

I stood up to rinse my dishes, but as soon as I turned on the faucet, Mr. DeVos shook his head and took them from me. "You'll make a mess," he said, and pointed to a small puddle of water I'd created beside the sink. "Wipe that up." He placed the dishes in a large machine on his left, then added Stephanie and Sofie's dishes. It was strange to see a white man cleaning up after himself. I'd never even seen Gervais wash a plate, and he'd been a child.

I wondered if the black man would eventually be replaced in Africa as he had been here.

"You must be tired," said Sofie, smiling as my eyes fluttered closed again and again. We sat in their living room, the moon high in the sky, and I could feel my body sinking into the soft cushions of their couch.

"Yes," I said. "It's been a long day."

"A long couple of days," said Mr. DeVos. "You should get to bed. Sofie and I have to work tomorrow at the refinery, but you're welcome to sleep as long as you like."

"Thank you," I said, sitting up. "Thank you for everything."

The night was freezing, and I managed to turn the heater on full. Still, the air seemed to seep under the covers and creep into my bones. I'd never experienced cold before, and didn't know how to combat it. I woke the next morning with a headache and a dry throat, bundled in nearly every item of clothing I owned.

How can people live in weather like this?

I got up and walked around the apartment, relieved to find it empty. I hadn't been comfortably alone in many weeks, and the mental space was good for me. I took out the trash and began to clean the apartment. I figured that if they were paying the bills and being gracious enough to give me a room to myself, it was the least I could do.

Three days passed in this fashion.

I was too scared to go outside, too nervous that I would get lost. As most people spoke Flemish, the language barrier was high, even though my French was perfect. Mr. DeVos worked from home much of the time, but didn't always speak to me while we were in the apartment together. In fact, if he said anything at all, it was usually to correct something that I'd done. He would watch me closely, chastising me if I didn't wipe the counter after brushing my teeth or if I failed to make my bed properly.

I began to grow self-conscious about my habits and cleanliness. If I took a shit, I would spray deodorizer all over the room, then wait ten minutes before opening the door, just to ensure that the smell was gone. I wiped up every drop of water, straightened every rug, washed every dish, and took out every scrap of garbage.

Still, he found things to complain about.

I owed this man a great deal and worked to meet his demands, struggled to keep him happy. I was rarely successful.

Eventually, I began to feel trapped in the apartment.

It was time to get out.

It was time to contact Marielle.

I took a number of deep breaths. This was the day I'd dreamed about. I would call Marielle and tell her that, against all odds, I'd escaped from the Congo. I would leave Mr. DeVos behind and I would go to Marielle and we would be married and live in Europe for the rest of our lives.

Her face flashed through my mind and I closed my eyes for a

few seconds in order to see her more clearly. I said her name out loud a few times, just to make sure that my voice was strong and masculine.

I took out a neatly folded piece of paper on which I'd copied down the number given to me by her father months ago. I walked over to the phone.

She picked up on the second ring.

"Hello?"

"Marielle? It's me."

"Tchicaya?" Her voice was strangely distant, as if we were talking through a long tunnel.

"Yes! I'm in Europe!" I waited for the shout, the shriek, the explosion of joy that I knew was coming. I could feel my cheeks stretching, grinning in anticipation.

"Okay," she said. There was a strange silence. "How did you escape?"

"I got help. Where are you?"

"Berlin." Her voice was cold, but I couldn't figure out why.

"When do you want me to come?"

"I don't know."

"You don't know? What do you mean you don't know? I came all this way to be with you, Marielle. When can I come?"

It was then that I heard a voice in the background. It was a man's voice, asking something in German. Marielle paused, but said nothing.

I swallowed, the smile fading from my face like the sunset. "Marielle, who is that?"

Her voice was flat, disconnected. "My fiancé."

It was worse than being shot. My chest constricted and I felt my hand start to shake. I searched for the right words. "Your fiancé? What about me?"

"I didn't know you were going to make it. I had to get on with my life." She paused. "I'm happy. I'm living with him."

I wanted to throw the phone against the wall, but couldn't let myself show weakness. I glanced into the mirror, watching as my skin changed from black to gray. "Okay," I said.

She didn't say anything.

"Okay," I said again.

In that moment, I felt all my hopes, my dreams, my plans dissipate into thin air.

"I have to go," she said, and I heard a soft click as the phone line went dead.

I sat there, staring at the wall, not moving, too sad for tears, too broken for expression. I relived every moment we'd shared in the Congo.

The dial tone began shouting, and still I did not move.

I felt like a bubble with nothing inside, hovering above the earth, thin and empty.

I felt worthless.

The day passed in a haze, and I cuddled up beside the space heater, wishing desperately for sleep to come.

Mama Nicole, my mother's sister, had married a black Frenchman a few years before and had moved to Paris to live with him. She'd since gotten divorced, but had been given her citizenship and been allowed to remain in Europe. I called to let her know that I was alive, that I'd made it. I needed to speak to someone who understood what I'd been through.

"Tchic, it's so good to hear your voice!"

I forced a smile. "Yes, I'm here. I'm staying with Mr. DeVos in Belgium."

"Is it okay?"

"It's . . . okay."

"I have news, Tchic. Bad news."

I shook my head, wishing I hadn't heard her say those words. I didn't think I could take any more bad news. I remained silent.

"Tchicaya, your father was arrested."

"What?"

"The day you left, he was arrested for antigovernment activities."

"Because he helped me escape." My voice was flat, toneless. I couldn't help it. Guilt swirled around my head like a rainstorm.

"Yes . . . and other things. This was just an excuse, you know that. It was only a matter of time."

"Colonel Bemde?"

"Yes."

I cursed. Bemde was a Cobra militiaman and had risen to power along with Sassou-Nguesso. It wasn't surprising that he had put my father in prison. And I'd given him all the reason he needed.

I swallowed. "Is he okay?"

"I haven't spoken with him, but I know they don't plan on releasing him."

I tried to think of something positive to say. "Okay" is what came out.

"I'm sorry."

"I understand."

She paused. "If you ever want to come to Paris, Tchicaya, you can stay here with me, okay?"

"Thank you," I said.

"I mean it."

"Okay. I'll talk to you later."

I hung up the phone, numbness tracing through my body. My father was in jail for helping me escape. He'd willingly traded his freedom for mine. I knew what happened in Congolese prisons, and tears sprang to my eyes as I thought of my father enduring torture at the hands of the militias. But I couldn't go back. I couldn't save him.

I was stuck in Belgium.

Alone.

I sank to the floor, out of ideas, out of hope, out of steam.

Everything I'd planned for had disappeared, everything I'd wanted had fallen through my fingertips. Part of me wished that I could vanish from the earth, that I could die and never return. Life was too hard and offered too little reward. Marielle was gone. Gervais was gone.

I closed the door behind me and fell onto my bed.

For once, I let the tears come, doubling over as my body was racked with sobs. My stomach clenched, forcing the water from my eyes in streaming torrents.

Everything poured out of me, all the events I'd witnessed but hadn't mourned for. Mama Ntsiangani, Mama Julice, my mother, the baby who had died in my hands, the women I'd seen killed, the children, the men, the boys, the country disintegrating into greed, violence, and despair.

I'd left them all behind, but for what?

For a lifetime of sadness and solitude.

Eventually, the tears slowed, but I slept that night on a pillow-case wet with regret.

CHAPTER 26

I took to wandering the streets, simply to get out of the house. Mr. DeVos and I had stopped speaking entirely, and I could feel resentment suffocating the tiny apartment.

As the only black man in Bruges, I quickly grew accustomed to stares, whispers, and constant pointing. Silence greeted me every time I entered a restaurant or business. I began to enjoy the notoriety that my skin color brought me, and would walk around town, smiling and waving at all the stunned faces.

These walks became the highlight of my days, as I was fast becoming nothing more than a slave at the apartment. I was responsible for the cooking, cleaning, and shopping. I took out the garbage, made the beds, and ironed the clothes. When I wasn't doing chores, I avoided the awkward silences by staying in my room.

One morning, I decided to speak up. I didn't have any specific plans, but was desperately trying to explore my options.

Something had to change.

"That ten thousand dollars that Mr. Thibaut wired to you. Can I have it?"

Mr. DeVos shook his head. "Don't worry about the money. You don't need it here. We'll take care of you."

"But I'd like to get it."

He seemed annoyed. "Are you planning on leaving?"

"No, but I'd like access to my money."

"If you aren't leaving, then you don't need it now. It's silly to even bring it up."

He walked away, leaving me confused. I didn't doubt his sincerity—after all, the man had helped bring me from the Congo and let me stay in his house, trusted me with his family. They'd made me feel like an outcast, a pariah, but I didn't believe them to be dishonest people.

It was troubling.

A month passed.

The days dragged on, and the nights were even longer.

I decided to get a job. As an unemployed black man in Europe, I was less than nothing. I also thought that it might help my situation to get out, interact with people, and, I hoped, learn a bit of the language.

I mentioned my thoughts to Mr. DeVos, and he said that he knew the manager of a nearby McDonald's and would see what he could do.

A few days later, I put on my nicest suit and took the bus down to the restaurant.

"You can't work near the food," said the man, his jowls hanging near his collar.

I forced a broad smile. "No problem."

He scratched the graying hair around his temples. "You'll have to clean. Is that all right?"

"That's fine," I said.

He grunted. "All right, then. I'll call you."

But the call never came.

I began spending every free moment searching for employment, but the language barrier and the racism I encountered severely limited my options.

Meanwhile, things were only growing worse at the apartment. I wasn't allowed to leave behind any traces of my existence. After I drank out of a glass, I would have to wash it, dry it, then check it for spots. I would make sure everything in the kitchen was angled precisely the way I'd found it. I learned to clean the shower after every use, drying the walls with my towel.

Nearly every night, I would hear Sofie and Mr. DeVos arguing loudly in Flemish, and I knew I was the subject of their debate.

It was time for me to leave.

"We need to talk," said Mr. DeVos.

"Okay."

We sat down across from each other.

He cleared his throat. "Your attitude in the house has been unacceptable. You're not at all social, and you bring a negative energy to the apartment."

"Mr. DeVos, I don't feel comfortable here."

"What do you mean?"

"It's mental torture. I have to watch everything I touch, wipe every drop of water, cook, clean, shop . . . I feel like you don't really want me here."

"Tchicaya—"

"Just give me my money and I'll find my own way."

"Without us, you can't find your way. This isn't Africa."

I looked up, grabbing his eyes with my own. "I've already been through the worst part of my life. I'm not scared."

"I realize you're not afraid, but that doesn't mean you're ready to be on your own."

We fought for hours, eventually separating and going to our rooms with nothing resolved.

I woke early the next morning and walked the city for half the day. When I returned, I knocked on the main door as usual, nodding as the cameras spotted me.

No answer.

I knocked again, sure that Mr. DeVos and Sofie were home.

Still, no answer.

After about ten minutes, one of the neighbors exited the building to walk her dog, and I snuck in.

I walked up the stairs and turned the corner to find most of my things piled outside the door.

I rang the doorbell.

No answer.

I rang it again, then knocked.

"I don't mind that you asked me to leave. I understand, and I'll go without causing any trouble. But it's cold outside and I need the rest of my clothes." I waited. "Please. I'll only be a few minutes. I need the rest of my things."

And my money.

I knocked a few more times, then heard the lock sliding back.

As the door opened, I tried to slip inside, hoping to grab my belongings.

Mr. DeVos reached out with one hand and gripped my neck, pushing me against the doorframe.

I stood there, staring at him. I kept my voice level. "We both know I'm stronger than you. I don't want to fight. I saved your life. You saved mine. We're even. Just give me my money and I'll leave."

His eyes searched mine nervously. "I'll call the police if you don't get out of here."

"Fine," I said. "Call the police. I'm not leaving without my money."

I thought he was bluffing, but he walked to the phone and began dialing. I shrugged and sat down in the middle of the kitchen floor.

The police came, and fortunately were conversant in both Flemish and French. They asked for my ID and I handed it over.

"You live here?" they said, reading the address on the card.

I nodded.

"He was a guest of ours," said Mr. DeVos. "But he's grown belligerent and refuses to leave."

One of the officers turned to me. "They don't want you to live here."

I did my best to keep my voice level. "I don't *want* to live here! I just want my money, and I'll be more than happy to go."

We argued for a few minutes in front of the police, but when it became clear that I wasn't going anywhere, Mr. DeVos threw up his hands and went into his bedroom. He returned immediately, holding a thin, white envelope.

"Here," he said, shoving it into the hands of the first policeman. "Here is his money."

The officer looked at me and raised the envelope. "Here's your money. Let's go."

"I want to count it first."

The officer shook his head. "You can count it outside."

I didn't want to cause any more trouble and risk losing the support of the police. After all, I was still technically an illegal immigrant. "No problem," I said.

They escorted me outside.

"Do you have a place to stay?" asked the taller, whiter one.

"No."

"Get in the car. We'll take you to a shelter."

I didn't argue. There was no point.

When they dropped me off, I counted the money and found only four thousand dollars.

I called Mr. DeVos from a pay phone in the lobby.

"Where's the rest of my money?"

"What do you mean?"

"There was ten thousand dollars. Where's the other six thousand?"

"You had to cover the expenses of living here. Food, rent—"

"You charged me rent?"

"Yes, I—"

"I could have gotten my own apartment and my own food for much less than six thousand dollars. I haven't even been here two months!"

"Tchicaya, I'm not going to argue with you. If you want to involve the police again, we can."

I slammed the phone down. It was useless. I looked around at the dingy walls of the homeless shelter and made an instant decision. I had four thousand dollars, and I needed to get out.

It was November, and the snow glistened in the moonlight as I dragged my suitcase to the train station. The clock in the main square chimed ten.

I found that the first train didn't leave until 5:00 ?,к . the next day, so I curled around my bag and shivered until the sun came up.

Navigating the language barrier was still a problem, but I was growing used to it and managed to get myself to Brussels, the capital of Belgium. Exhausted, I got off the train and went straight to the immigration office to apply for political asylum. It was the only thing I could think to do under the circumstances. I couldn't risk being sent back to the Congo, and I no longer trusted Mr. DeVos to keep my illegal-immigrant status a secret.

Two white men in suit jackets looked me up and down as I stepped into the tiny building. I straightened my posture, realizing that I should have cleaned up and gotten a good night's sleep before taking such a risky step. After all, if my request was denied, they could have me arrested.

When they asked for my ID and passport, I handed over my ID card and hoped for the best. When they pressed me for a valid passport, I made the mistake of handing over the French document with the name Yven Mahonza on it. Clearly, this didn't match my ID card. My exhaustion and fear had betrayed me, and I nearly shouted with frustration at my idiocy.

I was denied on the spot.

They gave me two weeks to leave the country. If I was found after that, I would be forcibly deported back to the Congo. I'd have to use a good chunk of my remaining money to get to Paris and put myself at the mercy of Mama Nicole—something I was embarrassed to do.

I walked onto the street, the snow covering my eyelids with quickly thawing bits of ice and crystal. I shivered, dragging my suitcase through the mud and slush.

I sat down on a wet bench, fighting back the tears. The snow piled up on my legs and my teeth chattered like the beats of the *bôda*.

I'd worked so hard to escape the Congo, risked my life to save enough money to take care of my family, and now it was all gone.

Marielle had left me.

My father was in prison.

My mother was recovering from a brutal assault.

My family was split, scattered, disbanded across the Congo.

I was homeless and nearly penniless in a frozen wasteland where I didn't even know the word for "help."

It struck me that I hadn't changed my circumstances all that drastically.

A bullet isn't the only thing that can kill you.

PART 8
THE WILD, WILD WEST

Now let me welcome everybody to the wild, wild West . . .
. . . Sacramento, Sacramento where ya at?

—*TUPAC SHAKUR AND DR. DRE*

Brazzaville, Congo
August 22–25, 2004

Sunday–Wednesday

On Sunday morning, I begin to hear faint echoes of safety.

Everything that enters my mouth is first tasted and approved by my "bodyguards." They take their job very seriously, and I know they'll help me in any escape I attempt, should it come to that. The gendarmerie soldiers aren't allowed near me unless I okay it, and I've clearly expressed my intention to stay in the cell no matter what. I can never be alone, for I know that is the moment I will be killed. Throughout the day, the voices outside the jail only grow in number, and it sounds like an entire army has gathered to protest my arrest.

"There's a hundred people," whispers a voice.

"Two hundred," says another.

"There will be a riot."

I shake my head in the darkness. I need my captors to grow complacent, not fearful of rebellion. If I am to escape, my only reasonable weapon will be surprise, for I know my body has deteriorated rapidly under these conditions.

"The *mundelé* will alert America," I say. "The Marines will come, and I'll tell the world what's happening here."

"You will tell them for us," says a voice.

"Yes," I say, breathing in the thick scent of fear and doubt.

But even as I say this, I'm planning my escape, for there is no one in the world I can trust with my life.

The grate squeals open and Colonel Niama peers in through the bars of the cell door. He stares at me, spits on the floor, then turns to leave. I swear that a strange smile crosses his face.

A shudder courses through my body, and I recognize it as fear.

Light streams into the tiny room for nearly half an hour until two guards slam the grate shut, throwing us into darkness yet again.

I grow accustomed to the smell of the cell, the sound of my supporters, the growl of my captors. My life falls into a steady and painful cadence, and the hours pass slowly. The prisoners have unified in my defense and I know that, in this room, nothing can happen to me.

But beyond these walls, their power ends.

My mother begins to sleep outside the prison, her feet left bare in mourning. Day and night, she will stay by my side in silent support. I can't see her or speak to her, but I know she is there and this is comforting to me. I feel her presence.

I resolve to make cautious friends with the low-level gendarmerie soldiers who patrol the cell blocks. My escape plan will hinge on their trust, their complete lack of suspicion. The appearance I begin to affect in front of the guards is one of relaxed resignation, as if I know that the Americans will come to rescue me.

In reality, I spend all my time plotting and planning.

If the *mundelé* can't help me escape, I'll have to take matters into my own hands. I wait anxiously for Monday.

I only hope my body can endure as long as my mind.

The grate slides open, the door to the cell is unlocked, and two soldiers enter. Their names are Sergeant Gando and Sergeant Massasi, and I nod at them, establishing myself as a friendly, nonthreatening prisoner. Still, in this room, they fear me for the power I have over the other captives.

I say a silent prayer, thankful that the visitor isn't Colonel Niama again. There's no doubt in my mind that he is one of the men who tortured my father years ago, and that he would do the same to me, given the chance. I must escape before those who wish me harm manage to sway the minds of the more rational.

My cell mates ferry me to the back wall, beside the hole in the floor that functions as our toilet. Shit is piled around the rim, and flies buzz above it like spectators. I keep my expression neutral, careful not to incite the men. In the last twenty-four hours, tempers have grown short among the prisoners, and I don't want to be the cause of any more violence.

That will come soon enough.

The soldiers show their hands to be empty, then push through the crowd of filthy inmates. I notice that they don't push too hard or too fast.

They stand in front of me and I stare back at them, a curious smile on my face. One grabs my arm, clearly feeling the heavy gaze of twenty angry men behind him. He pulls out a key and unchains my wrists.

My breath catches in my throat and I try to suppress the growing swells of hope that cascade through my stomach.

It could be anything.

I resolve not to leave the cell for any reason but freedom. My captors turn to go, and my gut sinks in disappointment. Still, I take it as a positive indication of trust.

Maybe Tim Morano is doing some good, I think.

"Wait," I say, breaking the strange silence.

The soldiers turn, staring at me.

"You can't leave this cell until you unchain everybody."

This is a risk, but a calculated one. My allies here are not the soldiers, but the prisoners. I must stand up for my men. I must be a leader. I hear scattered rustlings around me, and I can tell that everyone is waiting for the soldiers' response.

I can make it difficult for them or I can make it easy.

I lower my voice and try again. "It's a simple gesture. There's nowhere we can go. We can't escape. Unchain the men, or you can put my own cuffs back on." As I say this, I raise my arms, offering myself to the soldiers.

I know they've been given specific orders to unchain me and that they can't go back to their superior without having done so. The decision is difficult, but they make it immediately, and begin unchaining all my fellow prisoners.

Air slowly hisses out of my mouth, and I nod. I've gained something for the men who've stood up for me.

I've also increased the likelihood of a successful escape.

The grate slides closed, and I'm surrounded by a rush of whispered thanks.

I don't acknowledge them, but stand at the back wall and listen to the distant sound of singing and the pounding thump of the *bôda*.

I feel, somehow, that morning will never come.

Through the small hole in the ceiling, I watch the sun peek a wary eye into the cell.

Monday.

I breathe deeply and center myself, ready to run if I must.

Today, the American consul will return, holding my fate in his hands.

I wait.

And wait.

Lunch arrives.

Then dinner.

And slowly, the tiny pinpoint of light moves across the floor, extinguishing itself before it reaches my filthy legs.

As darkness falls, I shake my head, silent. I don't speak with the other prisoners, don't answer their questions. Tim Morano hasn't come, and I take this as a very, very bad sign.

I don't sleep that night, horrified that he's forgotten about me.

Tuesday comes, then goes.

The sounds of singing outside the cell have grown every day since my capture, and those voices are the only thing that is keeping me alive. Inside this cell, I feel abandoned, alone, frightened. My body has begun to ache with every movement, every breath. I worry that I've somehow managed to contract malaria.

My exhaustion is becoming unbearable. Every squeal of the door, every muffled footstep is my death knell.

I drop in and out of sleep, my rest continually broken by images of decapitated heads, bullet wounds, and stacks of decomposing bodies. I do calculations in my head to pass the time and keep my mind sharp. I constantly fight the urge to attempt escape.

Colonel Niama accompanies the gendarmerie soldiers who bring us our dinner, and I can't help but feel he's sizing me up, waiting for weakness to overtake my body, waiting for my will to crumble. Again, he leaves without uttering a word, but again, he's managed to say plenty.

The darkness haunts me, and I try to project my thoughts into the ether, across the Congo, into the mind of Tim Morano.

He is my only hope at survival.

And he is nowhere to be found.

I wonder if I've finally put my trust in the wrong *mundelé*.

I watch the tiny prick of light form itself on the floor.

Wednesday.

I wait, but it's without much hope.

I feel defeat settling in, and let my head drop against my chest.

Tim Morano has abandoned me. I'll have to attempt an escape on my own, and I am not confident about my chances. My body is weak, my mind, confused.

Still, I would rather die running for freedom than waste away, confined in a prison.

The guards have grown comfortable around me, and I've narrowed down my potential targets to three gendarmerie recruits.

I spend the first half of the day planning different attack strategies and wrapping my mind around the pros and cons of each exit route.

After a few hours, I hear murmurs outside the wall, then a car stuttering to a stop.

My heart swells, but I don't let my hopes grow too high. I can't afford the disappointment that could bring.

Another hour passes, and footsteps echo through the hallway.

The sharp squeal of the outside grate sounds and I stand tall. My cell mates press ahead of me to confront the soldiers.

The light pours in and we all shade our faces, squinting to make out the cowboy hat of Tim Morano. I nearly faint with relief.

Finally.

"Tchicaya?" he says hesitantly, wrinkling his nose against the smell and squinting against the darkness.

I step forward. "What did you find? What took you so long?" I want to scream at him, to let him know that I'm dying inside this cell, that I'm sick with fever, that my wounds are festering. Instead, I stand still and watch him, searching his face for any clue to my future.

His skin is covered in a sheen of moisture and he keeps touching his forehead with a white handkerchief that he has balled up in his hand. He shakes his head.

Behind him, I see my aunt, staring into the cell. She says nothing, but her eyes are wide. She nods at me.

I nod back.

Tim Morano clears his throat. "There's over fifty people outside," he says to me.

"They're my family," I say.

"All of them?"

"Yes," I say. "All of them." I gesture to the other prisoners. "These men are also my family."

"I see." He pulls out a few papers. "The negotiations have been . . . difficult. Sorry for the delay. The general is standing by his initial claim of forty-five days."

"How?"

"On the grounds that you're a deserter from the Congolese army, and—"

My blood boils. "The gendarmerie was disbanded during—"

He puts a hand against the metal bars, as if to placate me. "Quiet," he whispers, and I comply. "I know that. I'm aware of that. But we're not dealing with American laws here. We're in the Congo. And under Congolese law, all we can do is negotiate."

"I'm an American!" I feel desperation leaking into my voice, and I hate myself for it. I must maintain control. My men are behind me, watching, listening.

"Yes. And we'll get you out. But my hands are tied right now, all right? I need more time."

I grab his hand through the bars and pull him to me. "They will kill me tonight," I say, whispering with as much ferocity as I can muster. "They will take me out and tomorrow I will be a memory to you. And there will be riots in the streets. Is that what you want? It gets worse every day—"

He doesn't look away, and I respect him for this. "Of course that's not what I want. But I don't have any options right now. I'll get you out, all right? Give me time."

"I don't have time."

"You have to hold on. Let me do my job."

"If you don't do your job, I'll do mine," I say, staring with all the intensity I can muster. He must believe me.

He takes one last look at my battered face, nods, then pulls away. My aunt pushes against him and reaches out a hand to me, using the consul's body as cover from the prying eyes of the soldiers. She squeezes my fingers tight and closes them around something hard. I don't look down.

She forces a smile. "Strength, Tchicaya."

I push my face against the bars of the cell and whisper quickly. "Get a canoe tied up at the Congo River. I'll find it."

The consul pulls her away, but I know she's heard me.

The grate is slammed into place, and darkness falls yet again.

My heart pounds as my fingers explore the object.

It's a mobile phone.

I move toward the rear of the cell. I realize this isn't my phone, because that was crushed in the first escape attempt. My brain begins cycling through every phone number I've seen, but the only digits that register are those to my apartment in Fillmore.

My roommate.

I'll call her and she can alert the authorities. If Tim Morano is powerless, I'll go to someone with power.

"Tchicaya, are the Americans going to get you out?" says the darkness.

I nod, but no one can see me.

Still, the singing continues. It's odd, but sometimes the joyful songs of my family and friends sound suspiciously like the melody of a funeral dirge.

I force myself to count to two hundred before opening the phone. The light glows in the darkness and murmurs start around the cell. I recognize it as Mama Nicole's cell phone.

"What is—"

"Shhh," I say, and silence reigns. "Come close." I breathe in the smell of twenty men and nod again. "My aunt has given me a phone to use, so I can call America. But if the guards find me with this, they'll kill me, and they'll kill my aunt. Do you understand?"

Murmured assent.

"I need your help. Can you protect me while I make my call?"

Chirps of bravery and muted battle cries lift me up. I dial the only number I know, saying a prayer with every button I touch.

I crouch, masking the phone's light as much as possible. I feel others crowding around, putting their bodies between me and the door.

The phone rings. And again. And again. The room is silent, tense, waiting.

"Hello?"

"Jessica, it's Tchicaya," I whisper.

"Hey! I was wondering—"

"I don't have time to talk. I'm in a jail cell in the Congo. They're going to kill me. Call the news. Call CNN. Call nine-one-one. You need to tell everyone, or I'll be killed here. Here is my number." I recite my aunt's cell phone number from memory. "Does this show up on your caller ID?"

"Yes, but—"

"Then call this number. Hurry. I don't have much time—"

The sound of pounding footsteps jars my senses and I hang up the phone, stuffing it into the waistband of my shorts.

No one speaks, but a cell mate touches my arm slightly and I feel him nod. This has given him hope.

And right now, hope is more important than food, water, or medicine.

Hope is the only thing that will keep me alive.

Paris, France
Frankfurt, Germany
Chicago, U.S.A.
Sacramento, U.S.A.
1997–98

CHAPTER 27

Three days of cold, weary travel took me to Rue Saint-Denis in Paris. Mama Nicole shook her head when she saw me, freezing and shivering on her front step.

"Tchicaya, get in here," she said, hugging me tight. I shook my head, relieved to finally see a friendly face. I was nineteen years old, and not wholly prepared for the sheer scope of the world, or the hardships it had to offer.

Her apartment was barely the size of Mr. DeVos's living room, but it had a roof and a heater, and that was all I needed.

We sat down and I began explaining how I'd gotten to her, the terror, the exhaustion, the mind-numbing violence. She listened without saying a word, which was exactly what I wanted.

I concluded by holding up my remaining cash. "I need to get a job."

She pursed her lips, and I hoped that there would be more options in France than there had been in Belgium. Here, at least I spoke the language.

"Africans in Paris generally work security or move boxes," she said, drumming her fingers. Her eyes lit up. "Oh, I know! A friend of mine, Mustafa, has a freight company. I'll send you down there tomorrow."

"Thank you, Mama Nicole."

"If that doesn't work, we'll keep looking, okay?"

"Okay."

I fell asleep that night on a few thin blankets. The hardwood floor felt like a block of ice underneath my body, but I dreamed of hot monkey stew and boiled cassava and was strangely content.

"Tchic," she said, shaking me awake.

"Hmm?"

"I have to go to work, but I wanted to give you the address and directions to the freight company. Mustafa said to come down there as soon as you can."

I sat up, shivering in the stale air. "I'll go now."

She smiled. "Take your time. Get dressed."

"I am. I'm wearing everything I own."

We both laughed and she went on her way. I stared at the ceiling for a few minutes, collecting my thoughts, then took to the streets of Paris.

My jaw dropped.

Now, this was a city for black people!

I saw Africans on every street corner, selling music, food, clothes, drugs . . . anything imaginable. They were dressed in the finest clothes money could buy—leather shoes, fine silk suits, tailored hats. Despite the bitter cold, I found myself smiling.

It appeared that the racism of the Congo didn't extend this far north.

But as I walked, I noticed something curious. There were no blacks *inside* the shops, only on the corners. The streets were filled with my people, while the shops were filled with *mundelé*.

Strange.

Mustafa was a barrel-chested man with stubby legs. His face was covered by a mask of thick spiderweb veins, and he moved in quick, jerky motions. He looked me up and down, then nodded. I was working within the hour.

This, I found, wasn't necessarily a good thing. My job was to stand outside in the subzero temperatures and unload boxes of frozen foods. I was given a pair of threadbare gloves and a hat, but I quickly forgot they even existed. It was like standing in a cold river, lifting cubes of ice over and over and over again. We would work for three hours, take thirty minutes to thaw out inside the warehouse, then work another three hours.

I tried to make conversation with the other workers, but they kept their heads down and mouths shut as they ran from truck to dock, truck to dock. I learned a few of their names and where they were from, but not much else.

I stumbled home that night exhausted.

Mama Nicole put on some hot water to thaw me out and smiled. I knew that her day had been as hard as mine, so I couldn't show weakness, couldn't complain.

"How was it?" she said.

"Good," I said. "Thank you for helping me find a job."

"Of course. You save that money and stay as long as you need."

I thanked the gods that I had such family in my life. I knew I would be nothing without them.

Still, I couldn't help but wonder what was next for me. I couldn't see this as a permanent existence.

I worked twelve-hour shifts, which left very little time to explore the neighborhood. However, after a few days, my restlessness got the best of me and I began to wander.

The first thing I observed was the massive amounts of dog shit everywhere. Well over half the people in Paris had dogs, and no one picked up after their animals. This, I later learned, was the responsibility of the black sanitation workers.

The second thing I discovered was the fierce nationalism displayed by the French. Their motto was *"La France aux Français,"* or "France for the French," and it applied to every sector of the city. White nationals got the prime jobs and white immigrants got the second-tier jobs, while black nationals were relegated to relatively menial tasks. Black immigrants had it the worst.

Every job I saw appeared to be clearly divided along racial lines. There were black jobs, and there were white jobs. Very few professions fell into both categories.

The segregation ran even deeper, separating white from white and black from black. West Africans would carry boxes, clean streets, and do more service-oriented work. Central Africans generally worked security. The divide here seemed to be cultural—Central Africa, where I'm from, values fine clothes, education, and fighting, while West Africa places the emphasis on hard work and family support.

West Africans were the freight-yard workers. Central Africans were the ones on the street corners, wearing six-hundred-dollar shoes and starving to death.

I realized that Mama Nicole hadn't put me with my own people, but I didn't care. Money was coming in.

Within a few short weeks, the toll on my body was already evident. I had back problems every morning, shivers even in the warmth, and I noticed it was taking an increasingly long time to regain the feeling in my hands after work. Some shifts, I wouldn't even realize I'd pissed myself until I was walking home.

There has to be something better, I thought.

I resolved to continue working hard so I could pay part of Mama Nicole's rent. Meanwhile, I kept my eye out for any opportunity to escape the winter hell.

• • •

The whistle blew and I wiped my forehead. Somehow, I'd managed to break a sweat, even in the frigid weather. The droplets felt like icicles and I shuddered. We were unloading crates of frozen fish that day, and the smell permeated every breath I took, every inch of my body. As I stepped into the warmth of the warehouse's back room, I nearly gagged on my own scent.

I fell into a seat and grabbed a cup of tea.

West African men love to watch TV and drink tea. It's part of their social life back in Africa, and they carry these habits with them wherever they go. I grew accustomed to spending the thirty-minute breaks with my eight coworkers, silently sipping weak tea and passively watching whatever happened to be on that day.

I stared at the screen, my mind empty and my body worn.

For weeks, all I'd been thinking about was going somewhere else, anywhere else. I was tired of being a second-class citizen. I'd gotten a taste of equality on my flight to Europe, and couldn't rest until I had it every second of every day.

MTV was on, and strange songs accompanied even stranger images. I watched with about 10 percent of my brain, conserving the other 90 percent for brainstorming and self-pity. The screen cut to black, and a strange, futuristic scene faded in. I found myself looking at a bunch of people in crazy, militaristic costumes . . . all of them dancing, and all of them African. The beat started, followed by the words "California Love."

My cup never made it to my mouth. I heard the words "Welcome everybody to the wild, wild West."

Everybody.

The environment looked hot and sweaty, like the Congo.

Dr. Dre and Tupac Shakur.

Beautiful women.

California love.

It was like gazing into paradise.

I watched the entire song, the wheels in my mind spinning wildly. There, it seemed, a black man could be free. There, at least, was opportunity. There, the color of your skin didn't matter. There, talent and drive were what defined individuals.

By the time the last note of the song played, I'd made up my mind.

I would go to California.

CHAPTER 28

I worked even longer shifts every day for the next two months. I had my passport, but needed to raise enough money for a plane ticket and travel expenses. Only about two thousand dollars remained from the money Mr. DeVos had given me.

This would be the biggest risk of my life, and I found myself asking advice from every person who would listen to me.

"You have to go during the holidays," said one coworker named Tulivu. "Americans don't pay as much attention on those days."

"Which ones are the best?" I asked.

"Doesn't matter too much, as long as it's a big one. Christmas, New Year's, Valentine's Day, Easter."

I did some quick calculations. I'd never save enough money by New Year's, so I set my sights on Valentine's Day, 1998.

"You have to shave your head," said another coworker.

"Why?"

"If the picture on your passport has hair, most white Europeans won't be sure if it's you or not. They can't tell us apart. Just smile real big and swear that it's you."

Another man chimed in. "And make sure you know what's on that passport. You have to know everything about the guy you're pretending to be."

"Yeah," said the first. "Europe's easy, but America's hard. That's what I heard."

Every piece of advice was absorbed, practiced, memorized. I became more serious about this journey than I had been about anything in my life.

It was one shot, one kill.

All or nothing.

I bought a used CD player and listened to "California Love" on repeat every day while I lifted those frozen boxes. It kept me focused, got me through the coldest winter of my life.

Welcome everybody to the wild, wild West.

It was as if he was speaking directly to me.

It was difficult to suppress the growing resentment that I felt. Every day, I would watch black people across the city hustle for change, while the whites sat in heated cafés, smoking cigarettes and drinking coffee. It was impossible to avoid the feeling that I would never make it in Europe, not because I wasn't capable, but because I was black.

My initial positive impressions of Paris were dead wrong, and the reality of the city began to color every interaction I had.

I stopped talking to whites altogether, putting up my defenses whenever I encountered one.

I became rough, angry, lean.

My life was on the line, and I fought tooth and nail for every penny.

By the end of January 1998, I'd saved a total of nearly four thousand dollars. It would have to be enough.

One morning, I woke up early and shaved my head bald before going to work. I asked two of my coworkers, Kimya and Ipyana, to cover me for an hour while I went to the travel agent.

I nervously approached the small office, reeking of sweat and rotten fish. My only pair of gloves was the one I wore at work, so I couldn't take them off without freezing my fingers.

I opened the door and inhaled the warm, humid air that spilled out. Inside this office, at least, it was a paradise. The long line intimidated me, and I went to sit down in one of the few open chairs. As I did, the white woman sitting to my right turned, grimaced, then got up and moved across the room.

I wanted to scream, to shout, "The only reason I smell is that I'm moving your food for you!" but I didn't. There was too much at stake. I wasn't going to let anybody or anything get in my way.

Eventually, the line dwindled and I stood up.

"Can I help you?" asked a young blond woman.

"Yes," I said. "I want to go to California."

She looked confused. I didn't break eye contact, because I wanted her to know that I wasn't a man who could be dissuaded or robbed. She glanced to her left, at the other travel agent.

For some reason, this made me nervous and angry. "What don't you understand?"

She blushed. "Where in California do you want to go?"

I couldn't understand why she was treating me this way.

My racism boiled, and I struggled to lower my voice. "Listen, lady, I don't know what your problem is. I have my money and my passport. I want to go to California." I pulled out my plastic bag of cash and my papers, slamming them onto the counter.

This white woman would not stop me from achieving my dream. I'd worked too hard for anything to stand in my way.

"Sir, I don't—"

Her voice was quiet, but mine had grown loud. I couldn't contain it. "I want to go to California, and you will not stop me!"

"Do you realize that California is big?" she said, her cheeks flushed and her voice taut.

I leaned across the counter. "You will not stop me. Tupac is waiting for me, and you white people will not stop me."

She took a few steps backward, and a manager walked over. He looked perfect, like a mannequin, and a gigantic smile covered his face. "What seems to be the problem?"

I took a deep breath, realizing I was blowing my chance. "She doesn't want to sell me a ticket to California."

He approached her computer terminal. "Well, where do you want to go?"

I shook my head. "I don't know. It doesn't matter."

"Hmm, okay. Let me see what we have available." He tapped a few keys on the computer, and I watched the green glare of the screen reflect against his perfectly sculpted face. I realized that everyone in the office was staring at me, but I didn't care. They were nothing. This was my life.

After a few seconds, he looked up. "How about Sacramento?"

The song lyrics played in my head.

Sacramento, where you at?

"Yes," I said. "Sacramento is good."

"And what day did you want to leave?"

"February 14," I said.

He smiled. "Valentine's Day?"

"Yes."

He tapped a few more buttons, then looked back up at me. "Leaving out of Paris on February 14 to Sacramento, California. That total comes to . . . 20,853 francs."

A thin panic went through my body. I pulled out my Ziploc bag and opened it, the warm fish smell permeating the office. I hurriedly counted my money, finding only 20,850 francs. The rest of the cash had been given to Mama Nicole so that I'd be sure not to touch it. It was my travel money for America.

"I have 20,850 francs," I said. "Is that enough?"

The man frowned and shook his head. "Not quite. I'm sorry, sir."

"But it's only three francs."

"That's the price, sir. There's not much I can do for you. If you want to come back this afternoon with the rest of the money, you're welcome to."

I gathered up the cash, shoved it back into the bag, and left the office.

I ran all the way back to Mama Nicole's apartment and proceeded to tear it apart, searching for loose change. I looked in the carpet, between the couch cushions, under the bed, in the bathroom. In less than thirty minutes, I'd managed to scrounge together an extra three francs. I poured the change into another Ziploc bag and ran out the door.

When I got to the travel office, I was out of breath. I pulled on the door and found it locked. I rang the doorbell, but the office was empty. There was a small sign posted, indicating that the office was closed from eleven to two for lunch. It was eleven-thirty. I sat down in the freezing cold to wait.

I wasn't going to leave without my ticket.

At two o'clock, I heard the lock turn and I stood up, my face only a few inches from the door. It swung open, and the woman who had first greeted me took two steps backward, a gasp escaping her lips.

"Oh," she said. "You were here this morning."

"Yes, ma'am," I said.

"You scared me." She paused. "Do you have an appointment?"

"To buy my ticket?"

"To be here. After lunch, you have to have an appointment to come in."

"No one told me that."

She thought for a second, and I wanted to punch her or bite her nose off. "We're pretty much booked, but if there's a cancellation, I'd be happy to take care of you."

"I'll wait," I said, walking into the office and sitting down. The room was empty.

The woman shrugged and walked behind the counter, picking up a tiny bottle of nail polish and the phone receiver. She dialed and proceeded to talk and laugh loudly while painting her nails.

I approached the desk. "Can I buy the ticket now? There's no one else here."

"Hold on," she said into the phone, then tucked it against her shoulder. "There's a two o'clock appointment scheduled. I have to wait and see if he shows up."

I turned and sat back down, my temper boiling.

At two-thirty, a man showed up. He was the second scheduled appointment of the afternoon, and was helped immediately. My patience was wearing thin. The smell of fish was making me sick, and I worried about taking such a long break from work. I couldn't afford to lose my job now.

I walked up to the counter again, but the woman was engaged with her new customer and ignored me. Finally, around two-forty-five, the manager came out of the back.

"Hello," I said, relieved.

"What's going on?" he said.

"I have my money and want to buy my ticket."

"Ahh," he said. "Usually we only take appointments at this time of the day, but I did tell you to come back. I apologize. Let's see what we can do."

He walked to the computer and punched a few keys. "Paris to Sacramento on the fourteenth, right?"

"Yes," I said, clutching my Ziploc bag.

He frowned, hit a few keys, then frowned again. A sinking feeling filled my stomach. "The price has gone up a bit," he said.

"I can't afford a more expensive ticket," I said.

"Well, that's the cheapest I can get you to Sacramento. Unless you're willing to leave from another country."

"Yes," I said. "Fine."

He tapped the keys, then nodded. "Frankfurt, Germany, to Sacramento, California, on the fourteenth. Layover in Chicago. I can do it for the original price."

"Here," I said, and opened both Ziploc bags, pouring bills and change onto the counter.

The man and the travel agent turned to stare at me, while the manager began using the back of his hand to count the dirty money.

I watched, resolving not to leave without guaranteed passage to America.

Finally, I left the office, a round-trip ticket clutched in my fist.

Well over half my money was gone, but I had a ticket to America.

I would work extra hours every day until I left.

I knew I needed all the money I could get my hands on.

"You don't speak the language, how are you going to live?" asked my aunt.

I shook my head. "Paris is not for me, Mama Nicole."

"You can make a living here," she said.

"But it's not the kind of life that I want. I want to go to California. There, I can be free. Tupac is waiting for me."

It was her turn to shake her head, slowly, as if she knew something that I didn't. "Remember," she said, "if you leave, you might not be able to come back. Your passport isn't real."

"I know," I said. "I would rather risk everything than stay here." As if to punctuate my statement, a loud wind blew outside, rattling the windows. "There's no future for me here."

She pressed her hands together and looked down. "You are a man. I'm not going to stop you. Just be careful."

"I will," I said, then stood and wrapped my arms around her.

I realized I wasn't making things easy for anyone, but a fire burned inside me. I couldn't rest until I'd gotten somewhere I could be comfortable, could be equal, could be myself.

I began doing research—watching as many American movies and television shows as I could. I became obsessed with programs like *Baywatch* and *Diff'rent Strokes*. I spent many nights contemplating the marriage status of Pamela Anderson and thinking about a country where two little black boys could be raised in the lap of luxury. America, it appeared, was the great equalizer.

I did my best to mimic the habits I saw on these programs, acclimating myself to the rhythm and sound of the language. My excitement doubled every day, and all I could think about or talk about was my upcoming trip.

I was going to America.

CHAPTER 29

On February 12, 1998, I woke up, said good-bye to Mama Nicole, and took the train from Paris to Lille, the bus from Lille to Berlin, and the train from Berlin to Frankfurt.

Not once during the twenty-four-hour trip did my passport leave my hands. I memorized every crease, every tear, every word. I practiced the signature thousands of times, often until my hand cramped up and would no longer hold the pen.

When I arrived in Frankfurt on the thirteenth, I first went to the airport to scout my battleground. Then, I checked into the nicest hotel I could find. I had to appear well rested, confident, natural. I wouldn't make the same mistake I'd made when applying for political asylum. The price was irrelevant. I deserved it and it was necessary.

If my plan didn't work, the money would be useless anyway.

There's a saying in the Congo: *Before a warrior goes to battle, he needs to have a good sleep.*

I walked into my hotel suite and slowly set my bag down. I slipped my shoes off and dug my toes into the thick carpeting. I walked across the room and felt the fine silk of the drapes. Polished wood and spotless mirrors greeted me everywhere I turned. For tonight, all this was mine.

It was the first time in my life that I would have a king-size bed all to myself.

My shower lasted nearly an hour, and I tested myself to see how hot I could stand the water.

I shaved my face, then shaved my head again.

I curled up into the plush sheets and felt like a human being. I called the front desk and asked them to bring me some food.

White men cooked my dinner and brought it to my door, and I was happy to pay for it. I didn't want to leave my room until I went to the airport the next morning.

I needed to focus, to prepare for my journey. I spent another hour practicing my signature, then turned on the television and fell asleep watching an American movie that I didn't recognize.

I woke the morning of the fourteenth around five o'clock and took a long, hot bath. My flight didn't leave until 1:00 ᴨᴋ., so I had plenty of time to prepare myself.

Today is the day, I thought.

Breakfast was brought to my room by a pale *mundelé*, and I ate every morsel. I chose to wear my African clothes on the trip so that I could highlight my accent instead of attempting to hide it. Yven Mahonza was clearly from Central Africa and wouldn't be ashamed of that fact.

I arrived at the United Airlines ticket counter at about 10:30 ?,ᴋ. and waited in line.

When it was my turn, I held my head high and put a large smile on my face. I handed my ticket and passport to the Indian man sitting behind the counter. He looked at me, then looked down at the passport. And again. His eyes narrowed. "I'll be right back," he said, and left his seat.

A few minutes passed and I struggled to project an image of calm confidence.

I glanced to my right and saw him returning with two huge German police officers.

My feet started to move, but I stopped them. *If I run here, I'm done*, I thought. *This will either work or it won't, but this is my last stand.*

I turned toward them, a wide smile on my face.

When a leopard is angry, he never retreats. He only goes forward.

I knew that in white countries, a person was innocent until proven guilty, so it was their word against mine. I just had to believe that it was me in the picture, that I was Yven Mahonza.

There was no going back.

They approached me and placed handcuffs around my wrists.

I remained calm. "Why are you handcuffing me?"

"Sir, we have to take you in for a few questions."

"Okay," I said. "No problem." I even smiled at the men and shrugged.

They sat me down in a small cubicle just behind the main ticket counters. They left the handcuffs on.

One of the officers removed his hat and set it on the table. He addressed me in French. "Where did you get that passport?"

I feigned ignorance. "I don't know what you mean. It's my passport."

"That is not you in the picture."

Now I let anger creep into my voice, but it was purposeful, controlled. "What a racist thing to say! I'm a French citizen, sir, and would like to speak to my consul. You have no right to stop a French citizen from traveling!"

The other officer picked up the passport and showed it to me. "This man is nearly twice your size! How can you say it's you?"

I shook my head, forcing another smile onto my face. "It's only the weight that's different. Just because I lose weight doesn't mean it's no longer me. I'd like to speak to my consul."

They stepped to the side and began whispering quietly in German.

I took this as a good sign. I'd created doubt in their minds. Now I just had to finish what I'd started.

One sat down opposite me. This time, his demeanor was more relaxed, more polite. I smiled, but didn't let down my guard for a second.

"Can we ask you a few questions?"

"Of course."

"Where were you in March of 1995?"

I knew immediately what the passport said, but let my face go blank for a second. "Let me see . . ." I let my eyes wander up as I pretended to think. "March of 1995, I was on a business trip to Switzerland. It lasted about . . . a week and a half."

The man's eyebrows went up and I knew that I'd answered the question correctly. "What business are you in?"

"I work in the fish business," I said.

The man nodded. "Okay, what about June of 1996?"

"Hmmm, June 1996. Ah yes, that was a pleasure trip. I was visiting my girlfriend in Spain. That was a much shorter trip. Business always takes longer than pleasure." Here, I laughed, forcing my voice to relax into a natural cadence.

"Why are you going to America? For business or pleasure?"

I was glad they'd asked, because it gave me the opportunity to reveal my secret weapon. I reached into my pocket and placed a diamond ring on the table. It was fake, but I was sure they wouldn't be able to tell.

"Pleasure," I said. "It's Valentine's Day, and I'm flying to Sacramento to ask my girlfriend to marry me. So you see, I can't miss my flight."

They asked a few more questions, every one of which I answered correctly without hesitation. The clock was ticking now, as my flight was scheduled to leave in less than an hour. I hoped that the ring had been enough.

The second officer stepped forward. "Okay, Mr. Mahonza, just one more thing before you go. Can you sign this piece of paper for us?"

I didn't let them see the tremble in my hands. I relaxed my fingers and just let the pen flow across the paper as it had thousands of times over the last week. It was hard to keep the smile off my face. It was perfect.

They picked up the paper and compared it to the passport.

"Are you happy now?" I said.

They stood up. "Yes, sir, Mr. Mahonza. Our apologies. You're free to go."

"No problem," I said, standing and smiling at them. "You're right. I have lost a lot of weight."

I picked up my bags, which had been searched and carefully repacked, and approached the counter again. I handed my ticket and passport to the same Indian man as before. This time, he let me pass without a word.

I stopped briefly in an airport shop to purchase a dozen red roses and a small teddy bear, then made my way to the departure gate.

I walked down the long tunnel, waiting to see the tarmac and the stairs, but again somehow found myself on the plane.

The white stewardesses showed me to my seat, and I sat down, satisfied.

I'd beaten the Congolese.

I'd beaten the French.

I'd beaten the Germans.

Now I just had to beat the Americans.

CHAPTER 30

We will be landing in ten minutes," came the booming voice. I woke up with a start, amazed that I'd slept at all.

America.

I leaned over to look out the window and gasped at the sight. The sky was black, but below me were lights as far as the eye could see. Millions upon millions of tiny yellow and white spheres turned the night into day. Truly, the white man was a magician if he could accomplish such a feat.

The view was so incredible that I forgot to be frightened, and by the time I felt my heart pounding, the plane was safely on the ground.

I took a deep breath, steeling myself for what I knew would be my most difficult battle yet. I stretched my face, planning to smile at everyone I saw. Once again, I attempted to decipher the strange form given to me by one of the stewardesses, but gave up and stuck it into my pocket.

I walked out of the airplane tunnel into an incredibly massive airport. The ceiling appeared to go on forever, and huge crowds swarmed around me as I walked to the international customs line. The sweet sounds of English filled my ears, reminding me of the movies I'd watched as a child.

Once more, I took a deep breath. I held my bag, a dozen red roses, and a teddy bear. I was clean, washed, and well dressed. There would never be a better time to face my destiny. I stepped forward and handed my passport to a white woman.

I smiled.

She didn't look up, and said something in English.

I told her, in French, that I didn't understand her question.

She looked up, squinted at me, and asked a different question.

I told her that I didn't speak any English, but again wasn't understood.

She held up the strange form that the stewardess had given me, and I nodded, raising my identical blank one. She stared at me, picked up my passport, then grabbed the receiver beside her. I forced the enormous smile to stay on my face.

Out of the corner of my eye, I saw two large black men in police uniforms striding toward me. They were each nearly twice my size.

This is it, I thought. *I'm going back to the Congo. I can fool the Europeans, but I'll never fool the Americans.*

Without a word, I was guided out of line and into an interrogation room.

I noticed that, unlike Germany, here I was not put into handcuffs. This energized me. In America, I truly was innocent until proven guilty. I had to be confident, charismatic, friendly.

We were joined in the tiny room by a French translator and an interrogator who sat behind a typewriter. Both were women. The officers stood in the back, watching silently.

The interrogator turned to the translator and said something.

"What are you here for?"

I smiled at both of them, then leaned back in my chair. "I'm flying in on Valentine's Day to propose to my girlfriend. I'm French. We do things like this. Do Americans not do these things?"

"What do you do?"

"I'm a businessman. I'm in the fish business."

They nodded. The interrogator looked at me and asked another question. I waited for the translation to come through.

"How long will you be here?"

"Two weeks," I said. "Unless the proposal doesn't go well." I forced a laugh, watching their faces closely.

"Do you have a round-trip ticket?"

"Of course," I said, producing my return ticket and thanking the gods that I'd planned this far ahead.

They nodded. Good. "How much money did you bring?"

I pursed my lips, as if counting. "Probably about fifteen hundred dollars. I'm planning not to use my bank cards while I'm here."

"Can you count it for us?"

"Of course," I said, reaching into my plastic bag and pulling out the stack of loose bills. Truthfully, there was a little less than one thousand dollars there, but I began counting anyway. "Twenty, forty, sixty . . ." After a couple hundred dollars, they stopped me.

"Okay, that's fine." The translator and interrogator conversed in English for a moment, then asked me a few more questions about my travel plans and about my girlfriend who lived in Sacramento. They kept staring at the photo of Yven Mahonza. I needed to distract them from that passport.

Inspired, I reached into the bouquet of flowers and pulled out two red roses, handing one to each of the women at the table. "Tell the woman recording that I said she's beautiful. You are as well."

I couldn't understand the interrogator's reaction, but I knew exactly what it meant. She blushed a little, put the flower on the table, and went back to her typewriter. She said something to the translator, who smiled.

"What about your girlfriend?"

"She has a ring and a teddy bear. She'll be fine." Again, I smiled, trying to give the impression that this interview was merely a formality. This was extremely difficult, because I knew that my entire life depended on it.

I felt the energy in the room shift.

I smiled even larger, forcing my body to relax.

They asked a few more questions, but the grins never really left their faces.

"Is there anything else?" I asked, trying to sound as casual as possible.

"Happy Valentine's Day," said the interrogator, and stamped my passport.

They opened the door and sent me off to collect my baggage.

I forced myself to walk away from them slowly, waving casually with my atrophied bouquet of roses.

When I got to the baggage carousel, my bag was the only one rotating lazily around the huge silver island. I scanned the room for police or security, amazed that no one had stolen something so obviously unguarded.

America is a wonderful place, I thought with a smile, grabbing my bag and heading to the ticket counter so I could send it through customs and have it rechecked to Sacramento.

It was then that I turned the corner and encountered the biggest obstacle of my journey.

An enormous moving staircase.

My jaw dropped. Somehow, the white man had constructed stairs that moved on their own, ferrying standing bodies up and down the sharp incline. It was incredible.

I looked around for another way up the wall, but saw nothing.

I would have to face the beast head-on.

My skin prickled with nervousness.

A good hunter always watches, feels, smells, and only then attacks.

I stepped to the side and stared at the monstrosity, sweat beginning to bead on my face like tears. One by one, men and women walked up, put a foot on the stairs and grabbed the railing. Once they'd done that, they pulled the other foot forward. Person after person performed this simple maneuver, and I watched until I was sure I had it figured out.

I stood in place, mimicking their motions, not caring who saw me.

Three deep breaths.

I took two confident steps toward the metal teeth of the monster, arriving at the same moment as an older woman. I let her go ahead of me, losing my nerve and momentum in the process.

Thrown off, I quickly put my left foot and hand on the machine, gasping as I felt them being pulled up.

Turning to bring my right foot forward, I realized that I'd left my bag on the floor.

I reached out as far as I could, refusing to let go of the moving rail, and grabbed the bag with the tips of my fingers. I slid my right foot forward onto a step that was rising out of the floor like the head of a snake.

My groin felt as if it would snap at any moment.

I bit my bottom lip and rode up the enormous staircase in nearly a full split.

Though both my body and my ego were taking a severe beating, I sucked in a deep breath, relieved that I'd accomplished this gigantic task.

It was then that I realized I not only had to get *on* the contraption, but had to find a way to get *off* it as well.

Frantically, I watched as people lifted a foot, released their hand, and stepped.

Lifted a foot, released their hand, and stepped.

I approached the top, watching the stairs get smashed flat, one by one. I had a brief daydream of Tom and Jerry, imagining what would happen if my African cloak were caught between two stairs as they merged. The device would pull me in, grinding me through the metal teeth, flattening me like a sheet of paper.

I pictured myself coming out the other end, thin as a palm leaf, a frozen expression of surprise permanently etched onto my face.

Before I knew it, the moment of truth was upon me.

With a grunt, I hoisted my bag up, pushed off with my right leg, and leaped as far as I could. Fortunately, I landed on solid ground.

Everyone was staring at me, but I didn't care. I'd gotten past the French, the Germans, the Americans, and now, the moving staircase. There was nothing I couldn't conquer.

I slowed down, a rush of exhilaration passing through my body. I inhaled through my nose, bringing in the sweet smells of freedom.

America.

Women passed by in giggling clumps, and I did my best not to stare at their tight shirts and tight jeans. I was seeing bodies that I'd never imagined could exist in these numbers. It was an entire nation of Pamela Andersons.

I smiled.

My flight didn't leave for over an hour, so I walked slowly, amazed by the shops and signs and hordes of people.

I could do whatever I wanted, go wherever I chose. Nothing would stop me, nobody would care. Here, a black man had the same rights as everybody else.

Welcome everybody to the wild, wild West.

I came to a wall with a small gap in the middle, then froze as the two partitions slid apart. It was a door. And it had opened on its own.

Confused, I took two steps backward.

It hissed to a close.

Again, I stepped forward, more slowly this time.

And again, it slid open.

This, I thought, looking around, *is amazing. Surely there's a white man watching, waiting for me to get close to the door, then opening it for me.*

I stepped backward, then forward.

And again.

The mundelé *are crazy.*

This was incredible.

This was power.

Here, a black man was somebody.

Here, the *white man* opened the door for *me*!

I stood in the middle of the hallway, smiling broadly and reveling in my accomplishment.

That was the moment I finally realized I'd made it.

I felt the stress and sadness of Mr. DeVos and the travel agency and the boxes of fish and the immigration officers and the militias and the wars and the pain and the fear and the sorrow all dissipate into the popcorn-scented air.

I was free.

I'd fought my way to America, and had arrived unscathed.

It felt better than I could have ever imagined.

CHAPTER 31

My plane landed at the Sacramento International Airport at 10:00 N,K. on February 14, 1998.

I got into a cab, pulled out my French-English dictionary, and directed the driver to a "hotel—cheap cheap cheap."

He nodded and merged into traffic.

I sat back and watched the streetlights fade into hazy globes in the night sky.

America.

It was beautiful.

The longer we drove, the darker the streets grew. I saw men sleeping beside garbage cans. I saw a woman standing on the corner, looking lost and alone.

The buildings were crumbling and I counted more broken windows than whole ones.

None of this bothered me.

I checked into the hotel using my French-English dictionary and paid for thirty days up front at twenty dollars a night. This left me only a little over two hundred dollars, but I'd bought myself an entire month to make more.

The room was small, the sheets looked used, and I saw a rat or two, but it was nothing to me. *American rats*, I thought, *are better than rats in the Congo.*

I lay down and stared around the room. Never before had I seen a door that required two locks, or as many spiderwebs on a ceiling.

I smiled and finally let myself relax. Sleep came easily that night, because it was the sleep of a conquering warrior.

I had accomplished my mission.

Now the fun would begin.

. . .

The next morning, I got up early to take advantage of something called a "continental breakfast." It wasn't much, just some fruit and assorted cereals, but I packed in as much as I could. Between the roof over my head and this breakfast every morning, I knew that I could survive for at least thirty days.

I crammed my pockets full of food and gathered my things. I didn't feel comfortable leaving any belongings in the room, and had decided to take them with me to the American version of a shopping center, something called a "mall." Using my dictionary to communicate in pidgin English, I managed to get directions to the nearest mall from the new hotel desk clerk.

There's a saying in the Congo: *When you go to a village, if everyone is dancing on one leg, then you dance on one leg.*

I needed to learn how the blacks in America dressed, how they acted, what they sounded like. It was time for me to become an American, and I'd decided that the mall might be the place to accomplish this.

I slipped the remaining money into my pocket and took the bus down to the Florine Mall, which, as it turned out, wasn't far from my hotel.

After getting over the shock of walking into roaring waves of air-conditioning, I found a bench in the middle of a high-traffic area and sat. From that vantage point, I absorbed the attitudes and actions of American blacks. They wore baggy jeans that they pulled up every five to seven seconds. They wore baseball caps on their heads, but sideways. Tags covered their clothes, as if the items had just been purchased. Their shoes were usually labeled "Timberland," and were rarely laced up. It struck me that it would be remarkably easy to catch a black man if he were running from you. If the shoes didn't get him, the pants certainly would. In America, I learned, the clothes don't fit the man, the man has to fit the clothes.

People did not greet each other with handshakes. Instead, they slapped their hands together, pounded their chests, and gave some sort of signal with two fingers. When they walked, it often looked as if they were injured, or had some sort of deformity. I stared at black man after black man as they limped through the mall, underwear exposed, hat tilted to the side. Their language was melodious, as if they were always rapping. Words flowed from their tongues in staccato patterns that reminded me of Tupac. Everything they said was punctuated by large hand movements, as if that were part of the communication.

Some of them had hair that extended nearly a foot from their heads. Others looked as if they'd forgotten to remove their combs.

I saw enormous gold chains, gigantic rings, diamond earrings, bracelets.

I took a deep breath.

I could do this.

I could learn to fit in anywhere.

I walked into a store and purchased a pair of jean shorts that I had to pull up every few seconds. I also bought a baseball cap that sat awkwardly on my bald head.

I picked up my bag and walked down to the bus station, this time to watch how blacks moved on the streets. In the Congo, there was a difference between how people acted in restricted private places and how they acted downtown in the open air. I sat and stared, amazed by the cars that bounced by themselves, the silver rims bigger than the tires they were designed to protect, the men who drove from a nearly horizontal position. Music blasted from practically every car that crept by, the thumping bass notes obscuring the harsh roar of the engines.

A few smaller cars drove by with neon lights on their undercarriages, illuminating the ground as if they were floating on carpets of light.

I shook my head and laughed. It was too much for one day.

I felt drunk on the sights and the sounds and the energy.

This was where Tupac was. Where the black man had rights.

I stood up, ready to return to the hotel, excited to process what I'd learned. It was almost too much to hold in my brain at one time.

My shorts began to drop, and I grabbed them, wondering what I would do if I had to use both hands to hold something. Would I have to let my shorts fall to the ground? There was a great deal that needed to be figured out before I'd be accepted as a local, but I was optimistic.

I took a step toward the bus, but was intercepted by a large black man. His eyes were more red than white, and his voice sounded as if he was chewing gravel. He smelled of shit and piss, and only a few rotten teeth hung in his mouth.

"Do you smoke?" he said, but I didn't understand.

I turned and reached for my French-English dictionary. As I twisted back around, I felt the familiar sensation of cold metal against my cheek.

"Nigger, give me your wallet."

Again, I didn't understand the words, but when someone points a gun at you, it always means the same thing—they want what you have.

I raised both hands to indicate that I would cooperate. I could have fought him, but any time there's combat, both men lose. I couldn't afford to risk my life on my first day in America. I'd come too far and risked too much.

Slowly, I handed over my money and my bag. He turned and ran, leaving me with only my dictionary, some loose change, my baggy jeans, and my new hat.

An old woman who'd witnessed the robbery rushed over, blabbering in English. She indicated that I should stay where I was, so I did. A few minutes later, she returned, followed by two policemen.

My heart began to pound.

She pointed at me, then pointed in the direction the other man had gone. A steady stream of words poured from her mouth. The policemen nodded and asked me a question, but I couldn't understand.

Finally, one looked at me and said, "Welcome to America."

This, I understood.

Welcome everybody to the wild, wild West.

I nodded at them and stepped onto the bus, emptying the last of my change into the meter.

Even paradise appeared to be afflicted by its inhabitants.

But, as my father used to say, "If you love dogs, you love fleas."

I was determined not to get depressed or overwhelmed.

It's your bad days that make your better days, and I was in America with my life intact. Things could have been worse.

The bus rumbled and more of my father's words flashed through my brain. "When there is a problem, the solution is always next to you."

I stared out the window at the brick buildings and mostly black inhabitants of Sacramento.

Five minutes into the ride, we passed by something called the Thompson Taekwondo Studio. Inside, I saw people training and fighting.

Martial arts. This was something that I knew. I'd been training in Mpongo since I was seven years old, and my skills had grown considerably.

This was an American job that I could do.

I resolved to return the following day and show them what I had to offer.

I leaned back in my seat and decided to take even more food from the following day's continental breakfast.

· · ·

The studio was packed.

People in uniforms were crammed onto the practice mat, and the smell of sweat brought me back to my own training days.

Immediately to the left of the door was a reception desk.

"Can I help you?" asked the receptionist, brushing her blond hair to the side.

I opened my dictionary and flipped to the word "job," then pointed to it, smiling widely.

She looked confused, so I found the word "fight," then pointed at myself.

"You want a job?"

I pointed again at the word "job," careful to keep smiling. The way I saw it, this was one of the few opportunities I would have at an actual paying job without drastically improving my English.

"You have training?"

I didn't understand, so I let her take the dictionary and find the words that she wanted.

I nodded, then found the words for "black" and "belt," again pointing at myself.

"Ahh," she said, finally understanding. She looked at me as if I were crazy. Using the dictionary, she asked if I had a certificate.

I told her that Tchicaya's house had burned down, so he had no certificate.

"Who's Tchicaya?" she asked.

"Good warrior," I replied, pointing at myself. I danced a few steps and made a couple of monkey noises. I flipped through the dictionary. "Tchicaya clean, fight, teach—"

"You fight?" she said.

"Strong," I said. "Fight."

With a half smile on her face, she walked into the back room. She returned a few minutes later with a uniform and a white belt. She handed them to me. I'd been a black belt for many years, but didn't argue with her. She was going to give me the opportunity to fight for a job.

I took off my baseball cap and baggy jeans, then slipped into the uniform. It hung loose on my frame, and I cinched the belt as tightly as I could. I took a deep breath. I knew that if I wanted something, I would have to prove that I deserved it.

I would attack like a leopard and dance like a monkey.

She led me out to the mat and placed me in the center. A circle gathered around me and I watched as she talked with a few of the men. One stepped forward—a black belt.

He assumed a fighting stance, so I did the same.

If this is my job interview, I thought, *you'll have to kill me, cook me, and eat me, because I'll eat you raw. I'll eat you alive.*

Tupac rang in my ears. *It's me against the world.*

I sized up my opponent, hoping to gain any information I could. A warrior can always recognize a good hunter by the way he stands, walks, and talks. I stared at the man's feet, noticing that they were too clean, too perfect to belong to a hunter. My opponent was soft.

The match began, and I immediately received a strong kick to the chest. I didn't lose my footing, but stumbled backward a few steps, the wind almost knocked from my body.

I settled into my fighting stance again. This time, I knew how much power he had. I could take three, four, even five of his kicks. But he didn't know how many blows he could stand from me.

The man began jumping, executing complex flying kicks, driving me backward. I went into monkey mode, crouching low and scampering across the mat, barking at him with high-pitched squeals.

I opened my eyes wide and bared my teeth. I shook my butt in the air, watching as students from around the studio stopped what they were doing and surrounded the makeshift ring.

Now I would have to prove myself.

I began to put on a show, aware that I was a strange African man crawling across their studio, fighting the best student in their school. I saw people shaking their heads, confused. Others laughed or pointed.

My opponent leaped into the air again, but this time, I didn't retreat. I leaped forward, planting a kick in his midsection the moment he landed. He dropped to the floor.

I leaped on him, lifted him into the air, and slammed him to the mat.

The fight was over.

I danced around on all fours, shouting my victory to the heavens.

A couple of students clapped their hands.

I stood, searching for the blond receptionist. I'd beaten the man she'd chosen for me and was ready to claim my job.

Instead, I discovered a stocky man leaning against the door and staring at me with a strange, concentrated gaze. He waved me over.

"I'm Master Thompson," he said, and I understood.

He looked me up and down. "How much do you weigh?"

I grabbed my dictionary and handed it to him. He smiled and flipped through, searching for the right words. He pointed to "weight," but I knew the answer only in kilograms and that seemed to confuse him.

I flipped through the pages and pointed to the word "job," then at myself. I smiled as wide as I could, and took a step backward.

He asked me if I had my papers.

"No," I said.

He nodded, then sized me up again. "I need a janitor—$3.75 an hour," he said, writing the figure on a piece of paper. "You can work every day."

When I figured out what this meant, I was ecstatic. My third day in America and I already had a job—and at almost four dollars an hour! It was almost too good to be true.

I hooted like a monkey, smiling again as he laughed.

. . .

For the next twenty-seven days, I spent all my time at the studio. I cleaned the floors, wiped the mats, and washed the uniforms. I worked hard for the money that Master Thompson was paying, and I was happy to do it.

My English slowly improved, and I began to help out with some of the classes as an assistant instructor. I became known for my ability to make the students laugh and to make them sweat.

Master Thompson was aware of my living situation and told me that I was welcome to sleep in the supply closet of the studio after the rent at the hotel had run out.

He laid down a long piece of cardboard for me as a bed, and I nodded happily. It was warm in Sacramento, and I no longer had to worry about freezing to death at night.

A few months passed and I began teaching classes in my own style of Mpongo, training the young *mundelé* as I had trained Gervais so many years before. Rarely during this time did I have to buy food for myself. Parents and students would always bring in cakes, cookies, meats, and bread for me to eat. Clearly, they knew that I was living in poverty in the back of the gym, but they didn't make me feel guilty for my situation. Instead, they were generous and kind to me, thankful for the attention that I showed their sons and daughters.

Each time a student entered the gym, I would say "five," and they would have to immediately drop and give me five push-ups. Quinze would have been proud. Some of the parents told me that before I started teaching, their children would have plenty of energy after class to run around and play. With me as the instructor, every child went home and went straight to bed.

After six months, Master Thompson promoted me to full manager of the studio.

I was in love with America.

Truly, this was a country that would allow a man to rise to his potential.

I learned how to run the studio, how the accounting worked, how the leases in America were negotiated, how a small business functioned in this new country. It was not unlike my father's hotel along the banks of the Djoué.

I began daydreaming about opening my own business.

The opportunities appeared limitless.

Still, there was no way I could have predicted the next offer I would receive.

It was my childhood dream, fulfilled.

PART 9
FOREIGN SOLDIER

If you can't find something to live for, you best find something to die for.

— *TUPAC SHAKUR*

Brazzaville, Congo
August 26, 2004

Thursday

The phone springs to life, vibrating noisily. I clamp down on it, gritting my teeth as the steady buzzing echoes against the stone walls. The soldiers have just delivered the first meal of the day and are hovering outside the cell door.

I close my eyes and cough loudly, doing my best to drown out the awful sound that I'm suddenly sure is audible for miles.

The phone goes silent, its screen fading once again to black.

I shake my head and listen carefully to the voices of the soldiers for any indication that they've heard something.

The prisoners pace nervously around me.

And the phone erupts again into a blast of light and sound.

I slump against the back wall, holding the device between my hands and thighs, struggling to make the buzzing stop. I can't answer while the guards are nearby.

"Noise!" I whisper to my men, and they begin shuffling and stomping their feet. A few of them talk loudly, while others break down into strange coughing fits.

The grate squeals backward just as the phone falls silent and goes dark. A soldier leans his head against the bars of the cell, the tip of an AK-47 just below his chin.

"What's going on in here?" he shouts.

"Nothing," says a large, dark inmate named Dion. "There was an argument, but it's been settled."

The soldier stares suspiciously at the group, then slides the grate closed.

I release another batch of air.

This cell phone will kill me before it has a chance to save my life,
I think.

Time passes, and the pinpoint of light above our heads fades to
a dull glow. The voices of the soldiers are long gone, and I will the
phone to ring again.

I stare at the tiny object, sending all my energy into it as if the
sheer force of my will can somehow alter the state of the universe.
There is only one bar remaining on the battery life, and I wonder
what I'll do if it falls dead.

It shudders in my hands, and I blink, disbelieving.

The light from the phone floods the darkness, and I open it,
pressing it against my ear.

"Hello?"

It's my roommate, Jessica. "Tchicaya, I'm here, the sheriffs are
here, talking with me. What do you need us to do?"

I thought the police would have ideas, and I struggle to for-
mulate a plan. I assume that Tim Morano is trying to release me
through bureaucratic means, so I latch on to the press as a possible
option. "I don't know, let the media know, you know what I'm saying? It's all about the media now. Because I'm an American citizen."

I hear a man's voice in the background. "Ask him what prison
he's in."

"What prison are you in?"

"Brazzaville."

The man's voice again. "Why is he being held?"

"And you're being held because why?"

"I'm being held in Brazzaville, in the gendarmerie."

The man's voice was louder now. "Because you're an American?"

The connection fuzzes out.

"Hello?" I say, terrified that the call has dropped, that I've lost
my chance.

"Hello?" says the man. "This is the Sheriff's Department. Why are you being held?"

"Sir, I'm being held in Brazzaville. I got shot in my leg. Right now, my health is not good, and I've been here for five days. So I don't know, right now, what to do. The consul was here, there's nothing that he can do, so I just don't know."

Jessica must have handed the phone off to the sheriff, because his is the only voice I hear anymore. "Okay, but you're being held for what reason? Just because you're an American?"

"Because I'm an American, because I'm a U.S. Marine. That's it, sir, that's it. I've done nothing wrong."

"Okay, and they shot you?"

"I got shot in my leg, yes. Because when they arrested me, I tried to escape and I got shot in my leg. Right now, I am having malaria and am being held in the commission of . . . I have no clue. It's just . . . I'm being tortured, all that crap. It's terrible right now."

"If we contact your Marine unit, would your Marine unit be able to do anything for you?"

The connection buzzes, and I can't hear what he says. "Say again, sir?"

"Would your Marine unit be able to do anything for you?"

"I don't know," I say, talking faster now, struggling to say as much as possible as quickly as possible. I don't know how much time I have. "Something has to be done in the media, call CNN or do anything, somebody has to do something, I have no clue. I'm an American citizen, I'm overseas. I used to be a Congolese citizen, I came down here to see my family, and then . . . that's it. You know, I got arrested for being an American citizen and being a U.S. Marine. Right now, I don't know what to do."

"Okay, what we will do is we will contact the State Department and get them involved."

The phone fuzzes out and I try not to scream with tension and frustration. "Say again, sir?"

"We're gonna contact the State Department."

That's a good start, I think, struggling to be polite with this man. If Tim Morano falls through, this phone call is likely my only chance at rescue. "Okay. If you can contact the State Department or the Pentagon, that would be wonderful."

"Okay, do you have a phone number for your unit in Encino so we could contact them as well?"

I bite my lip to contain my growing anger. "Sir, there's no way—I don't have—the only phone I have right now is my . . . my friend's phone. The only phone I can get to—they took everything from me."

"Okay."

"Right now, I'm using someone's phone in jail, right now. They don't know that we are hiding a phone in jail."

"Okay, okay, well, you need to preserve your phone. So what we'll do is we'll contact the State Department and we can give them this phone number in case they need to talk to you. But we've got the name of the prison that you're in, and we'll try to get you some help."

I try to convey my desperation one more time, in case he doesn't understand the enormity of my situation. "I don't know what to do. Right now, I'm just here, I'm just waiting."

"Okay, well, hang in there, we'll try to get you some help."

"Okay, thank you, sir, I appreciate it."

"All right." I hear him handing the phone to Jessica. "You want to talk to him?"

Her voice comes on, heavy with concern. "Call when you can."

I want to speak with her, to let her know that I can't talk, that time is running short, but I hear footsteps coming down the long hall toward the cell and I hang up the phone, shoving it into the waistband of my shorts.

The grate slides open and my stomach sinks. I know that I've been found out, that I'll be beaten and killed.

Colonel Niama sticks his head in and stares at me. My blood runs cold.

He lifts a hand into the cell, but then changes direction and scratches his head.

He nods at me slowly, murmurs something under his breath, then turns to leave.

The grate squeals to a close.

Shivers shoot up my spine. I can't tell if he suspected anything or not, and I begin to sweat, there against the cold stone of the cell.

"Shit," I say, and the man beside me laughs.

"That was a close one."

"Yes," I say, aware of how weak my body has grown. "It was."

The hour grows late, and I feel my nerves beginning to fray. I don't sleep. I rarely eat. Every time the grate squeals, I worry that my time has come, that they're coming to get me, to torture me for my supposed desertion from the Congo.

I know the mind of the general, and am sure that he'll kill me rather than release me, if he can find a way to do it without incurring the wrath of the Americans. I'm wary of "accidents," so I make sure to stay in the cell at all times.

Here, at least, my men can protect me.

It's time to make a move, I think. *Tim Morano missed his chance.*

Colonel Niama won't bide his time much longer.

I've noticed that the soldiers follow a set rotation, and I've carefully picked out their weakest link—my target—a young gendarmerie recruit named Issou. For days, I've smiled at him, doing my best to reassure him that I'm not a threat. I'm happy to see how much his body language has changed.

I can't wait any longer. I need to start making my move.

"Hey," I say to Issou as he delivers our dinner.

He smiles nervously at me, but doesn't say anything. This is the first time I've tried to engage him in conversation, and I don't expect him to reply.

"It's okay," I say. "You don't have to talk. I know you have orders. I was gendarme as well. First class back. Did they make you sit in the pig shit, too?"

The soldier's eyes light up, despite his best efforts to suppress the reaction.

I smile widely. "I think my arms are still sore from all the push-ups I did that year. You're still a recruit, right?"

"Yes," he says quietly.

I shake my head. "They called me *morpion*."

He laughs, then covers his mouth with one hand. The food is sitting on the floor, but he isn't moving toward the door, so I keep talking. "I graduated, then escaped to America. I'm a Marine now. And the physical training in the Congo is much harder," I say. "Don't let anybody tell you anything different. The Congo has the strongest soldiers in the world."

Issou edges a little closer to me, clearly anxious to get back outside the cell, but overwhelmed by curiosity. "What's America like?"

I smile, relaxed and calm. Unthreatening. "Amazing," I say. "Plenty of black people own cars and houses and businesses. It doesn't matter what you look like. You just have to work hard. And there are lots of beautiful women there. Everyone looks just like Pamela Anderson. Big boobs. Blond."

"Really?"

"Yes. Have you ever thought about going there?"

He steps even closer to me. "All the time."

I nod and act as if I'm thinking hard about something. "When I get out of here, maybe I can take you over. I know a lot of people."

"You're an American now?"

"I am."

He shakes his head. "Why did the general have you arrested? I've been talking to the others, but no one seems to know."

This is a good sign. "It's a mistake. My father was one of his rivals in the old Sassou-Nguesso military. I came back to see my mother, and the general suspected me of spying."

"But your father didn't send you?"

"I'm an American now. I'm here for my mother. That's it." I point to the door and smile. "You should get back. I don't want to get you in trouble. We'll talk more later."

He nods, then murmurs, "Thank you," as he slides the grate closed behind him. I feel the stares of the other men, but don't acknowledge them. If Tim Morano fails, and the Fillmore Sheriff's Department falls through, I may be forced to attack an innocent man.

Twenty-four more hours, I think.

I'll give them one more day.

Sacramento, California
Camp Pendleton, California
Camp Lejeune, North Carolina
Mediterranean Coast

1998–2001

CHAPTER 32

Brian, a regular student of mine, disappeared from classes one day. When he returned three months later, my jaw dropped. He was lean, muscular, confident, and dressed neatly in a Marine Corps uniform.

I watched him walk around the gym, nodding deferentially and saying "Yes, sir" and "No, sir," to the instructors and parents. He'd never been a stickler for politeness when I'd known him, nor had he been in particularly good shape. I was impressed by the dramatic changes.

He smiled at me. "Tchicaya! How are you?"

"Good," I said, still struggling with my English. "Where did you go?"

"Boot camp. I'm a Marine now." I couldn't help staring at his uniform, admiration plastered on my face. A strange look came into his eyes. "Have you ever thought about joining the military?"

I shook my head. "Congolese military. Many years."

"This is different. I'm talking about the Marines."

"I always want to be a Marine. I watch *Full Metal Jacket*."

He grinned. "Well, why don't you?"

"I don't know how. I'm not allowed."

He thought for a second. "I'm going to bring a recruiter over. Is that okay with you?"

I didn't know what "recruiter" meant, but nodded anyway.

"Good," he said. "You can talk to him about the Marines."

"My English is not good, I don't know—"

"Don't worry about it. He's a great guy. I want him to meet you. I think you'd be great."

I did my best to keep expectations low. There was very little chance I could ever be accepted into an American fighting force, and I was gradually learning to be happy with the job I had. Still, I felt that familiar itch to get out, to do more, to see more.

A few days later, I was teaching one of my regular classes, when I became aware of two men in Marine Corps uniforms watching me from just inside the studio. One of them was Brian. The other was a short, muscular man with choppy blond hair. His uniform looked as if it had been sewn onto his body.

I pushed the students even harder, shouting loudly, letting my voice echo off the walls of the gym. Out of the corner of my eye, I saw the new man nodding.

This, I thought, was good.

After class, I wiped my face with a towel and walked over to them. The new man took a step forward, hand extended, and Brian said, "Tchicaya, I want you to meet Staff Sergeant Kowalski."

The man smiled and grabbed my hand in a viselike grip. I smiled back. This *mundelé* was tough.

"Nice to meet you, Tchicaya. Heard a lot about you. Hear you might be interested in joining the Marines."

"Yes, but my English is not good—"

"Not a problem," he said, releasing my hand. "You have your GED?" I turned to Brian, confused. "Your high school diploma?"

"No," I said.

Kowalski shook his head. "I'm sure it'll be fine. We can work something out. You think you'd be willing to come down and take a little test for us?"

"Okay."

"Just to see how good a fit the Marines would be for you. No stress."

"Okay."

He smiled largely, and I noticed how perfect his teeth were. "Great. You have a car?"

"No."

"No problem. I'll come and pick you up myself. Where do you live?"

I thought frantically. He couldn't know that I slept in the studio, or he might not want me in the Marines. "You pick me up here," I said. "I come to work early."

"That's what I like to hear. I'll be here tomorrow at ten. Sound good?"

I nodded, shocked that a white man was going to pick me up to apply for a job.

After clearing my absence with Master Thompson, I retired to my room and tried to get some sleep. For hours, my brain scrolled through the subjects I thought they might test me on. Math and physics and chemistry and mechanics and English and martial arts ability . . . I eventually fell into a light slumber and dreamed of the first gorilla I'd killed and the proud look on my father's face.

"Put your seat belt on," he said, and I attempted to figure out the strange strap.

The car was a sleek, government-issue gray sedan. It smelled of trees and fruit, and I listened as Staff Sergeant Kowalski talked to me about the world and about America and about the Marines.

When we arrived at the recruiting headquarters, I noticed separate offices for the Army, the Air Force, the Navy, and the Marines. Kowalski followed my confused stare and shook his head. "Don't worry about these other groups," he said. He pointed to the Navy office. "Those guys are the squids. They're our bitches. Their job is to cook for us, clean for us, take us around the world. They're our ladies on the ship."

I nodded. I didn't want to be a lady on a ship. It was strange that there were so many different armed militias in the same office. I wondered if they ever fought each other.

"Over there," he said, pointing to the Air Force office, "is a bunch of civilians wearing military clothes. Bright blue coats, no training—they're weak." He pointed to the Army office. "Those are a bunch of knuckleheads who want to be like us, but can't. They're not strong enough." He paused as we crossed the threshold into the Marine office. "The Marines are a combination of the other three branches of the military—land, sea, and air. We're the strongest, the smartest, and the bravest. The first to fight. The kings of the war."

"Like *Star Wars*?" I said, giving up on deciphering the word "knuckleheads."

"Yes," he said. "Like *Star Wars*. The best of the best."

I stared around the office at four men, all in perfect, neatly pressed uniforms. Each of the men was in excellent shape and appeared poised, confident. They wore their uniforms, the uniforms didn't wear them.

I liked this.

They all stood up to shake my hand, smiling largely as Kowalski introduced me. I watched the camaraderie between the men, the easy banter, the mutual respect, the *pride*. It was the closest I'd felt to my gendarmerie brothers since I'd left the Congo.

They put me into a back room with a piece of paper and a pencil.

It was a three-page exam and I shook my head. This was the test to join the military? I thought back to the intensive examinations I'd had to undergo to join the gendarmerie. America was a strange place.

I skimmed the test, answering the math, chemistry, and physics questions with relative ease. Those subjects didn't change much from country to country, as long as the wording was minimal. The English questions, I either guessed at or left blank, as I could barely read them.

The most amazing part of the exam was that they gave me answers to choose from, something they called "multiple choice." It seemed impossible to fail a test where the correct answer was given to you, right below the question. In the Congo, this was unheard of, but I certainly wasn't going to complain.

They graded the test while I waited, then pulled me into the office again. "You got a 78," said Kowalski, giving me a thumbs-up. "Looks like you're ready for the military."

"Shit," I said, smiling.

"Sit down," he said, and I did. "What's your status?"

"What do you mean?"

"Are you a citizen?"

"No," I said. "I'm a refugee."

"How long have you been here?"

"Almost a year."

He nodded, and I understood why. After a year, refugees were eligible to apply for a green card. "We need to spruce up your paperwork. But don't worry—we'll help process your citizenship application."

I could hardly contain my laughter. The white men were going to help make me an American! I'd spent many nights wondering how I would ever apply for a green card with no money, no government contacts, and only a rudimentary grasp of the language. Now these Marines were going to take care of it for me.

My brain called up images of Tom Thibaut, and I wondered why all these white people wanted to help me.

I truly was blessed by the gods.

The next three months were spent studying for a test called the ASVAB (Armed Services Vocational Aptitude Battery), and waiting for news of my green card application. As it turned out, the tiny three-page test was just a precursor to the major entrance exam for the United States Marine Corps.

I began to carry my ASVAB study manual, or "Bible" as Staff Sergeant Kowalski called it, everywhere I went. The process reminded me of memorizing Yven Mahonza's passport in Europe, and I worked as hard as I possibly could to absorb the information. I knew I wouldn't be given many opportunities in America, and I wanted to ensure that I made the most of each and every one of them.

Every day after class, I would retire to my back room where I'd write out every question and every answer on blank sheets of paper. When I got through the book, I would start over at the beginning and do it again. I didn't understand what many of the words meant, but I learned to recognize them, and learned what answers they usually indicated.

Wherever I went, I began telling people that I was going to be a Marine. It excited me to see their eyes light up, their posture straighten. As Tchicaya, I was nothing in America, but as a Marine, I garnered instant respect from those around me. I checked the mail every day, waiting for the letter stating that my green card application was being processed. According to Kowalski, once I had that letter in my hand, the Marines could step in and guide me the rest of the way.

Kowalski and other Marines began to visit me at the studio and take me out to dinner. At least twice a week, I'd be visited by a

Marine who appeared genuinely curious about me and my life. It was a whole new group of friends and, for the first time since I'd left the Congo, I felt as if I was developing a true family.

I opened the letter with shaking hands, skimming it as quickly as I could. "We have received your application for residency . . ." This was it! I immediately called Staff Sergeant Kowalski and told him the good news.

"All right! I'll get down there as soon as I can. That might just be your passport to boot camp."

He picked me up the following day in the gray sedan and drove me over to the immigration office in San Francisco. I'd heard about the immigration process, and knew that people often stood in line overnight to be seen. The line extended past two city blocks, and I noticed a few tents erected right on the sidewalk.

It looked like a refugee camp.

Kowalski parked the car, got out, and slipped his cover on. A few women walked by, staring at him. He turned to me and smiled. "Women love Marines, Tchicaya. You think you're ready for all the women you're gonna get?"

"Shit," I said, and he laughed.

I was worried about the long lines, because it had taken over an hour and a half to drive from Sacramento and I had to be back to teach class that night. I followed Kowalski as he walked toward the end of the line . . . then past it. "Follow me," he said, and we bypassed everyone who'd been waiting in line for hours, even days.

This made me nervous, and I scanned the line, searching for angry faces or disgruntled applicants, but found only slight reactions.

When we came to the main doors of the building, two men opened them for us and a number of immigrants moved out of our way.

"This," said Kowalski, "is the power of the uniform."

I was impressed.

We walked in and he took me directly to the head of the immigration office. We sat down and Kowalski pulled out my letter. "Is he eligible?"

The director of immigration pulled my file up, scanned it, then nodded. "I don't see any major problems."

"Great," said Kowalski. "All we needed to hear. Would you mind?"

"Not at all," said the immigration director, and stamped the letter with a strange red symbol. I stayed quiet, observing the interaction.

Five minutes later, we were back outside. "The actual process can take up to two years," said Kowalski, "but we don't want to wait that long. If he says you'll get approved eventually, that's enough for us." We got into the car. "You ready to apply for boot camp?"

"Yes, sir."

"How long do you need to prepare for the ASVAB?"

"I'm ready," I said.

He frowned. "We really have to work on your English."

"I'm trying."

"I know. How's next week sound?"

"Fine," I said. "It sounds fine."

With the threat of an actual test hanging over me, I realized there were many things in the study manual I didn't have the slightest clue about. I began to stay up even later, memorizing every strange word, every multiple-choice answer.

I was exhausted, sleeping only three or four hours a night, but continued to give 100 percent to the classes I was teaching. I couldn't afford to let down Master Thompson, as there was a very good chance I would still need the job.

The morning of the exam, I ate a large breakfast in my back room, made a few sandwiches, and packed them in my bag. Supposedly, this was an all-day affair, and I would need to keep my strength up.

Staff Sergeant Kowalski picked me up, and this time I put on the seat belt with no trouble. "You'll do fine," he said. At the office, he introduced me to a new set of Marines. They all smiled and shook my hand, all of them in perfect shape, all of them happy to see me.

"You ready?" asked one of them.

I nodded.

Kowalski looked serious. "We only take the best of the best, Tchicaya. Do well."

I matched his stare. "I will."

"Good luck."

I was escorted into a different back room and placed in front of a computer. My palms began to sweat. I'd never touched a working computer before, and didn't have the slightest idea how to operate it. In fact, my first thought was, "Why do I have this TV in front of me?" The computers I'd seen the *mundelé* carrying through the streets of Brazzaville looked old-fashioned and ancient compared to these sleek machines.

There were at least twenty other people in the room, and I stared at them, searching for a clue about how I was supposed to take the exam. I moved the small handheld device located to the right of the keyboard, watching as the screen lit up.

That was a good start.

A small arrow moved wherever my hand did, and I figured out how to use the button on the device to select certain things on the screen.

The first part of the test was only two hours long, and I used at least thirty minutes of that time struggling to decipher the computer.

I began the test, quickly realizing that I wasn't allowed to go back to previous questions once I'd moved on. I would have to answer them all as I went and be sure of my choices.

"Shit," I muttered.

I paid extra attention to the math and science questions, realizing I didn't have much of a shot at the English section anyway. All around me, people began getting up and leaving, their tests completed. I was nowhere near finished, and this made me incredibly nervous.

Finally, a man put his hand on my shoulder. "Time's up."

I looked around the room, surprised to find that I was alone.

My eyes burned. My heart pounded. I had no idea how I'd done. I needed to pass this test—my future depended on it—but suddenly it was out of my hands. There were about thirty questions that I instantly wished I'd answered differently.

Since Kowalski was my ride home, I sat in the waiting room while the results were processed. It was an excruciating time, and my brain worked its way through all the possible directions my life could take.

The door opened, and Kowalski poked his head out. His face was solemn and my heart sank. He stepped into the room, closing the door softly behind him. He sat down beside me.

I remained silent.

"We processed your results," he said.

"Yes?"

"I'm not supposed to tell you directly. We have to mail them out to everyone."

"You can't tell me?"

"I could make an exception, I suppose."

"Well?" I couldn't stand the suspense. This was no time for games or jokes.

"You got a 36."

I stared at him, not knowing what that number meant, but realizing it was extremely low. Had I really done that poorly?

"To get into the Marine Corps, you need to score at least a 32." Suddenly, that familiar smile overtook his face and he grabbed both my shoulders. "You passed! You're in!"

"But I got a 78 last time," I said. "Why did I do so bad?"

Kowalski shook his head. "Tchicaya, there are people who were born in this country, who went to high school in this country, who fail this test three or four times. You passed it on your first try! You did great!"

Slowly, I let a smile work its way onto my face.

I'd done it.

I was going to be a Marine.

Kowalski laughed and shook my hand. "Now you just have to pass the physical part of the exam. Can you do that?"

"Shit," I said. "No problem."

He smiled. "You're the shit-man, aren't you? That's your word."

I nodded. "Shit."

The physical test was a joke. I hadn't been in this kind of shape since my days in the gendarmerie, and decided that I would beat all the other potential recruits in the tested areas of sit-ups, pull-ups, and running. At the track, I peeled off my shoes and began to leap into the air, preparing myself to race. The Marines and the other applicants stared at me, but I didn't care. Once the race started, I knew they would realize my bare feet were stronger than their covered ones. I imagined I was chasing a zebra through the grass and sprinted around the track, finishing over a minute before the second-place applicant. When we were tested in pull-ups, I challenged the active-duty Marines, and emerged victorious. What I lacked in test-taking ability, I resolved to make up for with my physical prowess.

The medical exam was awkward, as they had me stand naked in front of an old white man who put on rubber gloves and touched me in strange places while asking me to cough. In the Congo, a man never touches another man's balls, and here, this old *mundelé* was rubbing my testicles as if they were a toy. I didn't understand what my balls had to do with my ability to be a good soldier, but I didn't complain.

They asked all the potential recruits to pee into different tiny bottles, and I didn't understand this either. It became even more confusing when a fellow recruit asked me to pee into his bottle as well as my own. I shook my head, turning away from the strange request.

The last thing they asked me was what area of the Marines I wanted to be placed into. Staff Sergeant Kowalski had been in the infantry, and I thought that might be good for me, but my friends at the studio had given me different advice. They said that special forces/recon was the best job, and I requested this. However, I didn't have citizenship, or even a green card, and was denied. The man behind the desk thumbed through some papers and said, "What about supply?"

"Okay," I said, not even knowing what the word meant.

It didn't matter.

I was going to be a Marine.

CHAPTER 33

On March 26, 2000, I was sworn in as a U.S. Marine recruit and flown down to San Diego, where I was put up in a four-star hotel before being picked up in a long white bus. The driver was a white woman who was short, but tough. Despite her size and sex, I noticed that she inspired instant respect, and I admired her for it.

The heat was sweltering and I stared out at the concrete scenery streaming past my window. The bus was noisy with roughhousing and conversation, but I sat alone, retracing my journey, replaying the moment my father had dropped me off at the gendarmerie. I didn't know what to expect over the next few months, but I knew I wouldn't fail. I couldn't. It seemed that every day was life or death, every new experience was one shot, one kill. It was both invigorating and terrifying. I'd been working without a viable Plan B for years, and I worried what that pressure was doing to my brain.

Master Thompson had accepted my resignation with pleasure, disappointed to see me go, but excited that I was moving on to something so honorable. The gym, with my students, their parents, and the other instructors, had become the first place since I left my country that even remotely resembled a family, and it had been hard to leave behind. I wondered, just for a split second, if I was making a mistake.

As we passed under the archway to the Marine Corps Recruit Depot, or MCRD, everyone fell strangely quiet. I looked around and saw a busload of tense, nervous expressions. A small smile crept onto my face.

It was quickly erased as an enormous man in fatigues leaped onto the still-moving bus and began shouting at the top of his lungs.

"Listen up! You are now on MY base. You are now MY property. For the next three months, I OWN you. I tell you when to eat, sleep, shit, and breathe. If you don't hear me tell you to breathe, I better not see any GODDAMN air going into your GODDAMN lungs. Is that understood?"

The bus echoed with the reply. "Aye, aye, sir!"

"What was that?"

"AYE, AYE, SIR!"

"Now you have five seconds to get off of my limousine, and put your nasty feet on my yellow footprints. Do you understand me?"

"AYE, AYE, SIR!"

"Five, four, three—"

The bus erupted into movement as the men threw themselves over the seats, struggling to get outside. It looked like a herd of goats being chased by a leopard.

I understood hardly any of what had been said, and began to worry that this would be an enormous problem. I followed the others off the bus, and did my best to blend in with the crowd. When in doubt, follow the herd.

Monkey see, monkey do.

The next thirty minutes were a complete wash of sound and motion. We were lined up butt to nuts outside the bus and continually harassed for no apparent reason, sometimes by as many as three drill instructors at once. It was worse than *Full Metal Jacket*. It was worse than the Congo. My brain rang with fear and doubt. I looked down to see an enormous wet spot growing on the pants of the man beside me. The drill instructors leaped on him like gorillas.

We were sent running in all directions, and I found that I could get by as long as I wasn't given any individual orders. I couldn't understand a single word that they shouted, and just hoped that someone near me spoke better English than I did. When two people performed different actions, I just imitated the one who looked the most reliable.

We didn't sleep that first night. The drill instructors took us to the barber for our first Marine haircuts, made us do push-ups, taught us to march, and ran us into the ground. I pushed myself harder than I ever had before, thankful that I was in much better shape than most of the other recruits.

The gendarmerie was physically tough, but the Marines were mentally tough.

For the first time in my life, I worried that my mind wasn't strong enough.

I began to compensate for my lack of understanding by always being the fastest and loudest person in the platoon. No one shouted "Aye, aye, sir!" louder than me, and no one would ever beat me to the finish line. This didn't keep me out of trouble, but it appeared to ease the pain and redirect the fury of the drill instructors.

They seemed like animals to me, madmen, worse than anything I'd encountered in the Congo. It was incredible—the sheer amount of fury they managed to work up in a short period of time, especially for such inconsequential issues.

"Shaka Zulu! Are you eyeballing me?" The drill instructor stood two inches from my face and tried to make eye contact, while I tried to avoid it.

"Aye, aye, sir!" I shouted, as this was generally the best guess when asked a direct question.

"You are!? You're eyeballing me? Sergeant Jacobs, get over here. Shaka Zulu thinks he's funny. Do you think you're funny, Alphabet?"

"Aye, aye, sir!" I shouted again, hoping for better luck on this question.

"You do?!! Well, we got a regular joker on our hands, don't we? T-15 here thinks he's a comedian!" And the merciless shouting would continue, leaving me wondering what exactly I'd done wrong.

The mental cacophony created by three drill instructors simultaneously shouting at full volume was absolutely incredible. In the gendarmerie, you never had more than one person yelling at a time. Here, anywhere between one and five people would be doing their best to tear your head off and spit down your throat.

Somehow, through all this, I was assigned to be the platoon guide, or the de facto leader. During formation training, I would hold the guidon and lead the marches.

In this position of leadership, the language barrier became an enormous problem. I would miss direct orders, confuse commands, and even turn the opposite direction from the rest of my platoon. It was not uncommon to see me hoisting my guidon and taking off alone across the deck, unaware that there was not a single recruit behind me. The drill instructors made it their mission to teach me the difference between left and right, but I could never understand a single word they said.

I thought their hearts were going to explode.

As the leader, I was punished for any mistake made by a recruit under my command, and my arms and chest were constantly sore from all the push-ups.

Within two weeks, I was contemplating giving up.

This wasn't for me—the abuse, the torture. I'd joined the Marines for the camaraderie, for the pride, for the honor. I was sick of being shouted at. I was tired of being harassed during every waking moment.

Everything was done by command. You didn't shit unless ordered to. You didn't eat unless ordered to. You didn't sleep unless ordered to.

Each morning, I would spring out of bed as enormous metal garbage cans slammed down the hallway of the barracks.

Each night, I would pass out, exhausted, in my rack, listening to the sound of taps being played on a bugle outside my window. They made sure we got at least eight hours of sleep a night, but it never felt like more than one or two.

The mental beatings began to weigh heavily.

Drill instructors holding magnifying glasses to my face during inspection and saying, "Damn, Kunta Kinte, you're one ugly motherfucker."

Drill instructors running alongside me shouting, "Shaka Zulu, this isn't Africa! You need to wear shoes!"

Every waking moment became filled with dreams of freedom.

One of the duties of the guide was to report the platoon to the chow hall for breakfast, lunch, and dinner. I was expected to bang the enormous wooden door of the hall three times, then shout, "Guide for platoon one thousand fifty four requests permission to bust the hatch [open the door], sir!" Of course, my English was still slim to none, and I rarely got this right.

Drill instructors would gather around when they saw my platoon approaching, waiting for me to screw up, excited for me to mispronounce a word or, worse, forget one entirely. Everyone knew when Shaka Zulu was coming, and they would taunt me even before my palm touched the door. Some days, I would knock, open my mouth, and forget how to speak any English at all. My nerves grew thin.

Not surprisingly, I was fired from my leadership position after about three weeks.

I considered leaving, but images of my father flashed through my brain and I knew I couldn't let myself be beaten by these *mundelé*.

I was stronger than this.

So, instead of quitting, I found a fellow recruit, an English teacher named Michael, who was willing to help me learn the language. We sat down together one night after lights-out and he handed me the *Marine Corps Recruit Manual*. "Read this paragraph," he said, pointing to a long string of tiny words.

I struggled through, watching him shake his head after just about every syllable. It was incredibly frustrating. My mouth simply didn't want to form the sounds that I heard in my ears and brain.

"This word," said Michael, pointing to the word "them."

"T-him," I said slowly.

"No, it's one sound. The 'th' makes one sound. 'Th.'"

"Tar," I said.

"No, 'th.'"

I tried again.

Michael sat back, pursing his lips, figuring out a way to explain the strange new sound. "It sounds like an 'f' sound. Can you make an 'f' sound?"

I nodded. "Fff."

"Good. Like that. When you see a 'th,' you can substitute the sound of an 'f.'"

"Okay," I said. "No problem."

"No," he said, "not 'no problem.' You say 'thank you' when someone does something for you. Thank you."

I worked through the word, substituting an 'f' for the 'th,' and said, "Fack you."

A strange grin worked its way onto his face, and he laughed. "Good," he said. "That's right. Fuck you."

"What is funny?"

"Nothing," he said. "You're doing great."

The next day at chow hall, I felt a new sense of confidence. My English was already improving. I had no doubt that within a few weeks I'd be reinstated in my guide position and leading my troops again.

The recruit on mess duty slapped down a ladle of mashed potatoes onto my tray. "Fuck you," I said, smiling widely.

He stared at me. "What did you say?"

I swallowed, then tried to pronounce it better. Maybe he hadn't understood. "Fuck you very much," I said. "For the potatoes."

A nearby drill instructor walked up, his mouth open. "Kunta Kinte, what did you just say?"

"Fuck you," I said, the smile no longer on my face.

"Who taught you that word?" screamed the drill instructor.

Still holding my tray with four fingers, hands shaking, I gestured with my chin to Michael, who was sitting nearby.

His eyes went wide as the drill instructor rushed him.

After that, Michael was assigned to be my personal English tutor, and was required to stay up with me every night for an hour after lights-out. We used the Marine Corps manual as an English textbook, and I began to carry it with me wherever I went.

Within a few weeks, I'd memorized the entire book, and could nearly pronounce every single word in it.

The familiar feeling of power began to trickle back into my consciousness.

Meanwhile, I was still excelling on the physical front. I ran faster, climbed higher, and pushed harder than just about any other recruit. I'm convinced that this is what kept me from getting kicked out in the first few weeks of boot camp.

One afternoon, we climbed a huge wooden platform overlooking a long pool. The drill instructor (DI) stared us down one by one. "All the whites to my starboard, all the blacks to my port!"

I didn't quite understand these words, but watched as the white people separated themselves out from the blacks. It seemed like some strange racism, but I hadn't thought this to be one of the racist DIs, who constantly used words like "nigger" and "spic." I squinted, trying to figure out what was going on.

He shouted a few commands at the whites, causing them all to leap off the platform and into the pool.

He turned back to us. "Now," he screamed, "which of you motherfuckers knows how to swim?"

No one raised a hand. I was relatively sure I understood the question, but it didn't make sense that no one around me could swim, so I kept my arm down.

"Not one of you can swim?"

Again, the word "swim," which I thought I understood. I tentatively raised my hand. The DI's eyebrows went up. "Kunta Kinte, you can swim?"

I nodded, still not totally sure I knew what he was asking.

"Everyone, get over here!" shouted the DI to the rest of the platoons on the ground. "Kunta Kinte's going to swim!"

And he pushed me off the platform.

I fell into the water and sank, thankful for the silence, thankful for the cool liquid against my skin, thankful for the dirt and grime that peeled away from my body.

It was the closest I had felt to Africa since I'd left.

I let myself sink for a bit before kicking back to the surface, but apparently during that time, the drill instructors became convinced that I was drowning. The next thing I knew, two men were holding me in vise grips and dragging me toward the surface. I struggled to get free, to kick toward the air, but they held me tight.

I heard one of the men shout, "Calm down!"

"Tchicaya swimming good!" I shouted, sputtering in the water.

A sharp blow struck me on the back of the head, and I went limp for a moment. "No!" I shouted, blinking the stars out of my eyes. "Tchicaya swim! Tchicaya swim!"

They must have understood, because they released me. I swam away as fast as I could.

I turned to see all the recruits and drill instructors staring at me.

I realized I was the only black man in a pool full of *mundelé*.

America never ceased to confuse me.

Weeks went by, and I grew happy that I hadn't let myself quit.

I felt myself changing.

I felt myself becoming a Marine.

The word "kill" forced itself into my vocabulary. It replaced basic words like "good" or "thank you."

A typical exchange between two recruits would be as follows: "How are you today?"

"Kill."

The word lost meaning.

I felt myself growing cold and hard, but this was a good thing.

I readied myself for graduation, realizing I'd made a mistake by signing up to be part of the supply department. I wanted the action, the battle, the glory, the honor.

I wanted to be a warrior, not a desk jockey.

Luckily, fate intervened.

"Your name is Tchicaya," said the sergeant major. His name-plate read "Kent."

"Yes, sir."

"Where are you from?"

"The Congo, sir."

He smiled and said, *"Sango nini."* He was greeting me in Lingala, the regional dialect of the north.

"Sango té," I replied, stunned. A *mundelé* who spoke Lingala? It was unheard-of.

He smiled. "I was stationed at the American embassy there for two years. I recognized your name and took a guess. What are you doing here?"

"I escaped," I said.

"I bet you did," he said. "Good for you. What's your MOS?"

"Supply."

He shook his head. "Supply? Is that what you want?"

"No. I want to be a grunt."

"Well, I'll see what I can do about that."

"Thank you, sir," I said, containing a smile as he walked away. Sometimes, the world worked in strange ways.

Hell Week arrived, and all the recruits were transferred to Camp Pendleton for our final testing. There, we were pushed to the limits, taught how to shoot, how to be a team, how to be Marines.

It was the hardest week of my life, and I felt as if I was fleeing the Congo again.

We were shoved into gas chambers and forced to breathe OC gas, or pepper spray.

We learned to drag each other's bodies across huge expanses of relentless terrain, how to secure a wound, how to provide CPR.

We were taught to survive with little to no sleep and hardly any food.

The concept of "teamwork" took on an entirely new dimension in this haze of pain and sound.

It was the first time I'd fired an M-16, and I was amazed by the precision it offered. I felt like Rambo, like Schwarzenegger. I wanted to return to Africa with my M-16 and chase monkeys with it. With that weapon, I felt that nothing could stop me. It made the AK-47 seem like a pistol.

I also learned that everything in boot camp had served a purpose, even the seemingly inconsequential activities. For example, all recruits were required to hold their food trays with only the first two fingers of each hand. Something that had seemed so stupid for months now made sense, as I used those two fingers every day to charge my M-16, and I was thankful that they'd grown so strong.

There was a reason behind the pain, a method behind the degradation, and forgiveness began to fill my heart.

The last three days of Hell Week are known as "The Crucible." We were allowed only four hours of sleep a night and one meal a day, while our bodies were subjected to incredible physical stresses. The final day, we were brought to the bottom of a sprawling hill called "The Reaper" and were marched up its steep, ten-mile face as a unit, each of us wearing full battle gear. There at the summit, we were given the sacred eagle, globe, and anchor—the symbols of the Marine Corps.

Tears filled my eyes and pride filled my heart as I held the gleaming devices in my hand.

I hadn't given up.

I hugged my brothers and stared up at the clear sky, thinking of my family, who had given so much for me to be there atop that mountain.

It was an incredible feeling, matched only by the "warrior's breakfast" the next day, where the recruits gorged themselves on every type of food imaginable.

America, I thought, only managed to get better.

Sergeant Wills, one of the most aggressive DIs in basic training, pulled me aside after the boot-camp graduation ceremony.

"Shaka Zulu, you're a good Marine. Keep doing what you did here, and you'll be noticed. Be the loudest, the strongest, the fastest. They won't have a choice but to make you a leader."

"Thank you, sir," I said.

"Godspeed," he said, and I felt a strange connection to this man who'd spent the last twelve weeks making my life a hell on Earth.

After graduation, I switched out of supply and went straight into infantry school. It was another chance for me to demonstrate my leadership skills, but this time, I understood the language.

Infantry training went by quickly and was a breeze compared to the general boot camp. Every weekend, my fellow Marines would head off base to get drunk, but I would stay in the barracks with the infantry manual, reading it, improving my English, studying.

I had no need for parties. I was creating my life.

It was important that I be the best of the best for my family. They'd given their lives for my dream, and I vowed to let my father's words guide every aspect of my training.

Always work harder than the man next to you.

I wouldn't be the smartest, the strongest, or the quickest, but I decided no man would ever work harder or be more persistent.

When the final tests came, I graduated first in my class.

Everyone was shocked that the only non–English speaker in the company had managed to finish at the top of the school, but to me it was no surprise.

The test was multiple choice. I didn't understand how anyone could fail.

On September 22, 2000, I was assigned to the Victor 2/8, Second Battalion, Eighth Marine Unit in the sand, swamp, and jungles of Camp Lejeune, North Carolina.

There, I was handpicked and trained to be a scout sniper.

I went through three days of mental, physical, and emotional hell, during which my toothbrush spent more time on the latrine than in my mouth, and then I began my intensive sniper training.

Our battle assignment was to deliver long-range fire from concealment positions in support of combat operations. We were the eyes and ears of our commanding officer, the infantry of the infantry, the best of the best.

I learned to trace, survey, and kill from long range without being detected.

We were pushed to fail at every step, but I'd given up the notion of failure. At this point in my life, there was nothing I could imagine quitting. There was no challenge too large, no enemy too strong.

The only road bump in my sniper training came in the form of a staff sergeant named Wilson, who made it clear that he didn't like me or my looks. I was the only black man in my unit, and I began to notice that I constantly received the shit duties—the cleaning, the cooking, the night watches.

I secretly worried that racism had found its way into my life, yet again. Still, I did what was requested of me and kept my head down.

One of the other Marines eventually reported Wilson after hearing him ask "where the nigger was at" on a number of different occasions. When I heard this, I took a deep breath and chose not to react. His opinions affected me only if I gave them the power to do so. Battles weaken both sides, and I had higher goals in mind. Staff Sergeant Wilson attempted to have me put into a different group for deployment, but his efforts were thwarted by the base commander, and I was allowed to finish training with my unit.

For two years, I would be part of this elite unit, but would never be officially recognized, because I wasn't a U.S. citizen. In fact, I still didn't have a green card.

In 2001, I was issued my first overseas deployment, on the USS *Kearsarge*. It wasn't a bad job, as our primary responsibility was patrol and presence along the Mediterranean sector.

The ship was incredible—it was a floating city, complete with restaurants, stores, movie theaters, basketball courts . . . there was more to do on that one ship than was possible in the whole of the Congo, and my jaw dropped almost daily as I discovered the nearly limitless resources at my disposal. I made as many friends as I could, and even began training the ship in kickboxing, Mpongo, and general physical fitness. My sessions on the hangar decks grew almost daily, until I was well-known around the *Kearsarge* as one of the best personal trainers on the ship. Even the captain became a regular attendee at my classes, and eventually awarded me the prestigious "Marine of the Day" title.

Life was good, comfortable, predictable.

But on September 11, 2001, we were issued a new set of orders.

PART 10
HOMECOMING

*I must confess that I have enjoyed being on this
mountaintop. . . . But something within
reminds me that the valley calls me in spite of all
its agonies, dangers, and frustrating moments.
I must return to the valley.*

—DR. MARTIN LUTHER KING, JR.

Brazzaville, Congo
August 27, 2004

Friday

The next morning, Tim Morano arrives with the sun.

"You've been working," he says, lifting his hat and scratching his head.

"Yes," I say.

"I don't know how you did it, but the State Department has been alerted, along with the FBI and the Congolese embassy. We're negotiating your release right now. They're hearing about your case from all sides, so nice work, however you got through to them."

"What does that mean?"

He lowers his voice, even though no one else in the compound speaks English. "It means that the Marines have plans to extract you tomorrow, unless we can negotiate a peaceful release. I don't want to endanger your life."

"My life is in danger every second that I'm in this country," I say.

He nods. "I understand. We're doing the best we can. Be ready tomorrow. If they don't release you, we may have to bust you out."

"Okay," I say.

"I'll let you know the second I hear anything, all right? Whatever you do, stay in this cell."

"I will," I say.

"Okay." He pats me on the shoulder and turns to leave. I find it strange how accepting I am of this *mundelé* who holds my life in his hands. Ten years ago, I would have laughed at such a notion.

I sit down, listening to the singing of the crowds beyond the cell wall. Mama Loukoula has joined my mother, and together they sleep on the hard ground while praying for my release.

I worry about their health to avoid thinking about my own.

My friends and family are my strength, and I don't doubt that I would have been killed days ago if not for the men and women surrounding the jail.

Clearly, my captors fear the uprising my death would cause.

I lick my lips grimly, thinking how much pressure the general would feel if the Americans showed up.

Issou drops our food off, and I smile at him.

"My family is going to have a party tomorrow," I say to him.

"What?"

"To celebrate my one-week anniversary. I'll let you know more soon. You hear all those people out there?"

He nods.

"They're going to have some of the best food and drinks you've ever seen. I'm just letting you know in case you want to join them, you know, to thank you for the kindness you've shown me. I know you don't have to behave that way."

"It's nothing," he says, looking down at the ground. "The general is having his own party tonight."

My ears perk up. "What?"

"A celebration of his command. In the main lobby. We're all required to go."

"Maybe you should bring me a drink from the party." I smile to let him know that I'm only half joking. This would be the perfect diversion, and the soldiers will be drunk.

I pat his shoulder, and he smiles back. "I don't know."

"Think about it," I say, guiding him toward the door. "Have fun."

He closes the grate.

I've sized him up and know that I can take him, even though I've lost more than fifteen pounds in five days.

Mama Nicole is allowed another quick visit, and explains that Sazouka has secured a canoe at the north end of the Congo River. It's a long shot, but my body will be worthless by next week. Something has to happen now. I cannot wait for others to rescue me when I am able to rescue myself. I cannot place my life in the hands of strangers, not when I have a clear mind and a functioning body. It is not how my father would behave. It is not how I will behave.

I sit and wait, preparing myself.

The other prisoners sense my mood and don't attempt to speak to me.

The next twenty-four hours will decide the direction of the rest of my life, and I can't help but think of everything I've been through to get to this point.

The wars, the checkpoints, the escapes, the moving staircases, the training—all are worthless if I die tomorrow in some shit- and piss-filled Congolese prison.

No matter what happens tomorrow, I think, *this is my last night in captivity.*

I lift my head and silently sing along with the chanting masses.

Mayélé mamé mayélé
O mayélé mamé
Tchicaya mayélé
O mayélé
Marine hé mayélé

.   .   .

As it gets later, the cell begins to stir, and I notice a strange, subdued silence.

Fear.

Worry.

Doubt.

I don't let these emotions cloud the hope I feel deep in the pit of my stomach.

It will be all right.

I have to believe this.

My ears are tuned to the sounds of life beyond the wall, and I hear no tanks, no cars, no boots on the ground.

I prepare myself for a fight. If I'm not released tomorrow morning, I've decided to either escape or die trying.

Minutes tick by.

We begin to hear sounds of revelry from the main lobby of the prison.

The party has begun.

Footsteps in the hallway.

The all-too-familiar sound of the squealing grate.

A new soldier unlocks the door and enters the cell. The room stands as one, and my men surround me.

The soldier points with his free hand. The other holds a pair of shower shoes. "Tchicaya. I need you to come with me."

"No," I say. "I will not leave the cell."

"We want you to take a shower."

"No," I say.

"You have to. It's an order." He takes two steps into the cell, freezing as the other prisoners match his movements.

"I will not leave the cell."

He stares around at the faces of my men, smelling the shit, the piss, the aggression. He clears his throat. "We want you to take a shower so that the general can see you."

"Then he can see me as I am." I picture the general smelling me now, smelling the blood, shit, and piss, and it brings pleasure to my heart.

"He needs to speak with you."

"I have no need to speak with him."

Now we're in a standoff, and I know that one of us is going to lose face. But this soldier's life isn't at stake, only his reputation, so he will not succeed.

"Tchicaya, I've been given orders to come and prepare you for release."

I stare at him, sizing him up. I can't decipher if he's telling the truth, don't know if I should wager my life on this man's word. I don't want to risk dying before the Marines arrive. I want to give Tim Morano the chance I promised him. But I don't want to anger the general if he's having a moment of weakness, of doubt.

So much rides on my decision.

I shake my head to clear the dust. "Tell the general to come to me."

He shakes his own head, and I see the strength that lies in this man. I understand why they've sent him for this task. "You don't want to miss your chance. The Americans have contacted him and demanded your release. He's going to give you to them to save face. If you disobey, he may change his mind."

It's a strong play, and I feel the weakness in my legs, the faintness of breath in my chest. I scan the eyes of my men. Some of them shake their heads. Others nod.

I walk forward so that I can stare into the eyes of the man who will either take me to freedom or betray me.

He holds my gaze and for some reason, I trust him.

"Come," he says, gesturing toward the hallway. "Let me take you to the general. You don't want to disobey him when he's in a good mood."

I don't move. "Did you know my father?" I say to him.

He blinks. "No," he says. "I didn't."

I nod, believing him. "Are you going to kill me?"

This time, he shakes his head slowly. "No. I give you my word."

We stare at each other and an incredible amount of time passes. The man hands me the pair of shower shoes. "Here."

I slide the shoes on. "I'm not leaving the cell without my family by my side."

The soldier sighs, knowing that this is a point he will have to concede. He gestures beyond the prison walls. "You can bring your mother with you."

I nod. "Get her for me. And my grandmother." I believe the general would kill me, but I don't believe that he would kill two unarmed women, especially with the sheer numbers that have gathered outside. It wouldn't make sense.

The soldier begins to protest, but then turns on his heel, locks the cell door, and walks back down the hallway.

He returns a few minutes later, trailed by my mother and Mama Loukoula. They run ahead to the cell and grasp my hands through the bars. My cell mates stay back a respectful distance and watch, wary.

The soldier opens the door and nods for me to step out of the dank cave where I have spent nearly a week. I notice that he doesn't touch me. This, I also take as a positive signal.

I walk past him and into the hallway.

It's strange to hear the echo of the grate from the other side.

Camp Shoup, Kuwait
An Nasiriyah, Iraq
Al Kut, Iraq
2001–4

CHAPTER 34

On September 11, 2001, I was exercising at the gym along with many of my fellow Marines on the USS *Kearsarge*. Out of the corner of my eye, on the TV, I saw smoke and papers falling from the New York skyline. The television showed people covered in soot, their eyes wide and white, their mouths open and red. I paid it little attention, thinking it to be part of a new American movie or TV show. When everyone around me stopped working out, I turned off my CD player, stopped the treadmill, and walked over for a closer look.

When the second plane hit, chaos erupted, and I knew that what I was seeing was real.

My stomach twisted into knots.

How could America, the greatest country on earth, be attacked like this? Beneath my feet, I felt the ship slow, then turn. The *Kearsarge* began to circle in place, awaiting orders. An hour passed in a haze of worry and frantic inaction.

Finally, the command came over the loudspeakers. "All Marines, report to your sections."

Sergeant Underwood walked past me and grabbed my arm. "Get your gear ready," he said. "We're going to war."

"Against who?" I said.

He shook his head. "Just get your gear ready."

We scrambled to our sections and began cleaning our guns and optics, stowing our ammunition. I noticed that the ship's stores were nearly depleted from our six-month mission patrolling the Mediterranean coasts. I listened to the groaning of the engines and felt the ship sway gently as we got underway.

We weren't going home.

Eventually, we were informed that the ship had been ordered to the Indian Ocean to provide support for ground troops in Afghanistan. I was excited. Word trickled down about this man named Osama bin Laden, who had claimed responsibility for the attacks, and I wanted revenge. He had attacked the country I'd worked my whole life to be part of, the country I'd risk my life to defend. I wanted his blood.

Unfortunately, because our ship had very little ammunition, we were ordered to simply patrol the waters until a replacement ship, the USS *Bataan*, could relieve us.

When I heard the news, I approached my commanding officer and asked to be transferred to the *Bataan*. I wanted to see action. I wanted to fight for my country. I wanted to go to war as part of the most sophisticated military force the world had ever seen.

It's every Marine's dream to go into battle with his brothers.

He denied my request, and I was shipped back to the United States with my unit.

At Camp Lejeune, my platoon watched footage of Afghanistan on the television and grumbled to ourselves.

We'd been denied the opportunity to fight for our country there, but a new situation was developing that we began to watch very closely.

According to President Bush, there had been weapons of mass

destruction discovered in a country called Iraq. These nuclear, chemical, and biological weapons were supposedly intended for use on American soil. In addition, Iraq's dictator, Saddam Hussein, had apparently helped to plan or fund the massacre at the Twin Towers.

We were glued to the television, awaiting our fate.

Time passed, but still we were not deployed. The Afghan conflict wound down, and talk of Iraq increased almost daily. Unsure of our future, we stayed in shape, honed our marksmanship skills, and kept our weapons clean.

I learned that waiting for battle is often more difficult than the battle itself.

In December 2002, I was issued two weeks of leave to visit Master Thompson and my other Marine friends in Sacramento.

On my second day there, December 30, I was awakened at 4:00 ?,K. by a phone call. It was First Sergeant Beith, my immediate supervisor. "Sergeant Tchicaya?"

"Yes, sir."

"Pack your shit and get on the first plane back here. We're going to war."

"Yes, sir."

I exploded into action, gathering my things and catching a cab to the airport. It was happening. I was being deployed.

It was the day I'd been waiting for.

I was an American, going to defend my country against those who had attacked us. I was going to defend the honor of those men and women who'd been murdered on our soil.

We gathered together, nearly five thousand Marines, in a parking lot in Jacksonville, North Carolina, and I watched my fellow warriors say good-bye to their loved ones. Wives, children, parents, friends, everyone crammed onto the hot asphalt and hugged each other, wept for each other, made promises to each other. I stood alone, watching from a distance.

"Don't you have any family?" asked a first sergeant.

"My family is the Marines," I said. "My family is coming with me."

The next day, we loaded onto the USS *Saipan*, and my jaw dropped at the sheer quantity of weaponry and ammunition on the ship. I'd never seen anything like it.

I thanked the gods that I was fighting on the side of the Americans.

We set sail and quickly fell into a routine. As a squad leader, I took responsibility for the preparedness of my men, and worked them extra hard in hand-to-hand combat, knife fighting, marksmanship, and physical fitness. We practiced regularly with our gas masks and facsimiles of the chemical suits we might be forced to wear. These were the men whom I would trust with my life, and I wanted them to be ready.

After one particularly grueling training session, I stood on the deck, staring out at the water. The ship was scheduled to land in Kuwait in a few days, and many of the men were nervous. Corporal Kevin McMillan, the leader of my first team and my best friend at Camp Lejeune, stood beside me, smoking a cigarette.

"Do you think we'll see combat?" he asked, taking a long drag and releasing the smoke into the air, watching as it hovered for a moment before being swept away.

"Probably not," I said. "Might be another Afghanistan."

"I was thinking the same thing," he said. We stood in silence for a while, enjoying the feel of the wind against our skin, the sight of the moon near the horizon.

"I hope we get sent in."

"Me, too," he said, turning his back to the ocean and stamping out the cigarette. "Me, too."

I stared into the distance and watched strange shapes climb out of the darkness. "What's that?"

He followed my pointed finger and squinted into the blackness. "I imagine we're coming up to the Suez Canal." He gestured to the right. "That, my friend, is Africa." Then the left. "And that is Europe."

I stared, eyes wide, probing the hulking landmass rising out of the ocean like a prehistoric beast. This was Africa. I'd stayed awake many nights wondering if I would ever see her again, and here she was, confronting me head-on. I wanted to leap off the boat, swim to her shores, and run naked through her jungles. I wanted to scrub my skin with the sand of the Djoué. I wanted to sit with my family around a campfire and eat smoked monkey and boiled cassava.

To my left was Europe, my halfway house, my temporary layover. I'd found so much pain there, so much hardship. But it had gotten me to America, my true home, so I was thankful.

It was a strange feeling, sailing through the Suez Canal at night, riding an American warship between the two segments of my past. Kevin patted my arm, then went below deck to sleep. I stayed up, turning my head from side to side, staring as far into the darkness as I could, hoping to see something, anything that would offer clarification to my strange new life, but I never did.

CHAPTER 35

We arrived in Kuwait around midday, and I nearly keeled over from the heat. I'd never felt sunlight like that before. We were assigned to Camp Shoup, which was less a camp than a few piles of sand scooped up to form makeshift walls. The orders came down to pitch our tents and dig in for a long stay, so we did just that.

Night fell and I nearly froze. It was the most inhospitable landscape I'd ever encountered. Sandstorms constantly came and went, destroying your tent, ruining your food, blowing tiny grains of sand into every crevice of your body. The storms were so thick that you couldn't even see your hand in front of your face, much less the person beside you.

Every night, the storms came, and I began to wonder how they expected us to fight in these conditions.

Nearly two months passed in this sandpit, and I realized we wouldn't be going into Iraq. We were merely a show of force, a supreme fighting machine designed to scare Saddam into submission. I grew disappointed.

We spent every day training in the harsh Kuwaiti environment, awaiting further orders and becoming comfortable with our gas masks and heavy packs. We slept on the ground with only our weapons and live ammunition as company. My sole female companionship was my rifle, whom I'd named Janet Jackson because she was black and she was hot. She wasn't a real woman, but she kept me safe and she kept me happy and she kept me warm when I was cold. It was the most I could hope for.

The boredom was interrupted one afternoon when we received word that NBC News was coming to do a story on our unit.

The cameras showed up while my squad was digging trenches. As usual, I was leading them in a series of African songs designed to keep morale up.

I felt the camera turn on me and I leaped up to it like a monkey, smiling into the lens, then returned to my men. It felt good to laugh, to be playful in such harsh circumstances.

The news anchor, a man named Kerry Sanders, asked if he could interview me.

I agreed, excited at the opportunity.

He asked about my background and my time in the Congo, and they shot extra footage of my men and me singing together.

Toward the end of the interview, his face grew serious and I felt the camera push close to my face. "You're not even an American citizen," he said. "Why are you fighting?"

I smiled at the question, because it was very easy to answer. "Some of the people born in America don't know what they have until it's gone. America stands for freedom. You don't have to be an American to fight for freedom."

Unbeknownst to me, this short interview played all over the world, rallying support for the troops. It wasn't my intention to be a motivating force for the Marines. It was my intention to fight for my beliefs.

It was a brief moment of excitement in an otherwise dreary, monotonous existence.

Then one day, the chemical suits arrived.

Those suits have a shelf life of only thirty days, so when I saw them, I knew that something was amiss. We'd acclimated ourselves to the desert conditions and were prepared to fight. In fact, we were clamoring for action.

On March 20, 2003, we gathered around a big television set exactly as I'd done years before in the Congo. Only this time, I watched as President George W. Bush gave the order to invade Iraq.

It was happening.

My first reaction was relief.

We gathered together, there amidst the swirling sands and roiling heat, and we bowed our heads. A chaplain began to lead us in a quick prayer service, absolving us of guilt if we had to pull the trigger. "God," he said, "forgive us for what we are going to do to the Iraqis."

I'd never prayed before killing.

It seemed strange.

My battalion was assigned to the first wave of attacks, and we joined a long convoy on the road to Iraq. Two days of travel brought us to the burned-out barbed-wire fence marking the division between Iraq and Kuwait.

Our constant companions were the aircraft delivering payload after payload to Baghdad and central Iraq. Day and night, 24/7, the planes flew overhead, until we stopped noticing them altogether.

Again, I was happy to be on the side of the Americans.

Every time we stopped for the evening, we'd dig a few feet into the ground to protect ourselves from grenades, bombs, and sandstorms. Our weapons, clothes, and skin quickly turned a dirty yellow from the constant barrage of swirling grains.

I learned that for three hours every day, there is no shade in Iraq. The sun is so intense that light somehow manages to shine everywhere at once, even underneath the vehicles. There was no relief, no respite, no showers, no toilet paper, and plenty of flies. My body rebelled.

I learned that men who eat exactly the same MREs (Meal, Ready-to-Eat) day in and day out eventually begin to expel identical waste. These food products, which quickly became known as "Meal, Ready-to-Excrete," became the bane of our existence. After a week, I found myself able to tell at a glance if shit on the ground was American, if it was from a Marine, and often, what company it came from.

Still, the only enemy we encountered was the environment, and nervousness set in.

Our convoy slowly rolled up to a city called An Nasiriyah, close to the southern border. Specks of sand swirled in sporadic miniature tornadoes around a sprawling mess of weathered brick and sagging architecture. I squinted through my goggles at the "skyline" of this poverty-stricken town and shook my head at the drooping power lines and decrepit roads. I couldn't imagine anyone living there who could put up a fight against the firepower we had at our disposal.

The Cobra gunships roared overhead, continuing the relentless bombardment.

First Sergeant Beith gathered us together for a briefing.

"All right, men," he said. "Expect to encounter heavy resistance. Recon picked up several hundred fedayeen filtering into most of the border towns. This morning, a convoy of Army soldiers was ambushed and killed. They took huge losses and we need to recover those bodies and scout for survivors. We need the roads and bridges north and south of the city clear so it doesn't happen again. Got it?"

"Aye, aye, sir!"

He looked in the direction of my platoon. "You'll be the first wave."

I nodded, my heart thudding against my chest like a captured animal. We'd been told that we were the reserves of the reserves, and here we were, some of the first soldiers into Iraq. I thanked the gods that I was being given the chance.

Stress mixed with adrenaline, and I took a deep breath to clear my brain.

I was a leader.

I couldn't show fear, because fear is contagious.

Beith approached me and issued specific mission orders for my squad.

"Aye, aye, sir," I said, then waved my men over. I nodded at Kevin, startled by the grim look on his face. He forced a smile. "Here we go," I said.

"Here we go."

I assigned Kevin to lubricate the .50-caliber machine gun on top of the seven-ton truck so it wouldn't jam during combat, then made sure that the rest of the squad was heavily armed with MK-19s, 240Gs, and plenty of ammunition.

I bent over and sketched a rough outline of An Nasiriyah in the sand. My men hunched around me, providing a brief moment of shade.

"We're going out to the ambush site, here. Our job is recovery and support, understood?"

"Aye, aye, sir," said my men.

"We keep these avenues of approach, here and here, open, and we won't have any problems. Intel says a couple of Army soldiers from the attack might still be alive. If they are, we're getting them out. The bodies, we take back with us. No man left behind."

"Aye, aye, sir," they said again.

"Let's move out." I spat on the sand and erased the makeshift map with my boot.

A couple of trucks split off the main convoy and headed north.

When we arrived, the area was still, silent. Even the omnipresent air attacks paused for a second as we stared at the burned-out wreckage of about twelve Army transport vehicles. Bodies scattered the ground like seeds, many too mutilated to even recognize as human. Some of the trucks had clearly attempted to flee, only to be ruthlessly gunned down by Iraqi RPGs or mortar rounds. The area smelled of death.

There were no survivors.

"Let's get these bodies loaded up," I said, and leaped down from the lead vehicle.

Sadly, this was something I'd grown used to.

I strode forward, staring at the mound of charred flesh at my feet. The man's dog tags were the only thing that hadn't been obliterated by the explosion.

I'm in the war now, I thought.

Somehow, up until that point, it hadn't seemed real, but I nodded slowly as everything came crashing down. I was staring at a human being who'd had hopes and dreams and a family. I had the strange realization that I was aware of this man's death, but his mother wasn't. Somewhere, she thought her son was still alive, and an Army officer in Kansas or Georgia or Alabama would be responsible for knocking on her door and informing her that her son had made the ultimate sacrifice for his country. That he had given his life in pursuit of freedom.

I resolved that I wouldn't go out the same way. I promised the gods that I wouldn't die without taking at least twenty enemies with me.

A Marine never dies alone.

I felt my mind focusing, becoming a deadly weapon.

I flashed back to the rescue of Tom Thibaut, and breathed deeply as my muscles tightened. I was trained for this work.

It was in my blood.

"Hurry up," I said, looking around. "Let's go."

When the bodies were loaded up, I gathered my men. Their faces were solemn, their bodies, still. "Today, I saw a dead American. Soon, his mother will be told." I paused, letting the words sink in. "I don't know about you, but I can't afford to die in this country. I can't die here, today, because I love to eat chicken. And if I die, then I'll never get to eat any more chicken." A few of my men smiled. "Let's avenge that soldier. Shoot to kill, two in the body, one in the head. If you don't do your job today, one of your friends will be killed, or you will be killed. I brought you guys to war, and I'll bring you home in one piece."

I lowered my voice and took a step toward them. "You are warriors," I said. "Listen, smell, feel, and attack. Look your enemy in the eye when you kill him. It is your life against his. We need to go home and eat chicken."

They smiled.

I stepped back. "Load up."

We dropped off the bodies, then headed back toward An Nasiriyah to join the rest of our unit. Our company had been instructed to support the Alpha Company of the First Marine, Second Division, as they'd come under heavy fire while attempting to secure a necessary bridge just outside the city.

It was March 23, 2003. Eleven soldiers had died in the first thirty minutes of the attack.

Friends of ours.

Brothers.

The expressions on my men's faces were grim.

Driving into battle is a strange feeling, and as we rolled down the "Road of Death" into the center of An Nasiriyah underneath the thundering blanket of Cobra gunships, I began to feel the nervousness growing in my own stomach. In the distance, we could hear the stuttering sounds of machine-gun fire and the soft pop of mortar rounds.

We crawled through an area of town perilously close to what was called "Ambush Alley," but weren't overly concerned. The fighting was audible, identified, distant.

We moved forward cautiously, but steadily.

Our trucks weren't armored, so we'd piled sandbags around the doors for extra protection. I saw my men hunching behind them, trying to expose as little of their bodies as possible. I wasn't sure if this was to protect them from the sun or from the enemy. I didn't ask.

I took a few deep breaths, struggling against the sensation that something was wrong, out of place.

The surrounding area was horribly quiet, and I watched the yellow and brown buildings fade from one into the other. Garbage littered the streets, and I noticed bullet holes in many of the brick façades.

I realized that I hated this place, its poverty, its filth.

A dull haze hung in the air.

The convoy began to slow, and I squinted.

People.

That's what was strange.

There weren't any civilians around.

Just as my brain processed the thought, the lead vehicle exploded.

I was surrounded by screams, and bodies fell around us like a rockslide.

Bullets streamed out of windows from all sides.

I saw nothing but fire, heard nothing but explosions.

Time slowed to a crawl and I imagined I could follow the trajectory of individual bullets.

"Out, out, out!" came the shouts, and I snapped out of my reverie, pushing my men onto the street. We scrambled for cover behind the trucks and around the sides of the buildings.

The fedayeen stormed out of the alleyways, and I watched as Kevin leaped onto the truck and manned the .50-caliber machine gun. I'd seen the gun rip targets to shreds, but had never seen the effect it could have on the human body. As the Iraqis turned away, Kevin directed the gun toward them and fired.

Du-du-du-du-du-du.

I watched as a man's left leg was blown completely off his body, his chest exploding in a puff of red mist. He fell to the ground, mutilated, decapitated.

I roared in triumph.

My heart was filled with bloodlust, and I aimed my own weapon at the fleeing Iraqis. My battle mind had taken over.

I saw children holding sawed-off AK-47s, men in civilian street clothes, men in traditional *dishdasha* robes, all hiding behind buildings, leaning out of windows.

The world had changed in an instant.

I tried to regain my composure amidst the blood and screams.

We secured the wounded and pulled them to cover.

I aimed my weapon at a few nearby windows and fired.

The confusion of the opening salvo had faded, but the danger was still very much real.

Gunshots surrounded me, and I lowered my head.

I would not die here.

Not in this desert.

Not in this shithole of a city.

Not in this war.

I focused my mind and gathered my men. Marines were scattered across the streets, leaving little hope of consolidation or group maneuvers.

We were trapped.

The firefight dragged on, with scattered explosions and sporadic machine-gun bursts lasting well into the night. Silence came only when the first rays of morning illuminated the blood and grime around our feet.

My men shivered and sat against the walls, their weapons raised.

Kevin stared at me and shook his head.

I said nothing.

All my men had survived the attack, but the same could not be said of our brothers and sisters.

We had officially entered the war.

CHAPTER 36

As the sun climbed, we began to move south, leaving our vehicles behind.

Our mission hadn't changed—we would secure the city and surrounding bridges, or we would die trying.

The going was slow and horrifying. I could see my men's faces beginning to settle into permanent expressions of terror, and this filled my heart with sadness. I wanted to reassure them, to make them safe, but I couldn't. The truth was that we were sitting ducks in the streets of An Nasiriyah, subject to the whims and fancies of every militiaman or civilian with an eye toward heroism.

Snipers and fedayeen hid around every corner, behind every door. What was supposed to be a brief mission had turned into a perpetual firefight for control of this small town. We slept at night, but only when we managed to secure an empty room we could adequately defend. Even then, everything was hurried—sleeping, eating, shitting.

We began moving from house to house, hoping to flush out the fedayeen and militiamen, doing our best to capture or kill them before they shot us. To secure the bridges and streets, the Marines would have to secure the city. That meant eliminating the enemy, and my squad took on that task willingly.

Days passed and we slowly began to realize the obvious. When the Iraqis fought us in the streets, they wore their uniforms. But once they got home, they became civilians. Faces began to haunt me from the battlefield, faces that I would see days later as husbands or fathers living humbly in tiny apartments.

Often, we would burst into normal-looking living quarters, only to find guns, ammunition, gas masks, and torture rooms barely concealed behind thin curtains. Nothing was what it appeared. Everyone was a potential enemy.

The confusion nearly made us unable to perform our duties. Prior to entry, we'd been given specific instructions to help civilians, not hurt them. But any male old enough to hold a weapon automatically became a suspect, and I knew I would willingly trade any Iraqi's life for the life of one of my men.

I noticed that every Iraqi fighter we flushed out would come back later with twice as many friends and twice as much firepower. The only recourse was killing everybody we met, but this was neither practical, nor moral, nor possible.

The official orders that trickled down were to shoot at anything that made us feel threatened. If we felt our life was in danger, we had specific orders—shoot to kill. Unfortunately, as time went on, there was little that *didn't* make us feel that we were in horrible danger.

We made the decision to begin taking prisoners as we stumbled through the mazelike inner sanctum of An Nasiriyah. We would slip zip-ties around the wrists of suspected enemy combatants and place bags over their heads. In this confusing environment, it was the only sure way we discovered to save Marine lives.

We learned quickly that many Iraqis had dogs as pets, and that these dogs would constantly bark, alerting anyone with ears that we were approaching. Within hours, we received the go-ahead to shoot anything that moved and began eliminating hundreds of dogs, cats, birds, rats—anything that could give away our position. Soon, the city was completely devoid of living creatures.

It was us or them, and I did not hesitate.

I was a killer, a warrior struggling for my survival.

We fought all day and all night, through strange rainstorms and blistering heat, through sandstorms and frigid cold.

After a week in these conditions, our nerves stretched to their limits, An Nasiriyah seemed no closer to stability than it had the day we'd arrived. To make matters worse, we received word that the Iraqis had cut off our supply line and blown up our food stores. The official estimation was that we'd be trapped in the city without food for four to five days.

It was alarming news.

I saw panic take hold in my squad. We began to spend hours of every day searching for anything even remotely edible.

Scraps, animal carcasses, decomposing vegetables.

Our grumbling stomachs became our worst enemy during silent night missions.

It felt as if we were trapped in *Full Metal Jacket*.

During the day, we'd sneak down to the nearby creek, brown from refuse and contamination, and scoop out bucketfuls. We'd drop in a few water purification tablets, then suck down as much as we could stand. Without access to food, liquids became incredibly important. I watched my men for signs of dehydration or hysteria.

One morning, while out on patrol, Sergeant Jackson stopped and leaned against a wall marked by bullet holes. "What are we going to do for food? We have to eat."

In the distance, I spotted an old rooster inching its way across a back alley. I picked up Janet Jackson, aimed, and blew its head off. "There's your dinner," I said.

We began prowling the area for more animals, eventually finding a small stash of taut, wiry chickens. We killed and roasted as many as we could, even though many of them were composed mainly of feathers and bone.

I stood over the fire, juice running down my chin, and smiled. "Men," I said, "I can't afford to die here—"

"Because I love to eat chicken," they all said in unison.

"Right," I said.

CHAPTER 37

For two weeks, we fought the Iraqis day and night. We slept when we could, taking turns as lookouts, wrapping ourselves in disgusting, ratty blankets to keep us warm in the frigid moonlight.

I'd been miserable in the Congo, but this was worse. It was the poorest city I'd ever seen, and every day was a new struggle against mosquitoes, flies, and Iraqis. Some Marines even believed that Saddam was using the flies as weapons, that he'd released millions of them on purpose, just to terrorize the troops.

As we expanded our sweeps through An Nasiriyah, my squad discovered a huge weapons cache in a warehouse on the outskirts of the city. Two men loitering nearby raised my suspicion, and we brought them over to us at gunpoint, binding their hands and shipping them off to be interrogated.

The men had revealed nothing, offered no information about the weapons or the fedayeen who'd relied on them. I stood in the entrance to the warehouse and stared at the racks of AK-47s and RPG launchers—weapons that had been used to kill Marines. I spat on the ground and turned around, waiting for backup to arrive.

Sergeant Lopez approached me. He pointed to an Iraqi civilian, an older man standing a few meters away.

"Sergeant Tchicaya," he said. "This man says he has information about an American being held prisoner."

I waved the man forward, scanning him for weapons. He approached, nervously eyeballing the rifles that my men had leveled at his chest.

"I'm a doctor," said the man. "There is an American soldier being held in the hospital."

I leaned over to Kevin. "Survivors from the ambush?"

"Maybe," he whispered back. "I thought everyone was accounted for."

"It couldn't be from the Army convoy, could it?"

"Yeah," he said, "it could."

The man continued. "There were two. One is already dead. I know where the other is being held. A woman. I can tell you how to get there."

I exchanged glances with my men, then nodded and clarified the location of the hospital with the Iraqi doctor. Afterward, I gave him a few MREs and some candy for his time.

I called the information up the chain of command and awaited our orders.

The Army alerted us that they had two soldiers MIA from the convoy and were sending in their Delta force to extract the remaining POW. We were assigned to provide support and cover during the rescue mission.

I was excited to receive this assignment, proud to support my brothers and sisters, relieved to be given a task with a foreseeable end. My men and I gathered ahead of the extraction team. We were a convoy of sorts, but this time, on foot.

We set off for the hospital in a staggered column formation, weapons ready, communicating silently via hand signals. As the squad leader, I was in the center.

The streets were quiet.

This area of town hadn't been secured, and was no doubt teeming with fedayeen.

I inhaled a slow, steady stream of air, senses alert, trigger finger tensed.

A few steps forward, halt, scout the area.

A few steps forward, halt, scout the area.

Silence.

I heard a tiny click and gave the signal to stop.

I looked around, weapon aimed.

Nothing.

My men froze.

The world took a breath.

Gunfire erupted from all around us.

Ambush.

Splinters of brick and mortar rained down on our position as the walls of the alleyway were blown apart by the chaotic shooting of the Iraqis.

"Go!" I shouted. "Repel!"

My men were well trained and began repelling backward through the alley, the second man in line providing cover for the first to retreat, and so on down the column. When it came to me, I held off the enemy, directing the rest of my men to take up defensive positions.

I would lead from the front, or not at all.

I took a few steps backward but was forced to the ground as the firing intensified.

I pressed my face into the dirt, listening as the bullets whizzed past my ear. The heat of their passage left my cheeks burning. I shouted for help, but no one could hear me.

Glancing to my rear, I realized I was alone in the middle of the road.

The firing doubled again.

And again.

It was a hailstorm of bullets.

I tried to crab-walk in reverse, but the bullets were too close, and I dropped back down.

I was trapped.

Suddenly, I heard the familiar *du-du-du-du-du-du* of a .50-caliber machine gun, and I knew that Kevin had run back to the convoy to provide cover.

RPGs and mortar fire erupted from behind me, and the Iraqi firepower tapered just enough for me to scoot backward on my stomach to the safety of the convoy.

My squad pulled me in, and I checked my weapon, breathing hard, heart pounding.

"Let's go," I said, and we turned as one toward the enemy, unloading our ammunition.

We were trapped in that alleyway for over an hour with nothing but the sounds of whizzing bullets and exploding grenades.

It seemed as if a week had passed.

A year.

Slowly, the firing dwindled and the Iraqi fighters slipped back into their roles as civilians.

No one can withstand the full force of American firepower, I thought. *You mess with us, you die like the rest.*

My squad inched forward, horrified by the damage. The Iraqis were well known for using human shields and for instigating dangerous firefights in residential areas. The casualties for the enemy were great, but the civilian casualties were far greater.

I shook my head as I stared at the carnage.

War was never good.

It was never simple.

But it was necessary.

We received word that we were being replaced as the Delta support squad, and were to secure the area.

That evening, the Army special forces successfully rescued the young woman who had been trapped in the hospital.

Her name was Private Jessica Lynch.

CHAPTER 38

A few days later, Central Command declared An Nasiriyah and its surrounding bridges secure and the 2/8 Marines were sent on to the next city without a break.

From firefight to firefight, our job wasn't to maintain tenuous peace, it was to push ahead, to destroy, to conquer.

We headed north, securing towns and cities as we went.

Nearly every road was lined with destitute Iraqis begging for scraps of food, trinkets, or fresh water. Children would approach us, saying, "Give me give me give me," holding out their hands and hoping for a piece of a cracker or some candy.

Women lifted their babies into the air, crying and screaming for help.

What we could spare, we did.

Still, we rolled on, staring at them through cloudy windows and half-closed eyes.

It struck me that there was one commonality among all the wars I'd fought in: The people who paid the real price were not the soldiers. They were the women, the children, and the elderly. The toll on the civilian population, no matter what the country, no matter what the war, was always staggering.

But you can't be sensitive during wartime, and our convoys rolled on, farther and farther north, until we received word that Baghdad had fallen.

Our mission had been accomplished.

We were ordered to Al Kut to provide humanitarian services to the locals there, tending to the sick, the injured, the homeless.

It was strange.

We'd become animals after nearly four months with no showers, no sleep, constantly on edge from never-ending streams of gunfire. Our job was to destroy, to annihilate. If one person shoots a Marine, we said, then the whole village is dead.

We were the Bastards of Peace, the Devils of War.

We were the Devil Dogs.

The first ones in and the last ones out.

Marines.

Brothers.

And now we were instructed to help, not hurt; save, not destroy.

It was difficult for the mind, damaging to the soul.

We were required to be all good and all bad.

Saviors and destroyers.

In Iraq, we were sent to protect. But sometimes, to protect, you have to kill.

Sometimes, you have to destroy others so that you may live.

We loaded onto the USS *Saipan* after nearly six months in the field.

Five thousand men, all unshowered, all unshaven, all with severe diarrhea. It wasn't pretty.

I stumbled into the shower and took off my clothes, turning the water as hot as it would go, smiling as it burned my skin.

I washed my body for the first time in months. I shaved my beard and let the steam infiltrate my nostrils.

It struck me then that I'd survived.

I'd made it.

I'd put my name in the history books and fought for the country that fed me when I was hungry, held me when I wept, took me in when I was homeless.

I'd shown my love for the country that had loved me.

Underneath the spewing droplets and clouds of steam, I smiled.

I'd fought for my beliefs, risked my life for my ideals.

The water poured over my face and I opened my mouth, drinking it in.

After a lifetime of struggle, I finally felt like I was going home.

When I arrived back at Camp Lejeune, I discovered a letter from the immigration offices waiting for me. My first thought was that someone had seen the news interview I'd done and I was being deported. I racked my brain, trying to remember if I'd said anything wrong, if I'd let on that I'd entered the country under false pretenses, somehow revealed that I'd joined the armed forces without officially receiving my green card.

I couldn't remember. I tried to reassure myself that everything I had done was legal, but I'd grown so accustomed to running, fleeing, and lying that nothing in my life seemed legitimate, even if it was.

With shaking hands, I tore open the letter, but it was simply an instruction to appear at the immigration offices on Friday of the following week. They requested that I wear my Marine Corps dress uniform.

Nervously, I did as I was asked and arrived full of equal parts hope and fear.

The date was August 1, 2003.

I entered the room, surprised to find news crews and streamers.

It was my swearing-in ceremony as an American citizen.

I laughed out loud, overwhelmed by the attention.

It was a huge party, and I felt like the governor, like the president.

I took my oath in front of a room full of Marines, martial artists, and a few other friends. I felt my chest bursting with pride at every word.

It was an honor to become an American citizen.

It is still an honor to be an American citizen.

News reporters interviewed me, soldiers shook my hand.

Staff Sergeant Kowalski laughed and hugged me tight. "Congratulations," he said. "You earned it. More than anyone I know, you earned it."

"I won't let you down," I said. "I'll keep fighting for this country. I'll keep believing in this country."

"You better," he said. "It's your job now."

I stepped to the back of the room, overwhelmed by the attention.

I was an American Marine.

My dream had come true.

I pictured that young boy on the golf course, touching the *mundelé* chicken skin and wondering how to achieve something so magnificent.

I pictured a scared teenager fleeing across the globe from country to country, hoping to find a home, desperate to find security.

I couldn't wait to return to the Congo and share the news with my mother. She had sacrificed everything to give me freedom, and now I'd achieved the ultimate expression of that gift. I'd fought for the greatest country in the world and been awarded my citizenship as a result.

I'd earned my rights, and no one could take them away from me.

After seven long years away from my family, I finally felt safe enough to visit.

It was time to return to the place of my birth.

I was an American. I couldn't be touched.

Marine meant more than *Ninja* or *Cobra* or *Cocoyes*.

It stood for power, independence, freedom.

I smiled and rejoined the party, putting an arm around my fellow soldiers, my friends, my brothers.

The next morning, I made plans to return to Brazzaville.

PART 11
AMERICAN

In my country we go to prison first and then become president.

—*NELSON MANDELA*

Brazzaville, Congo
August 27, 2004

Friday

I breathe deeply, flooding my brain with as much oxygen as possible.

This is my last fight, and I need all my wits about me.

My mother and grandmother hug me, conscious of my wounds and weakness. Tears trickle down their faces, and I do my best to smile, to reassure them that everything will be okay. I know that they could die today, but I also know that there are worse things that could happen.

The soldier walks forward.

I follow him down a long, dingy hallway. It's surprisingly empty, and I don't know whether this should fill me with enthusiasm or dismay.

He leads me up a flight of stairs, then turns the corner, ending at a large office door.

I memorize my location, and plot a route to the front door of the jail. If I have to escape, I'll do my best to take my mother and grandmother with me. I suddenly wonder if I've made a mistake by bringing them.

The soldier snaps to attention, then knocks on the door.

A man in a crisp uniform opens it and motions us in. "The general will be with you shortly," he says, gesturing for us to take a seat. He wrinkles his nose as my smell hits him, but says nothing else.

"The general's protocol," says the soldier.

I nod.

A second door opens and another man pokes his head in. He

gestures for us to enter, so we do. This is the general's cabinet director.

We're moved into a third room, with the general's secretary.

After half an hour, we are granted admittance into General Bemde's private quarters.

The soldier opens the door, waves us in, then follows behind us. He closes the door with a soft click.

I stare at the general, defying him by my presence, attacking him with my lack of weakness.

"So," he says amicably. "How you doing, son?"

I feel my muscles twitching from all the walking and the stairs. I begin to doubt my ability to run if I have to, and fight the intense claustrophobia falling down around me like a curtain. I wonder if I've made a terrible mistake by leaving the cell.

Tim Morano's words echo through my mind.

"I'm fine," I say.

"Good," he says, allowing an odd smile to settle on his face. "Now, why did you act the way you did?"

"What do you mean?"

"Escape. Why did you try to escape? That was unnecessary."

"Unnecessary? My life was placed into the hands of animals. They said they would kill me that night. I would rather die fighting than die in a prison for a crime I didn't commit."

The general nods. "We were just trying to scare you a little bit. Didn't mean you any harm. We actually planned on releasing you that night, originally, but you had to go and cause problems for my men. You're all right, aren't you?"

I see him glance down at my blood-spattered legs, now also coated with my own urine and feces. He shakes his head and looks up at me inquiringly.

"Fine, sir," I say through gritted teeth. I don't want to argue with the general. He would always be right, and I would always be wrong, no matter where the truth lay.

He reaches into his desk, and I tense, sure that he's about to pull out a pistol, but his hand comes out with a business card and a ten-thousand-franc note (about twenty dollars).

"Here," he says, reaching across the desk and handing me the tiny slip of cardboard and the money. "Take my card. If you need anything, let me know. There's some money for a cab."

I step forward and grab the items, confused, my mind not working well in my weakened state. I wait for the punchline, search for the gimmick.

Is he going to let me leave the prison, then shoot me for escaping? Are there men outside waiting to destroy me? Does the general plan on assassinating my entire family?

He waves at the door. "Go on and get out of here," he says. "The Americans want you back for some reason." I stare at him, watching his features darken. "I don't know why they want scum like you, but they asked, so I'll give you to them. Go. Don't make me change my mind." His eyes are barely slits in his face now, and I suppress a shudder.

I turn toward the door, nodding at the soldier as he opens it for me.

I allow my mother and grandmother to leave the office first. I can tell that they're elated, but are also experiencing the same torrent of emotions as me. Why would the general just let me go without a fight? Had international pressure grown so quickly?

We follow the soldier downstairs, ignoring the sound of the party in the next room. A member of the gendarmerie hands me my uniform, dress shoes, and ribbons. I notice that his gun is unlatched in his holster, and can't help but stare. It would be so easy to grab the weapon, eliminate the two soldiers, then flee to safety.

But my mother . . .

I bite my lip and do my best to keep my hand from shaking as I grab my shoes.

As we're led through the hallway, I wonder if I just signed my death warrant by not grabbing a weapon when I had the opportunity.

My cell mates, my friends, they're wondering where I am, waiting for the sound of a gunshot to echo through the halls of the prison.

Two new soldiers lead us through a side door and I inhale fresh air for the first time in nearly a week. My eyes water as the sun hits them, but I can't enjoy the moment.

I'm waiting for the bullet.

We approach an idling cab. "Here," says one of the soldiers, and holds the front door open. I scan the area, finding no visible snipers. But I do notice a number of perfect locations that could hide two or three soldiers apiece.

My mother is crying and tugging at my arm, overjoyed at my release. I try to comfort her, smile for her, but my military mind is in overdrive.

A free man doesn't need to be escorted outside.

I wonder if the car is rigged to explode.

"Get in," says the first soldier, and I tense my arms, wondering if I could take them both out before being shot.

I lead my mother to the front seat, put her in the car, and slam the door, wincing at the sound. I open the back door for Mama Loukoula and help her in. I turn back to the soldiers, running scenarios in my head. If I take them both out and commandeer the cab, I might have enough time to avoid sniper bullets. But I might not.

I don't know whom to trust. Nearly a week in prison has ruined my analytical mind. I don't want to make any mistakes here, so close to freedom. The sun is giving me a pounding headache.

I nod at the soldiers and slip into the backseat beside Mama Loukoula. She's smiling and crying, and my mother is turned toward the backseat, reaching for me.

"Turn around, Mama," I say gently. I slide into the car and position my body directly behind her. Mama Loukoula, I pull downward and in front of me. If the bullets come, they will come from the rear.

The soldiers don't move.

"Go," I say to the cab driver, sweat pouring down my face.

If it's going to happen, it's going to happen now.

He starts to pull away, and I turn to make eye contact with the soldiers.

They don't move.

The engine revs and we pick up speed.

I watch as the soldiers shrink into the distance.

The first ten seconds of the cab ride are the most frightening of my entire life.

But nothing happens.

The soldiers fade into tiny specks and, as the clock ticks, I feel my body loosening up, relaxing.

I am weak, beaten, bloody, and covered in excrement.

But I am with my family.

The rest of the car ride passes in a flash.

We pull up to my grandmother's house, and I see my entire family waiting for me. Somehow, the word of my release has traveled like fire across the town.

I step out of the car, woozy with hunger and excitement. Everyone begins cheering, crying, laughing. I raise a hand in thanks.

These are the people I've fought for.

My family.

My friends.

Children dance in the streets as I stumble toward the house.

They surround me, touching me, hugging me, kissing me, seemingly oblivious to my smell or the piss and shit coating my legs.

I raise my head to the sky and inhale a breath tinged with the smells of goat, smoked monkey, and boiled cassava.

In the distance, the *bôda* begins to play, and I want to shout, to scream with joy.

I turn around as the cab pulls away in a cloud of dust.

I watch a white car edge slowly forward, replacing it.

My warning bells erupt.

Tim Morano steps out of the car and smiles at me.

"Congratulations," he says, shaking my hand.

"I—I'm free?" I say.

"As free as they come," he says. "The Marines have a boat heading this way right now, ready to take you home. They're just glad they didn't have to bust you out." He shakes his head. "You certainly have a lot of friends over there worried about you."

I inhale again, more deeply this time.

I remember how beautiful it is to be an African.

How beautiful it is to be a *free* African.

My eyes fill with tears as I picture my two worlds colliding, my two families rushing toward me simultaneously. At this moment, I feel my heart expanding to encompass the entire world, and I know that freedom is on the march.

I am the connector between these very different parts of the world, but instead of feeling pulled in separate directions, I feel full, unified, complete.

I have been split into two, but somehow, it has made me double instead of half.

My brothers in uniform would give their lives for me, as I would for them.

My family would lay down their very existence to grant me access to my dreams.

Never before have I felt so blessed.

Every time I think that I understand what true freedom is, my eyes are widened by even greater experiences. I know my definition will change tomorrow, and the day after, but at this moment, I feel freer than I've ever imagined possible. My family hugs me and the smell of fresh mango hits my nostrils, and somewhere, not too far away, the sound of an outboard motor hums through the jungle as a boat of Marines comes to my rescue. Somewhere, Gervais is finding happiness. Somewhere, Marielle is finding true love. Somewhere, I know that my father smiles and weeps with joy at my release.

My time is now. My time is the future.

It is at this moment that I realize I have nothing to fear ever again.

Now I am an American.

Now I am untouchable.

Tim Morano pats me on the shoulder and turns me around.

"Let's get you cleaned up. You have some celebrating to do."

"Yes," I say. "I do."

I walk into the crowd and feel my smile growing. It is no longer forced, for I am no longer weary.

I am Tchicaya.

I am alive.

I am free.

EPILOGUE

Change will not come if we wait for some other person or some other time. We are the ones we've been waiting for. We are the change that we seek.

—BARACK OBAMA

Today, Tchicaya Missamou lives in Valencia, California, with his wife, his twin daughters, and his new son, Allan Kelvin Tamsi Tchicaya Missamou.

He is the proud owner and founder of The Warrior Fitness Camp, a chain of high-end personal training facilities that uses both American and Congolese military techniques to achieve fitness results. He hires only experienced U.S. Marines as trainers and gives 15 percent of all profits to wounded-veteran organizations. To this day, Tchicaya uses the business lessons of his father to create remarkable success for himself.

In addition to his fiscal ventures, Tchicaya still finds time to further his education. He holds a Master's in business administration from the University of LaVerne in Los Angeles, and is currently pursuing his Ph.D. in education.

On January 30, 2008, Tchicaya's mother joined him in Valencia as a permanent resident of America, and met her granddaughters for the first time. His father escaped from prison in 2003 and now resides in Lille, France, as a political refugee.

Tchicaya Missamou hopes to one day return to the country of his birth and free his people.

ACKNOWLEDGMENTS

Tchicaya Missamou would like to thank his father, Tchicaya Missamou, and his mother, Marie Collette, for their unconditional love. Their faith, spirit, and affection have made him the man he is today. Out of nothing, they have provided everything. He would like to thank his grandparents, who taught him the true meaning of life—sharing his gifts with friends and strangers alike. He would like to thank Mama Loukoula Madeleine, Pépé Nsienta Honore, Ntsiangani Therese, Mama Nicole, Mama Julice, and his brothers and sisters—Brigitte Tchicaya, Zabatou Tchicaya, Mireille Tchicaya, Juniore Linda Tchicaya, Michelle Tchicaya, Jurity Tchicaya, Carole Tchicaya, Francine Tchicaya, Magalie Tchicaya, Meme Tchicaya, Pascal Tchicaya, Dony Tchicaya, Sazouka Mampouya, Sandra Mampouya, Chris Kinata, and Mabakari Kinata. Thanks to the love of his life, Ana, his twin daughters, Marie Vangasi and Yana Simbasi, his son, Allan Kelvin Tamsi Tchicaya Missamou aka "The Legend," and his mother-in-law, Mama Vania.

Special gratitude is given to his friends Kevin McMillan aka "Showtime," Stuart Ambrose, Erika Grimes, Janet Rizzi, Djimon Hounsou, Tom and Maricha Grundy, Allan Rutta, Amadou Diaye, Christian Bwakira, Grand Master Lee, Master Clint Sr Robinson, Master Cedric Robinson, Durinda and Mark Evanoff, Adam Stern, Sylvie Ngangoue, Maria Rios, Terry Timmons, Judy and Howard Tons, Linda Roberts, Rebecca Golland, Tania Obeso, Bob Lederman, LJ Fay, Jaime Arroyo aka "Hot Sauce," Chase Rivera, Bonnie Lehigh aka "The Machine." The Ashjian family, Randy and Barbara Boliver, the Sidebotham family, Dana Bohlig aka "Dirty," Daniel

Ramirez aka "Delta Force," Eric and Sheila Holloway, Mercy Nolan, Tess Cozine, Stephany Garethy, Joni Young, Beatrice Edmondson, the Salazar family, the Ramirez family, Ed Galitz, Suzanne Foster, Cherryl Barndt, Wendy Oconnor, Barry Murphy, Laura and Paul Erickson, Lori and Michael Wikler, Joseph Jones, Traimaine Holmes, Svilen and Tuimi Kamburov, Gervais Loko, Olga Loko, Sergeant Major Taylor, Captain Jason Jones, Sergeant Major Anderson, Sergeant Major Beith, First Sergeant Acosta, Master Sergeant Scott, Master Sergeant Daniels, my fellow gendarme, class of 1995–96, Second Battalion, Eighth Marine Scout Snipers, Second Battalion, Eighth Marine Golf Company Third Squad Machine Gun, Second Battalion, Twenty-third Marine, all servicemen worldwide, the Santa Monica Police Department, the Fillmore Police Department, and all the members and staff of Warrior Fitness Camp for their support, inspiration, and trust.

Last, thanks to President Barack Obama for opening doors to those who have lost hope.

Travis Sentell would like to extend thanks to the following amazing women: Jo Sentell-Perez, for her unwavering love and unyielding support, Michelle Wolfson, first for believing and then for motivating, Amy Tannenbaum, for her careful guidance, and finally, to Carol Cregg and Barbara Ferguson for their friendship, time, energy, and relentless, priceless, and snarky feedback.

Special thanks to Stuart Ambrose, J. C. Aevaliotis, Ed and Sue Wirt, Everett Spear, Brent Perez, Brianna and Louis Pepiton, Alexis Perez, Tim Coston, Labid Aziz, Stephanie Reuler, Elliott Riebman, Eric DeSobe, Faisal Abou-Shala, Nir Eyal, Mike and Steffi Wickens, Lisa Gilbert, Ricky Marson, Mark Blankenship, Mike Garner, Merideth Kaye Clark, Jeff Lewis, Michael Siegel, Phil Johnson, Thomas Smith, Liam Kraus, Ed Glass, Ben Fletcher-Watson, Jamie

Wax, John Ammerman, Bill Fox, Taylor (M.) Dooley, Gabriel Viñas, Riz Ahmed, Jillian Quint, Matt Kellogg, Kalen Egan, Eric Ledgin, Sidewinder, the Bobby Jones Trust, the Emory Scholars Program, and the C Dubbers for their generosity, guidance, and support. Special recognition is due, as always, to his friends and family, without whose love it would be impossible to continue traveling such a strange path.